FABULOUS VOYAGER

James Joyce's *Ulysses*

BOOKS BY JAMES JOYCE

Ulysses

COMPASS BOOKS
Dubliners
A Portrait of the Artist as a Young Man
Finnegans Wake
Collected Poems

THE VIKING PORTABLE LIBRARY
The Portable James Joyce
edited by Harry Levin

BY RICHARD M. KAIN

FABULOUS
VOYAGER

James Joyce's *Ulysses*

NEW YORK · THE VIKING PRESS

FOR LOUISE

ACKNOWLEDGMENTS

Acknowledgments are gratefully made to my colleagues, Ernest C. Hassold, David W. Maurer, Mary Burton, and William S. Bowmer, of the University of Louisville; to Harvey C. Webster, of Fisk University; and to Ronald S. Crane, of the University of Chicago, for their patient reading and helpful suggestions. James T. Farrell's comments on my interpretation have been most stimulating. The acute sensitivity of Philip Manuel and Gavin Williamson, concert harpsichordists, has animated my feeling for Joyce's style.

The University of Chicago Press has aided substantially in the production of this volume. The staff of the University of Louisville Library; J. T. Windle, of the Newberry Library, Chicago; and Joseph Hanna, of Trinity College Library, Dublin, were of great assistance in securing materials.

TABLE OF CONTENTS

PREFACE TO REVISED EDITION

JOYCE STUDIES, 1947–1958

JOYCE'S richly allusive art continues to fascinate readers and to reward commentators. More than a hundred studies and reviews appear every year as new approaches and evaluations develop. The result has been that many of Joyce's preoccupations which once seemed eccentric have begun to take central places in the modern consciousness. The rhetorical devices of the newsroom chapter, for example, have come to concern modern textual critics, and what once seemed irresponsible parody is now understood as an insight into social levels of language, paralleling current interests of social anthropologists. Of the author's literary influence we cannot speak without surveying modern literature.

Meanwhile Joyce's public constantly enlarges, and university libraries are recipients of great collections (the Slocum collection at Yale, Joyce's own materials at the University of Buffalo, Stanislaus Joyce's at Cornell, Miss Harriet Weaver's Joyce manuscripts at the British Museum, the Spoerri, Hanley, Picher, and Croessmann books at Kansas, Texas, Stanford, and Southern Illinois Universities). *Exiles* has been revived, parts of *Finnegans Wake* have been staged, and an adaptation of the "Circe" episode proved to be an off-Broadway hit in 1958. Clerical opposition prevented the Dublin International Theatre Festival from staging Alan McClelland's *Bloomsday* in 1957 or 1958, but the Oxford Experimental Theatre Club presented it in November, 1958.

In the flood of studies there is inevitably much trivia, such as the revelation that John Henry Menton wore a hard hat! But, as Joyce punningly answered a complaint that many of his puns were trivial with the rejoinder that they were also

sometimes "quadrivial," we may look upon current research
as not entirely "old hat." In any case, the watershed remains
where Harry Levin located it years ago, at the boundary of
naturalism and symbolism, the meeting place of map and
myth. In the newsroom Myles Crawford had advised Stephen
to write "something with a bite in it," something all-inclusive:

> Put us all into it, damn its soul. Father Son and Holy
> Ghost and Jakes M'Carthy.

The episode is headlined, "YOU CAN DO IT!" Joyce certainly
could, and did. Even before the full text was published,
Richard Aldington wrote that *Ulysses* had "made realism
mystic." And T. S. Eliot's early pronouncement on Joyce's
mythic method has become classic—"a step toward making the
modern world possible for art."

The map and the myth, coordinates of naturalism and symbolism, have been diligently explored. The history of Joyce's
reputation in Marvin Magalaner and Richard M. Kain, *Joyce,
the Man, the Work, the Reputation* (New York: New York
University, 1956), can be brought up to date by the comprehensive checklist of Maurice Beebe and Walton Litz in *Modern Fiction Studies* (Spring 1958). Only the most important
findings can be mentioned here.

First, the myth. William York Tindall's *James Joyce* (New
York: Scribner, 1950) is especially rewarding in its treatment
of French Symbolism and the tracing of Joyce's basic themes
throughout the *œuvre*. The most convincing justification of
the symbolic method is Hugh Kenner's study of the influence
of the Thomistic concept of "signate matter." In *Dublin's
Joyce* (Bloomington: Indiana University, 1956) Kenner
showed how this theory of reality enabled Joyce to build an
aesthetic which found a true place for the artist's insight into
symbolic correspondences. Kenner should be supplemented by
Father William T. Noon's authoritative *Joyce and Aquinas*
(New Haven, Conn.: Yale University, 1957).

Meanwhile the map is being completed. Joyce's letters

(New York: Viking, 1957), especially those to Frank Budgen, deal with the gestation of *Ulysses*. Mary and Padraic Colum have recreated the Dublin of 1904, describing many who appear in the novel (*Our Friend James Joyce,* New York: Doubleday, 1958). The memoirs of "Cranly," J. F. Byrne's *Silent Years* (New York: Farrar, Straus, & Cudahy, 1953), include the reminiscence of a visit to Byrne's home, 7 Eccles Street, in 1909, by a distraught Joyce, a younger Bloom, in despair over a rumor of his wife's infidelity. The Jewish theme has been attributed by Herbert Howarth (*The Irish Writers*, London: Rockliff, 1958) to the literary and theosophical traditions of messianic expectation during the Revival, when the Jewish and Irish were often compared —witness the John F. Taylor speech quoted by Professor MacHugh in the newsroom. This speech, distributed in a four-page pamphlet of 1904 with the title *The Language of the Outlaw,* also impressed Yeats; and Joyce, despite his intransigence in politics, read this page of *Ulysses* for his unique phonograph recording. To the characters identified by Herbert Gorman in his *James Joyce* (New York: Farrar & Rinehart, 1939), additions have been made by Richard Ellmann ("The Backgrounds of *Ulysses*," *The Kenyon Review,* Summer 1954). Shakespeare allusion and the Shakespeare theory have been assiduously studied by William Schutte (*Joyce and Shakespeare*, New Haven, Conn.: Yale University, 1957). Joseph Prescott, J. Mitchell Morse, and A. M. Klein may be mentioned among the scholars who have uncovered so much material that a fully annotated edition of *Ulysses* at last becomes a possibility.

We are not here surveying biographical material, but Stanislaus Joyce's spirited memoir must be mentioned (*My Brother's Keeper*, New York: Viking, 1958). His shrewd insight and stubborn independence give a taste of what might have been forthcoming had he continued his account past the Dublin years through the time when he lived with James Joyce in Trieste from 1905 to 1915. His account of this creative period, of which we know so little, would have been invaluable, for these years were the making of the novelist. Then it was that *Dubliners* and the *Portrait of the Artist* were completed, and *Ulysses* begun. But even in death, Stanislaus remained a Joyce, dying on Bloomsday, 1955, and leaving the inception of *Ulysses* a mystery.

Turning now to the appendices of this book, with the regret at not making full acknowledgments to those who contributed information, I shall begin with the characters. Considerable ingenuity is necessary to discover that it was Vincent Lynch, not Lenehan, whom Father Conmee surprised, and that the field was at Artane, not the distant Clongowes Wood, which merely passed through the good Father's mind at the time. The characters from *Dubliners* should not include Joe Dillon or Jimmy Doyle, but must be increased as follows: "Lord" John Corley ("Two Gallants"), Crofton ("Grace" as well as "Ivy Day"), Bob Doran and his mother-in-law and brother-in-law Mooney ("The Boarding House"), Fanning ("Ivy Day" and "Grace"), Holohan ("A Mother"), Hynes ("Ivy Day"), Kathleen Kearney ("A Mother," "The Dead"), Leonard ("Counterparts"), and the Morkan sisters ("The Dead").

Among additional motifs in Bloom's stream of consciousness may be listed the following, which the curious reader can trace in the Miles L. Hanley's *Word Index to James Joyce's Ulysses* (Madison: University of Wisconsin, 1937): aconite, admirers, archbishop's letter, Beaver Street, Bennett Motor race, the bicycle of A. E., "Blood of the Lamb," Dr. Brady, Maud Branscombe, Cantrell and Cochrane, Capel Street library book, Boylan's red carnation, hag from Cassidy's, Chatterton, Cinghalese, St. Peter Claver, Coffee Palace, Comerford, Cormac, "Croppy Boy," Mrs. Dandrade, Dockrell's, "dreamy, creamy," Miss Dubedat, Miss Dunne, Dunsink time, "effulgence," Emmet, envelope of Martha's letter, Epps's cocoa, "Erin's King," Father Farley, Dr. Franks, Bloom's copy of the *Freeman's Journal*, Mrs. Galbraith, "gauging," "gentleman," Gilligan, Glencree dinner, the organist Glynn, Goldberg, Michael Gunn, Virag's Haggadah, hawhorn, headache, Hengler's circus, the Hill of Howth, impatience, "I.N.R.I.," Professor Joly, jujubes, Bridie Kelly, Marie Kendall, Keogh-Bennett match, Kismet, "Lady Cairns," "laughing witch," lottery, Lovebirch, Mary and Martha, Mario, Aristotle's *Masterpiece*, Mendelssohn, Mercadante, Mesias, Meyerbeer, Mirus Bazaar, Moisel, Mosenthal, Mozart, Dr. Murren, nannygoat, "naughty," octopus, O'Flynn, orangeflower, "opulent," Mrs. Palmer, par, poisoned, Prescott's, pugnosed driver, Rossini, rye, Salmon, "scaffold high," Scottish Widows' Insurance, showcart, Sinbad, sprained foot, staggering bob, statue, throstle, Tranquilla Convent, Turkish costume, Turko, Turnbull, Twigg, "Fair Tyrants," Vance, "Voyages in China," "Boys of Wexford," wonderworker, "world" as Martha's misprint for "word," X-rays, yashmak.

To the motifs associated with Stephen, the following may be added: algebra, Aquinas, Atkinson, Mulligan's aunt, backache pills, barbicans, "bawd and butcher," blemish, bullock-befriending, Columbanus, Cranly, costdrawer, "crooked smokes," crosstree, darkness-brightness, Deasy's letter, Delta of Cassiopeia, "down, baldpate," the man who was drowned, fambles, Fergus, Fetter Lane, *fichue,* frauenzimmer, gardener at Oxford, ghostcandled, goal, grandest number, Joachim Abbas, "Joseph the Joiner," "life ran high," link back, lookingglass, "lump of love," melon, "mighty mother," mockers, morrice, Mulligan's boots, *ogresse,* "old sow," "*omnis caro,*" one-handed, "paid my way," panther, pard, *per vias rectas, Pisgah Sight,* pluterperfect, possible, printed, Rosalie, ruddy, "seas' ruler," second-best, "see it," sentimentalist, "sinned against the light," *socialiste,* "he who stealeth," watercloset, "woman brought sin into the world."

The many occurrences of these motifs, together with the seven hundred listed in Appendix D, indicate Joyce's imaginative ingenuity and the mosaic nature of his art.

—RICHARD M. KAIN (*1959*)

FABULOUS VOYAGER

James Joyce's *Ulysses*

I TALKING ABOUT INJUSTICE: *JAMES JOYCE IN THE MODERN WORLD*

—Are you talking about the new Jerusalem? says the citizen.
—I'm talking about injustice, says Bloom.[327]

"FILTHY in word, filthy in thought, furious, raging, obscene"—how often these and similar charges have been leveled at Joyce's *Ulysses!* But it is not a modern critic from whom these words are quoted, nor is it Joyce who is being attacked; it is Thackeray misjudging the greatest satirist in the annals of English literature—Jonathan Swift.

The earnestness and honesty of satirists, their clear-eyed vision of evil, their moral horror, have ever been subject to misinterpretation by tender-minded readers. The weapons of irony and indirection are double edged and often return to wound the assailant as well as the victim. Since most twentieth-century authors use these weapons, it is not surprising to find that misguided zealots have accused modern literature of the very evils it attacks. Licentiousness, social irresponsibility, perversion—from these sins it is a short step to attributing to recent writing the decline of patriotism, the lowering of the birth rate, or the rise of Hitler. For the last it may be said that literature has no place in the discussion of fascism; the burning of the books was eloquent testimony to the power the Nazis feared most.

But it is hardly necessary to prove *Ulysses* a masterpiece of modern literature. It stands, an immense dol-

men, towering above the barren wasteland of twentieth-century culture. It has been savagely attacked,
and perhaps just as extravagantly admired. It cannot
be overlooked or by-passed.

In *Finnegans Wake* Joyce begs the indulgence of
the "ideal reader suffering from an ideal insomnia";
and, indeed, that work requires an encyclopedic
knowledge of philology, folklore, history, and metaphysics. No such extensive demands are made by
Ulysses. The work can be understood by the literate
reader. It requires patience and intelligence—above
all, sympathy and insight. The elucidation of minor
points, tracing of literary echoes, and other methods
of scholastic exegesis bid fair to discourage the public
who should read *Ulysses*. Just as Shakespeare has
often been ruined for schoolboys, so Joyce's brilliant
insights into the dilemmas of modern civilization are
too often smothered under a moraine of footnotes.

It is unfortunate, too, that Joyce is chiefly known as
a technician, a bewildering experimentalist. This kind
of fame is sterile; it creates of one of the most vital
and provocative of novels a preserve for graduate
courses in literature. It makes *Ulysses* a monument
of art for art's sake. The fascination of seeing a genu-
inely original and creative mind at work upon the factors of our culture is lost. Joyce is prophetic, as all
great writers have been prophetic. His is the clearest
and most incisive voice of our age, and we should do
well to heed him.

For *Ulysses* is a world book. The "Divine Comedy"
of our age, it brings an uncompromising intelligence
to bear upon the moral failures of modern civilization.
The dislocations of society, as well as the diseases of

the soul, are dissected with searing brilliance by one who was in a rare position to observe them, who possessed rare skill in analyzing them and rare courage in revealing them. Not for nothing were Joyce's heroes Swift and Ibsen. Like them he had the intelligence to see and the intrepidity to utter what he saw. The words of the young Joyce, in *Stephen Hero*, are pertinent: "Civilisation may be said indeed to be the creation of its outlaws."[178] As Swift mercilessly demolished the eighteenth-century idols of the tribe and Ibsen those of the nineteenth century, so Joyce has done for our day. We are all in his debt.

Nor is *Ulysses* as grim as this introduction might seem to make it. Joyce's humor is infectious, his gusto irrepressible. He has much of the "joyicity" of the grasshopper of *Finnegans Wake*.[414] Moralists who point to his "message" and moralists who lament his apparent lack of a "message" both fall into one misinterpretation. They forget that Joyce is a satirist, and a satirist without a sense of humor is as much an anomaly as a Dublin without pubs. *Ulysses* is fun to read.

The time is ripe for a reconsideration of this important monument of modern culture. Joyce's brilliant and unpredictable career has been brought to a close, and his last novel, *Finnegans Wake*, surveyed and annotated. One should be able to judge *Ulysses* more fully and justly than before.

Finnegans Wake, that strange nightmare epic, appeared in early May, 1939, at a time when the attention of the Western world was directed to other than literary matters. It aroused a brief flurry of excitement upon publication and a rebirth of interest in the summer of 1944, caused by Campbell and Robinson's *Skeleton Key*. At neither time, however, was more than a passing glance directed to the acknowledged masterpiece of twenty years' standing—and this despite the fact that *Ulysses* can be understood much more clearly in relation to the later work, for in *Finnegans Wake* appear the two basic themes of *Ulysses*—social criticism and philosophical relativity—the first somewhat submerged, the second considerably magnified.

The brief handbook, *James Joyce*, by Harry Levin, published in 1941, is not only an excellent guide to the entire career of Joyce but a masterpiece of judicial and perceptive criticism. His study of *Ulysses* is sound and challenging, though, of necessity, limited in scope. The indebtedness of the present study to the work of Levin will be apparent, as will be the modifications of his conclusions, particularly his charges that Joyce is deficient in human sympathy and in philosophical outlook.

Of earlier criticisms, Edmund Wilson's treatment of *Ulysses* in *Axel's Castle* remains an unsurpassable introduction. Important pioneer work was done by Valéry Larbaud, T. S. Eliot, and S. Foster Damon. Stuart Gilbert's elaborate commentary is more likely to terrify the general reader than to enlighten him, not to speak of providing a somewhat misleading perspective. His work suffers from two shortcomings: first, and less important, that the publication of the study before the novel was generally available necessitated extensive paraphrase (and expurgation) of the text. Of greater consequence is his exclusive preoccupation with esoteric symbolism, leading him to overlook many basic artistic and philosophical values. It will be necessary in this study to evaluate Gilbert's findings and to assess their aesthetic significance.

Readers of Joyce need not be told of the importance of the word in his style. No writer has used repetition, modulation, and permutation of single words so extensively or with such felicity. Hence the concordance to *Ulysses*, published in 1937 by Miles L. Hanley, is an invaluable aid to the fullest analysis of the novel.

Joyce has been the most bitterly attacked and grossly misunderstood of modern writers. The charges against him are numerous—that he is indefensibly obscure and indecent, that he lacks human sympathy, that his work is a formless and meaningless chaos, that he has no philosophy but cynical nihilism. Sometimes these opinions may be condoned, when they arise from a lack of understanding or sympathy on the part of the reader; but, more often, attacks are based upon deliberate misreading, misinterpretation, prejudice, or lack of literary and social perspective.

Joyce alludes to these charges in *Finnegans Wake*. His tone is one of irony, tinged with amusement, without concealing a justified contempt for the unappreciative public:

Sniffer of carrion, premature gravedigger, seeker of the nest of evil in the bosom of a good word, you, who sleep at our vigil and fast for our feast, you with your dislocated reason, have cutely foretold . . . . the reducing of records to ashes, the levelling of all customs by blazes.[189]

And when he refers to his "usylessly unreadable"[179] novel, "an epical forged cheque on the public for his own private profit,"[181] it is impossible not to feel his suppressed disappointment.

One cannot answer these attacks in a few words; indeed, the intention of this study is to provide a critical method by which the unique quality of the book may be appreciated and understood. Yet it is well to establish some basic principles of aesthetics as a preparation for the detailed analyses which follow.

First, as to motives of artistic creation. The imputation of sordid motives to the artist has long been one of the weapons of prejudiced criticism. Allegations of insincerity or incompetence follow as obvious corollaries. Hence we may never expect to see the end of such charges as that the artist is striving for notoriety, seeking money, or merely indulging in specious originality or exhibitionism at the expense of a gullible public.

Such amateur psychologizing is as difficult to prove as it is to disprove. But the nature of society, its innate conservatism and fear of change, makes it seem to the public that the burden of proof rests upon the defense rather than upon the prosecution. It was so in the days of Socrates; the charge then was the corruption of youth. Regrettably one must assume that it will be so in the future, no matter what form of government or social organization is adopted.

The root of the trouble lies in a misunderstanding of the function of art in society. So long as art is regarded primarily as a source of innocent entertainment or as a medium of escape, any artist who turns his attention to social criticism or personal analysis will be misunderstood. He will be labeled neurotic, scatological, nihilistic.

Yet no one acquainted with the history of culture can afford to make so naïve an interpretation of the nature of art. Whether or not the public knows it, even without the awareness of the artist himself, all art implies a certain standard of values. These standards may be taken for granted, but they are nevertheless present. Even Hollywood cannot escape acceptance or rejection of the mores of society.

There remain several attitudes possible for the practitioner of the arts. He may pander deliberately to the lowest level of taste in his potential audience, confirming their prejudices and accepting without question the demands made upon him. Such is the readiest way to financial success; it must be conceded that the advance guard of modern letters has failed miserably if the box-office is their goal.

The artist may sincerely be able to assume the basic rightness of the social pattern, seeing in it a compromise that is working more or less satisfactorily and which he feels no burning need to analyze or attack. This attitude can generally be adopted more readily in a society that is relatively stable, or one which is in the ascendant, rising confidently to its zenith; it may also be treasured sincerely by an individual who is jealously guarding the values of a society in decline. Of the first condition one can cite the example of Fielding or, with qualification, of Dickens; of the second, Doctor Johnson or Edith Wharton.

It is indeed difficult for the serious artist today to adopt this creed of wholehearted acceptance. The economic, political, and philosophical dislocations of the

twentieth century are so great that a perceptive observer can scarcely ignore them. He may, indeed,
proffer a positive solution, if he is happy enough to
have faith in any panacea; but such solutions are
difficult to find or accept. The more usual tone of
modern art is therefore one of scrutiny and self-exam-
ination, turning many times upon the artistic process
itself. This way lies skepticism, to be sure, but it may
also provoke a reorientation of basic values. Society,
clinging fearfully to its standards, finds it hard to accept or understand such an outlook; it fears what it
does not know.

One of the fundamental axioms of artistic appreciation is, in Coleridge's phrase, the willing suspension
of disbelief. In the present context the notion might
be better rendered as a willing suspension of distrust.
Adopt for a moment the frame of reference, the tone,
the code of values, which the artist implies; read with
an open mind, being sure that these intentions are as
well understood as possible. Then, and then only, can
one pose as a fair judge.

Let us turn for a moment to a brief survey of the
conditions of modern society. The entire world is today witnessing the convulsive death throes of the political and economic beliefs of the last century. The
future of capitalism and of liberal democracy seems
now to be at stake; and again the student of cultural
history is amazed by the uncanny prescience of writers who long ago sensed the imminence of the present
catastrophic changes in society. Ignoring the revolutionary spokesmen of the nineteenth century, as early
as 1900 Thomas Mann had examined with diligence

the decline of bourgeois standards of value in *Budden-brooks*. In 1912 an obscure German scholar, Oswald Spengler, penned the title of his philosophical master-piece, *The Decline of the West*, published in the mo-mentous month of July, 1918. From 1912 to 1924 Thomas Mann probed with increased powers of poetic sensitivity the problems of a young man of the pre-war generation, Hans Castorp of *The Magic Moun-tain*. During these years a similar task was under-taken on a colossal scale by Marcel Proust in France; and during these years Joyce wrote his panoramic *Ulysses*, depicting the disintegration of moral and philosophical values.

The intellectual finds that the long-vaunted in-tegrity of man, the keynote of humanism, has suffered from the depredations of evolutionary biology, of normal and abnormal psychology, and of materialist interpretations of history. Humanism has been dis-credited, so often has it been used to defend reaction-ary politics, authoritarianism, and the economic status quo, while a vigorous naturalism and relativ-ism in philosophy and literature seek a new basis for humane values. Likewise has the neatly geometrical Newtonian universe—the world view of classical physics and astronomy—been shattered by concepts of relativity, the quantum theory, wave mechanics, and the principle of indeterminacy. Marx, Darwin, Freud, and Einstein have brought into question bourgeois standards of value.

In his penetrating Introduction to the volume, *Books That Changed Our Minds*, Malcolm Cowley finds that the works selected by contributors as the most significant of recent years have one trait in com-

mon. Though ostensibly on diverse and seemingly unrelated subjects—logic, metaphysics, cultural history,
psychology, economics, and sociology—the works of
Darwin, Marx, Veblen, Freud, Bergson, and others
agree in refuting the accepted faith in rationalism.
Nineteenth-century liberalism was based on the su-
premacy of human reason, and its freedom from economic, national, or racial prejudices. From it stemmed
the hopes for continuous social and economic progress,
the belief in popular education, reform, democracy.
It is a matter not of cynicism but of clear-eyed observation to remark that these hopes are open to
widespread qualification today.

Of the three major writers of the twentieth
century—Marcel Proust in French, Thomas Mann
in German, and James Joyce in English literature—Joyce appears to be the one who faced
most unflinchingly the decadence of bourgeois society. Marcel Proust retired to the nostalgic
dreams of a social pattern from which he had been
exiled by ill-health—a society which was itself rapidly
passing away—and labored to render the aesthetic impressions left upon his memory. Thomas Mann grap-
pled courageously with the data of science and society, hoping to retrieve from destruction some of the
values of a world that was passing, and closed his
masterpiece with a pious hope that his faith in the
brotherhood of man might somehow be realized.
James Joyce alone felt the searing brilliance of
"time's livid final flame," on which Stephen reflected
throughout *Ulysses*. With microscopic exactitude
Joyce revealed the inherent contradictions and shortcomings of modern civilization. It is my purpose to

analyze and explain in detail his findings and the skill with which they are rendered.

In many ways Joyce was unusually qualified by temperament and circumstance to proceed with this necessary task of social analysis, necessary in the sense that no satisfactory social order can be successfully reared upon the dry husks and hollow shells of outworn beliefs. Raised under the strict dogmas of Catholicism and subjected to the discipline of a Jesuit education, he was plunged from the metaphysics of the Middle Ages into the practical exigencies of modern life. Thus, comparatively insulated during his early years from the basic contradictions of modern society, he found them all the more glaring, once they were exposed to his eyes. The situation inherent in so much satiric literature of the past—the visitor from a foreign land examining the customs of an age—was exemplified in the biography of Joyce. The young author, emerging from his scholastic education in 1902, was indeed a modern Rasselas, leaving the Happy Valley to judge the world.

Jesuit education not only provided Joyce with this perspective but was a source of additional isolation. In Joyce's excellent study of his mental development, *A Portrait of the Artist*, Stephen feels that his education, so assiduously cultivated, was itself an object of indifference or contempt in modern society:

it wounded him to think that he would never be but a shy guest at the feast of the world's culture and that the monkish learning, in terms of which he was striving to forge out an esthetic philosophy, was held no higher by the age he lived in than the subtle and curious jargons of heraldry and falconry.[209]

Another feature of Joyce's life deserves mention. One may question whether it is ever entirely possible to break away from the Catholic church. Readers of the *Portrait* will recall the urgent necessity to defend his position which obsessed the hero; an equally urgent necessity undoubtedly motivated the writing of the book. Stephen defends himself on the grounds of personal independence. The note occurs again and again. In refusing to sign a petition circulating within the university, Stephen responds to his schoolmates quietly: "You are right to go your way. Leave me to go mine."[232] "I shall express myself as I am," he answers another plea for conformity.[237] And in rejoinder to Cranly's efforts to return him to the fold of religion:

Did you believe in it when you were at school? I bet you did.—
    —I did—Stephen answered.
    —And were you happier then?—Cranly asked softly—happier than you are now, for instance?—
    —Often happy—Stephen said—and often unhappy. I was someone else then.—
    —How someone else? What do you mean by that statement?—
    —I mean—said Stephen—that I was not myself as I am now, as I had to become.—[283]

Levin says wittily that Joyce lost his religion but kept his categories,[25] but the matter is not quite so simple. Cranly remarks to Stephen in the *Portrait* that "your mind is supersaturated with the religion in which you say you disbelieve,"[283] and in the same discussion Stephen confirms this interpretation:

    —I imagine—Stephen said—that there is a malevolent reality behind those things I say I fear.—[287]

Now to renounce one's faith with misgivings such as these is to create within one's self a constant tension, a tension out of which a forceful art will be wrested. Far removed from a complacent acceptance of belief, Joyce, like Dostoevski before him, will be acutely aware of the ambivalence of the human mind, of the drawing-power of the forces which he wishes to reject or escape. Joyce's view of life will be that of an unhappy and homesick exile.

An exile in fact, too. In addition to the strains of uncertain disbelief will be those of loss of faith in his country. It has often been remarked that, though Joyce removed himself physically from Ireland, all his artistic work was devoted to the country he rejected. Again one finds the condition of aloofness and distance, so necessary to vital social analysis.

Ireland was in other respects a happy accident of Joyce's birth, for there the inconsistencies of modern economic and political practice were aggravated by a hated imperialism, centuries old. A revealing passage in the *Portrait*, apropos of a British teacher at University College, clearly shows this instinctive revolt from all things connected with the master-country:

—The language in which we are speaking is his before it is mine. How different are the words *home*, *Christ*, *ale*, *master*, on his lips and on mine! I cannot speak or write these words without unrest of spirit. . . . . My soul frets in the shadow of his language.—[221]

A national humiliation so long ingrained is bound to confirm one's innate tendencies to revolt and to sharpen one's eyes to injustice, chicanery, and hypocrisy wherever they are found. Nor was the rising Irish nationalism any more to the young Joyce's liking. He could never forgive the betrayal of Parnell. Whether it was attributable to provincial morality or to cowardice, it was unforgettable. Tim Healy, the politician who succeeded Parnell, was to Joyce little better than a traitor. It is said that he was the subject of a youthful polemic—"Et Tu Healy?"—written by Joyce at the age of nine. He appears in *Ulysses* as one of the hue and cry who pursue Bloom in a nightmare.[571] In *Finnegans Wake*, in a characteristic triple pun, Dublin becomes Healiopolis,[24] Egyptian home of the embalmed phoenix (Phoenix Park in Dublin was the scene of terroristic murders in Joyce's youth), as well as the city of the careerist politician.

Strict religious discipline, rejection of faith, geographical exile, and a strong sense of economic exploitation and political tyranny—add to these the natural independence and sensitivity of the artist. The conventional slogans of society were to Stephen merely wooden swords.[231] But they had a malignant power, too—an unseen, but nonetheless effective, ability to suppress and censor self-development. Conformity itself was dangerous. Stephen speaks of his fear of "the chemical action which would be set up in my soul by a false homage to a symbol."[287] Injustice can never be condoned. A diary entry at the end of the *Portrait* is as passionate as it is brief—"He said Bruno was a terrible heretic. I said he was terribly burned."[294]

The cost of such an attitude is loneliness, but there is also an ardent faith, a consciousness of mission. Stephen realizes this fully. Conversing with a college friend, he says:

When the soul of a man is born in this country there are nets flung at it to hold it back from flight. You talk to me of nationality, language, religion. I shall try to fly by those nets.—[238]

In an eloquent, yet uneasily self-conscious, statement of his artistic creed, the young Stephen asserts:

I will tell you what I will do and what I will not do. I will not serve that in which I no longer believe, whether it call itself my home, my fatherland or my church: and I will try to express myself in some mode of life or art as freely as I can.[291]

When the *Portrait* was written, it was still possible for Joyce to be optimistic about the reception of his work and the message he might bear to mankind. Grandiloquently, Stephen concludes his diary of the birth of the artist with the words: "I go to encounter for the millionth time the reality of experience and to forge in the smithy of my soul the uncreated conscience of my race."[299] Yet other disillusionments were to follow. The lengthy haggling over the publication of his relatively inoffensive volume of short stories, *Dubliners*, took its toll of his patience. Herbert Gorman's biography of Joyce recounts the tedious details of this process. All the author's delicacy of style, insight, and sympathy were overlooked; a few questionable phrases and political allusions were all that mattered to the publishers. The novelist was certainly justified in regarding it as one more sign of the impossible stupidity of the *bourgeoisie*.

Joyce never returned to Dublin after 1912, when he tried in vain to have his publishers release the volume. His books have been resented in Ireland; his native land has exiled him more fully than he was ever comfortable in exiling himself from it. Then, in 1914, when he was ready to start on *Ulysses*, the first World War began. Here was the cataclysm which revealed on an immense scale the inequities and inconsistencies of modern civilization. Here, indeed, was "the ruin of all space, shattered glass and toppling masonry, and time one livid final flame." Isolated in neutral Switzerland, Joyce consumed himself in the writing of an encyclopedic novel of modern life.

The complex personality of Joyce awaits a definitive biographer. To his friends he seemed jocose and flippant, little given to introspection, yet all his work is confessional. To what degree does it reflect subconscious motivations as well as the external causations here cited? The prurience may well be a form of inverted puritanism, the cynical acceptance of commercial values (as when Stephen demands payment for his writings in *Stephen Hero*,[182] the *Portrait*,[229] and *Ulysses*[211]) a painful sham, the scorn for country and church a desperate gesture. Like D. H. Lawrence, Joyce seems to have been fascinated by what he hated and repelled by what he loved. Is his psychological fiction, like Lawrence's, a series of psychological fictions, in the Freudian sense of the word, the disguised manifestation of latent personal tensions and desires? Or, to draw a closer analogy, the Joyce who embraces "silence, exile, and cunning" as his weapons and who builds his theory of static art seems more akin in spirit to Flaubert, whose artistic discipline was a bastion against a world he despised. Between the poles of Lawrence and Flaubert, between confession and repression, lies *Ulysses*.

Alienated from homeland, church, bourgeois society, local politics, and Empire allegiance, Joyce centered his masterpiece in the story of two homesick wanderers. The satiric imaginary travels of Gulliver, Candide, and Rasselas have here their modern counterpart, just as Bloom finds his ancient prototype in Odysseus, legendary voyager of the past. Indeed, as we shall see, one day in Dublin, June 16, 1904, is but a brief segment of that journey of man we call "life." The path of Everyman through space and time to infinity is the ultimate mystery. Man, finally, is the fabulous voyager.

II

DANCE OF THE HOURS: *THE TONAL PATTERN*

May's band played Ponchielli's dance of the hours. Explain that morning hours, noon, then evening coming on, then night hours. . . . . Poetical idea pink, then golden, then grey, then black. Still true to life also. Day, then the night.[69]

IN 1922, the Shakespeare Bookshop of Paris printed a limited edition of a strange work—a typographical monstrosity, with no chapter headings; with incomplete and unpunctuated sentences; with some episodes in dramatic dialogue, some in dialectical question and answer; with the type occasionally interrupted by newspaper headlines and frequently broken by snatches of popular songs. A glance would suffice to show *Ulysses* a work of extreme novelty.

The technique of the work has continued to preoccupy critics more than the interpretation of life that it affords. Actually, it is the most ambitious and monumental attempt in literature to render the inner lives of its three main characters—their thoughts, inhibitions, fears, and desires. *Ulysses* is, first of all, the greatest stream-of-consciousness novel in literature.

An interesting anticipation of this style is to be found in Tolstoy's first literary production, not translated into English until 1926, when it appeared in Tolstoy's *Stories and Dramas*, edited by Turin, Lucas, and Hogarth. Written in March, 1851, the unfinished sketch is significantly entitled "The Story of a Yesterday." Its purpose is stated in the opening sentence;

the idea emerged in the author's mind as an out-
growth of his inner religious struggles and was a fictional development of his diary habit. He writes, as he
says, not because yesterday was at all remarkable, but
because it would record the spiritual side of his life;
for, he continued, "how diverse and notable are the
daily impressions which occur to one, even as are the
thoughts aroused by those impressions." His only
fear was lest the manuscript be too long.

Tolstoy's story depicts an evening call on a young
woman (the same subject is used in Dujardin's
pioneer work, *We'll to the Woods No More*), and its
originality lies in an unspoken dialogue between the
lovers in the manner of *Strange Interlude* and a
Proustian associationism in the author's reflections
upon falling asleep. But its major importance is that
it so clearly anticipates the objectives and difficulties
of psychological fiction.

Seventy years pass; the work of the symbolist poets
and expressionistic dramatists and the novels of Dujardin and Dorothy Richardson appear. In 1922
Ulysses reaches the culmination of the stream-of-
consciousness technique. The utmost refinement of
sensitive perception is to be found here—the faithful
portrayal of those casual impressions which are the
essence of daily life and which are so often smothered
by the conventional narration of the traditional novelist. Here one may sense the subtle interplay of
thought and sense-impression in the human mind;
the amazing unpredictability of memory; the shifting
relations of individuals to one another; and the influence of nationality, environment, and experience upon
personality. In the creation of his background—the

city of Dublin on June 16, 1904—Joyce has achieved an amazing air of reality, a reality which proceeds not from ordinary external description but from a reliance upon the psychological sensations presented to the mind. Dublin is nowhere described; but, as the reader follows the characters through the streets, into lunch-joint, library, newspaper office, hospital, bar, and brothel, he feels that he knows Dublin as a resident would know it.

The story itself is slight. It is an account of the life of an average modern man on a characteristic day in an urban society. Leopold Bloom (whose profession, that of advertising solicitor, epitomizes the values of industrial civilization) gets breakfast for his wife; attends a funeral; visits a tavern, a maternity hospital, a brothel; and returns home, discouraged, in the early morning, accompanied by an acquaintance, the young artist, Stephen Dedalus, whose activities include teaching school and discussing Shakespeare with friends in the library.

Bloom's mind consists of a farrago of business adages, scientific half-truths, schemes for self-improvement, platitudes, lascivious desires, and frustrated hopes. Yet he is a kindly soul, with considerable intellectual curiosity, alertness of mind, and a secret longing for the poetic. Stephen, the contrasting character, is a helpless dilettante, a baffled intellectual, whose thoughts are a medley of scholastic concepts, poetic memories, and gnawing doubts. Having renounced the Catholic church, he flounders in a morass of skepticism, turning from art to philosophy, from philosophy to sensualism, in his desperate quest for faith. Bloom's wife Molly represents the earthy, pagan acceptance of life in all its sensual vulgarity. It is to the depiction of these three points of view that *Ulysses* is devoted.

Fiction which attempts to trace the flow of life in its most minute details falls into two dangers. One is the interminable length of the composition, a difficulty which concerned Tolstoy; the other is the chaotic formlessness of the material. The virtuosity of Joyce is exemplified in the mastery of these two problems in *Ulysses*. By limiting his scope to the time of one day and by restricting his attention to two major characters during this time, he has been able to create a microcosm of twentieth-century civilization.

Most obvious and most frequently discussed by critics of Joyce has been the adoption of the framework of Homeric episodes for his narrative. This is an intricate and elaborate procedure, as the detailed study of Stuart Gilbert has shown. But even to the reader who is unfamiliar with this framework, *Ulysses* has a narrative pattern of its own. It is created by a skilful modulation of the fictional tone, with styles appropriate not only to the time of day described but to the characters involved and to the implied philosophical outlook. Strangely enough, this feature of the work has never been fully interpreted.

The earlier *Portrait of the Artist* could have provided a clue to this interpretation, for it is written in three distinctive styles, reflecting the stages of youth, adolescence, and maturity. The opening pages give direct impressions of Stephen's childhood, throwing on the page the sights, sounds, and observations that first impinged upon his consciousness. The main body of the narrative, dealing with the youth of the artist, is written in a more romantic, impressionistic style, corresponding to the turbulence of his religious, intellectual, and personal revolt against his environment. The last few pages of Stephen's story are rendered by bald diary entries, reflecting the sober dedication of the hero to his calling as an artist in exile.

The pattern of *Ulysses* is both more elaborate and more interesting, for the successive styles correspond to the changing tones of the dance of the hours. Bloom conceives of the principle—"poetical idea pink, then golden, then grey, then black."[69] But, more than the changing tones of the day, the episodes bring to our attention changing points of view in regard to modern life—life as seen by the artist, by the sensual woman, by the man in the street; life as reflected in the confusion of machine civilization and the chaos of the continuous flux of personal contacts; life as seen from the vantage-point of the subconscious and from the cosmic perspective of astronomical space and time.

In the first three sections of the book we are introduced to the morning activities of Stephen Dedalus, hero of the *Portrait*, now returned from Paris for the funeral of his mother and temporarily teaching school. He arises and dresses at his lodgings on Dublin Bay, breakfasts with his friends who then swim in the bay. The second episode tells of his teaching at Mr. Deasy's school, receiving his pay and a letter which his master has written to the newspaper in regard to the hoof-and-mouth disease. The third scene reveals

Stephen's meditations as he walks on the beach before going to the newspaper office.

The style of the episodes corresponds to the morning hours which it describes. It is a style akin to that of the main body of the *Portrait*—a style of brightly flowing impressionism, keenly alive to the nuances of sound and color, turning with equal ease to external reality or psychological meditation. Sharpness of visual description is contrasted to the abstract indefiniteness of Stephen's stream-of-consciousness, which intervenes from time to time in the first two chapters and flows uninterruptedly in his walk on the beach. The opening of the school scene is characteristic:

—You, COCHRANE, WHAT CITY SENT FOR HIM?
—Tarentum, sir.
—Very good. Well?
—There was a battle, sir.
—Very good. Where?
The boy's blank face asked the blank window.
Fabled by the daughters of memory. And yet it was in some way if not as memory fabled it. A phrase, then, of impatience, thud of Blake's wings of excess. I hear the ruin of all space, shattered glass and toppling masonry, and time one livid final flame.[25]

In sudden contrast we are introduced to the second major figure, the middle-aged man of business, Leopold Bloom, who, we are told in the first sentence, "ate with relish the inner organs of beasts and fowls."[55] He is seen preparing breakfast for his wife, stepping around the corner for kidneys to grill, opening the morning mail—but, above all, reacting to the sounds, smells, and suggestions which come to his ever alert mind. As Ulysses, ingenious and observant, is to the weakling son, Telemachus, in the *Odyssey*, so is Bloom to Stephen. Joyce himself confessed partiality to Leopold, as Frank Budgen, his associate in Zurich at the time he was writing the novel, states in his volume on *The Making of Ulysses*. "As the day wears on," Joyce said, "Bloom should overshadow them all."

Bloom then goes off to the baths, walking through Dublin streets observing everything; passing the post office, where he picks up a letter from a Martha Clifford with whom he hopes to achieve intimacy; stepping into a church for a moment; purchasing a cake of soap at the chemist's. Next we read of Bloom's journey with a few friends to the funeral of an acquaintance, Paddy Dignam.

The style of the chapters dealing with Bloom's morning is sharp, staccato, in keeping with the alertness of the salesman's observing mind. Less poetic and rhythmic in style, the prose vibrates with concrete, objective impressions. It is much more immediate, clearer in focus. Bloom here receives his letter from Martha, as he notices a recruiting poster:

Answered anyhow. He slipped card and letter into his side-pocket, reviewing again the soldiers on parade. Where's old Tweedy's regiment? Castoff soldier. There: bearskin cap and hackle plume. No, he's a grenadier. Pointed cuffs. There he is: royal Dublin fusiliers. Redcoats. Too showy. That must be why the women go after them. Uniform. Easier to enlist and drill. Maude Gonne's letter about taking them off O'Connell street at night: disgrace to our Irish capital.[71]

Having thus been introduced to the two main characters, their personalities being contrasted by appropriate differences in narrative tone, we find the scene in the newspaper office a startling interruption. The reader is confronted with a chapter punctuated by frequent boldface headlines. Against the sensibilities of two individuals impinges the voice of the modern city—and that through its most blatant medium, the press. As if in confirmation of this impression, the chapter opens with the clanging trams at Nelson's Pillar, the central core of the city's traffic:

IN THE HEART OF THE HIBERNIAN
METROPOLIS

BEFORE NELSON'S PILLAR TRAMS SLOWED, SHUNTED, CHANGED
trolley, started for Blackrock, Kingstown and Dalkey, Clonskea, Rathgar and Terenure, Palmerston park and upper Rathmines, Sandymount Green, Rathmines, Ringsend and Sandymount Tower, Harold's Cross. The hoarse Dublin United Tramway Company's timekeeper bawled them off:
—Rathgar and Terenure!
—Come on, Sandymount Green![115]

This visual and vocal sketch of city traffic is followed by companion pictures which repeat the theme —the distribution of mail throughout the city, nation, and empire and the heavy thudding rhythm of the loading of barrels of beer, Dublin's principal export.

A new perspective is thus introduced into the epic of the city—the impact of modern commerce upon individuals. Beside its stentorian voice man is submerged. And, indeed, in this episode neither Bloom nor Stephen is prominent. They both come to the newspaper office, Stephen bringing Mr. Deasy's importunate letter on the hoof-and-mouth disease (so characteristic of the interests of citizens who address letters to the press), Bloom on an even humbler mission, that of negotiating an advertisement. Their paths cross but do not meet—possibly a symbol of the difficulty of establishing vital personal contact in the maelstrom of metropolitan life.

In the next two chapters we return to the preceding styles—those of Bloom and Stephen. Bloom is seen on his way to lunch, chatting with acquaintances on the way, his mind ever busy with his little thoughts and projects. Then we enter the library, where we hear Stephen discuss Shakespeare with certain members of the Irish revival group of littérateurs. Bloom also enters the library in quest of a design for his advertisement (note the contrast of interests) but is ridiculed by the group, except for Stephen, who does not notice him.

The first nine of the eighteen chapters of *Ulysses* thus present three, or at most four, distinctly recognizable styles. They are the impressionistic, rhythmical flow of Stephen's mind, observed in the first three scenes and in the library; the metallic prose reflecting Bloom's personality in his four morning episodes; and the jarring note struck by the scene in the newspaper office. A fourth style could possibly be found in the poetic stream-of-consciousness of Stephen in his morning walk on the beach.

Another abrupt change of perspective is introduced in the tenth episode. Just as Stephen and Bloom had earlier been submerged by the voice of the city in the newspaper office, so now they are lost in the constant traffic of persons on the streets of the city. In a chapter of eighteen separate scenes, capped with an ingenious coda, we are introduced to the daily activities of no less than fifty characters. The paths of these characters cross and recross haphazardly; their stories are narrated in most intricate counterpoint. Father Conmee makes pastoral calls; the undertaker's assistant reckons his accounts; a sailor begs in the streets; Stephen's sister waits for Simon; Boylan, Molly Bloom's lover, orders fruit; Stephen converses in Italian with a friend; Bloom rents for his wife a pornographic book at a bookstall which Stephen visits a few moments later; loafers are seen in the tavern. Finally, the attention of all is attracted by the cavalcade of the Viceroy of Ireland proceeding through the city.

Here the counterpoint structure (which has been successfully adopted by John Dos Passos) seems to imply that individuals are again submerged by the very size and complexity of an urban population. Their only common point of contact is the hated symbol of British rule, the Lord Lieutenant's procession.

"BRONZE BY GOLD HEARD THE HOOFIRONS, STEELY-RINGING,"[252] is the opening phrase of the next scene, one of the most musical in modern writing. With an overture of phrases taken from the chapter itself, we are introduced to the bronze- and gold-headed barmaids in the Ormond Hotel. Bloom enters, and as he eats his liver and bacon he listens to the strains of music drifting from the piano and the sentimental songs of Dollard and the elder Dedalus. His thoughts turn to his wife's infidelity, and with musical involutions the pains of longing and loneliness overwhelm him. Here we have the closest emotional identification with the dreams and desires of the man in the street, so often thoughtlessly ridiculed or ignored:

Quitting all languor Lionel cried in grief, in cry of passion dominant to love to return with deepening yet with rising chords of harmony. In cry of lionel loneliness that she should know, must Martha feel.[271]

The subjection of Bloom reaches its climax in the next scene, at Kiernan's bar. He has come to arrange with a friend for the collection of Dignam's insurance, but his attempt to lead the prejudiced discussion of patriotism and anti-Semitism into the light of reason results in a brawl from which he retreats ignominiously. A Dublin loafer tells the story in a racy vernacular, punctuated by Joyce with a transcript in heroic style of the details of the encounter. This is the first extended use of parody, a device so loved by the linguistic virtuoso. The desires and hopes of Bloom, emotionally rendered in the preceding chapter, are here viewed by the vulgar mind of the narrator, who sees in the humiliation of Bloom only an amusing encounter. The interposed parodies, of dubious artistic value to many readers, may be intended to reduce the stature of Bloom once more to the insignificant. The following passage is characteristic—a mock-heroic account of the escape of Bloom from the indignant barroom loafers:

And the last we saw was the bloody car rounding the corner and old sheepsface on it gesticulating and the bloody mongrel after it with his lugs back for all he was bloody well worth to tear him limb from limb. Hundred to five! Jesus, he took the value of it out of him, I promise you.

When, lo, there came about them all a great brightness and they beheld a chariot wherein He stood ascend to heaven. And they beheld Him in the chariot, clothed upon in the glory of the brightness, having raiment as of the sun, fair as the moon and terrible that for awe they durst not look upon him. And there came a voice out of heaven, calling: *Elijah! Elijah!* And he answered with a main cry: *Abba! Adonai!* And they beheld Him, even Him, ben Bloom Elijah, amid clouds of angels ascend to the glory of the brightness at an angle of forty-five degrees over Donohoe's in Little Green Street like a shot off a shovel.[339]

It is now twilight, and the breath of romance steals over the book. Bloom walks on the beach and reaches a climax of erotic excitement with a glimpse of the underclothing of Gerty MacDowell, a common shopgirl, who is sitting on the rocks watching a display of fireworks. Here Joyce's pathos, which is so often missed by his readers, verges close upon sentimentality, for we share Bloom's emotional starvation by now, and even Gerty feels that "the story of a haunting sorrow was written on his face."[351] Gerty's sentimental dreams of romance, couched in a prose abounding in clichés, seem to be a matter of ridicule:

Here was that of which she had so often dreamed. It was he who mattered and there was joy on her face because she wanted him because she felt instinctively that he was like no-one else. The very heart of the girlwoman went out to him, her dreamhusband, because she knew on the instant it was him. If he had suffered, more sinned against than sinning, or even, even, if he had been himself a sinner, a wicked man, she cared not. Even if he was a protestant or methodist she could convert him easily if he truly loved her.[351]

But when she limps away with her crippled gait, the pathos becomes poignant. There is an almost heart-breaking sense of loneliness as Bloom remains alone at twilight on the beach:

Chance. We'll never meet again. But it was lovely. Goodbye, dear. Thanks. Made me feel so young.[375]

The most elaborate tour de force in *Ulysses*, and
the one most open to question on aesthetic grounds,
is the parody outline of English literature utilized in
the hospital scene. Bloom has gone to the hospital to
await word of Mrs. Purefoy's lying-in. Stephen is
there, too, with his friends, the medical students.
Their conversation is general and need not concern us
for the present. But the style of this chapter, a series
of parodies of English prose from Anglo-Saxon down
to modern slang, seems to contribute nothing to the
spirit of the narrative. Stuart Gilbert would have us
believe that this series of parodies illustrates em-
bryonic development and hence is appropriate to the
subject. It may be questioned whether its effect on
most readers could be much more than amazement at
the linguistic virtuosity of the author and some sense
of his sheer creative gusto. Even if the earlier styles of
literature do suggest the growth of the embryo, they
are beside the point here, as we are concerned only
with the moments preceding delivery. For what they
are worth, here are the most important parodies which
have been identified: Anglo-Saxon,[378] Mandeville,[380]
Malory,[381] Elizabethan prose,[386] Browne,[387] Bunyan,[389]
Pepys,[391] Sterne,[398] the Gothic novel,[405] Charles
Lamb,[406] Coleridge,[407] Macaulay,[410] Dickens (one of
the most successful),[413] Newman,[414] Ruskin,[415] Carlyle,[416] modern slang,[417] evangelistic oratory.[420]

As the young medical students go off for drinks at
Stephen's expense, the prose tumbles into broken
sounds, echoes, and half-words, the closest approxi-
mation in *Ulysses* to the style of *Finnegans Wake*. It is
an amazingly successful rendition of the stupor of
intoxication:

Golly, whatten tunket's yon guy in the mackintosh? Dusty Rhodes. Peep at his wearables. By mighty! What's he got? Jubilee mutton. Bovril, by James. . . . .

Hark! Shut your obstropolos. Pflaap! Pflaap! Blaze on. There she goes. Brigade! Bout ship. Mount street way. Cut up. Pflaap! Tally ho. You not come? Run, skelter, race. Pflaaaap![420]

Stephen and Lynch enter the brothel district, followed shortly by Bloom. Strange figures emerge at the least suggestion; the specters of the subconscious take the stage. The thoughts of the day parade again before our eyes in a drama of hallucination.

Remarkably skilful is the technique of this scene. Just as in the past we have had human aspiration submerged by the traffic and confusion of the external environment, now it is menaced from within by the seething desires of the libido itself. In a lurid midnight atmosphere, with the underside of civilization revealing itself in slum and brothel, fumes of intoxication release the hidden fears and desires of Stephen and Bloom. The style—that of expressionistic drama—merges the characters, their dreams, and the setting in a phantasmagoria of weird shapes, sounds, and voices.

Possibly the most brilliant dramatization of Freudian psychology in literature, this chapter indicates a turning-inside-out of the point of view usual in the stream-of-consciousness technique, for, instead of the individual's remaining in the foreground accompanied by his many subconscious musings, here the hidden fears and desires become dramatized, as in dreams, and the individual fades into the background.

It is now 1:00 A.M., and the bleakness of the time

of day is reflected in the deliberately prosaic dulness of the prose. As Stephen and Bloom walk together to the cabman's shelter, Bloom makes several efforts to become more intimate, only to be regarded with cold-ness and indifference by his younger companion. The commonplace nature of the style is thus doubly sig-nificant, reflecting the distance between the two figures as well as the atmosphere of the hour. Bloom is timidly debating with himself whether or not to invite Stephen home:

Everything pointed to the fact that it behoved him to avail himself to the full of the opportunity, all things considered. His initial impression was that he was a bit standoffish or not over effusive but it grew on him someway. For one thing he mightn't what you call jump at the idea, if approached, and what mostly worried him was he didn't know how to lead up to it or word it exactly, supposing he did entertain the proposal, as it would afford him very great personal pleasure if he would allow him to help to put coin in his way or some wardrobe, if found suitable.[641]

They walk to Bloom's house together, where the host prepares some cocoa for his guest before retiring. The studied dulness of the preceding chapter is now reduced to the completely impersonal tone of ques-tions phrased in scientific fashion and answered in an equally cold manner. A new perspective is introduced here, in keeping with the scientific accuracy of the style. It is the meagerness of human existence as viewed from the point of material fact, whether that fact is the itinerary traced by the two walkers,[650] the boiling of water,[657] the relation of their ages,[663] re-flections on the stars,[683] or the contents of Bloom's locked drawer.[705] Here is the world of scientific reality, which a religionless world inhabits; here are its meager artifacts; here, too, the consequent coldness and impersonality of human relationships:

Did Bloom discover common factors of similarity between their respective like and unlike reactions to experience?

Both were sensitive to artistic impressions musical in preference to plastic or pictorial. Both preferred a continental to an insular manner of life, a cisatlantic to a transatlantic place of residence.[650]

The final chapter—Molly Bloom's soliloquy in the early morning hours as she lies in bed thinking of her erotic experiences—brings us once more to the realm of human aspirations. There is a rich lyrical flow to the prose, a pagan acceptance of life even on its most sordid sexual level. Molly is reflecting on her forthcoming concert tour with her present lover, Boylan:

well he could buy me a nice present up in Belfast after what I gave theyve lovely linen up there or one of those nice kimono things I must buy a mothball like I had before to keep in the drawer with them it would be exciting going around with him shopping buying those things in a new city better leave this ring behind . . . .[734]

Joyce, the greatest master of language since Shakespeare, often delights in the sheer exuberance of his satirical power. His later chapters particularly, beginning with the scene at Kiernan's bar, with its gigantic caricatures; continuing with the anthology of parody of the hospital, the extravaganza of the brothel scene, the ludicrous rendition of commonplace prose at the shelter, the extended travesty of the examination chapter; and culminating in the libelous picture of woman in the bedroom, seem far removed from any merely naturalistic intent. Like Rabelais, Joyce gives free rein to his sense of the ridiculous. Indeed, like Rabelais, who saw with amusement the crumbling of medieval ideals, Joyce portrays the decline of bourgeois values with the abandon of reckless laughter. *Finnegans Wake* goes even further in this direction. The work has its naturalistic basis in the rendition of the dream of Earwicker; it has, too, its philosophic overtones. But when we read its many fables, parodies, and digressions, we feel sure that Joyce is merely writing for the fun of it. The exiled bard, like a disobedient schoolboy mimicking his teacher, is expressing his disrespect with a thunder of mockery.

Indeed, without entering into esoteric problems of symbolism and Homeric correspondences, one must be impressed by the amazing technical skill of the writing, as well as by the deep human feeling that pervades it. The changing tones of the narrative fulfil the definition of decadence in art, so ably described by Théophile Gautier in his essay on Baudelaire. The style of decadence, he wrote, is "nothing else but art arrived at that point of extreme maturity yielded by the slanting suns of aged civilizations: an ingenious, complicated style, full of shades and of research, constantly pushing back the boundaries of speech, borrowing from all the technical vocabularies, taking colour from all palettes and notes from all keyboards, struggling to render what is most inexpressible in thought, what is vague and most elusive in the outlines of form, listening to translate the subtle confidences of neurosis, the dying confessions of passion grown depraved."

III

YEARS DREAMS RETURN: *THE EPIC STRUCTURE*

years dreams return[375]

THE Homeric parallels of *Ulysses* have preoccupied critics unduly. It has been shown in this study that, even without thinking of the Greek prototype, the novel has a tonal and structural unity of its own. Joyce removed the titles of the sections before publication, perhaps as a tacit implication that the book was far more than a modern paraphrase of the ancient epic.

With few writers is it so true as with Joyce that the successive books are variations and elaborations of already chosen themes. Each work anticipates that which follows it, and each throws new light upon its predecessor. The *Portrait* stands as an early study in the stream-of-consciousness technique and utilizes in a tentative fashion the principle of a changing tonal pattern. *Dubliners* introduces the milieu of Dublin, though much less naturalistically than *Ulysses*. Hence it should be possible to understand *Ulysses* more clearly now that the themes of *Finnegans Wake* have been probed.

Indeed, in regard to the Homeric overtones of *Ulysses*, we can interpret anew the reasons for this choice of framework. The dominant concept of *Finnegans Wake* is present in embryo in *Ulysses:* that basic experiences, characters, situations, recur throughout history. In the complex phantasmagoria that is the dream of Earwicker, the figures of Eve, Isolde, and Swift's beloved Vanessa merge, not to speak of hundreds of other correspondences. What has hitherto been regarded as an arbitrary framework, a literary tour de force or gigantic parody of Homer, can now be appreciated as an embodiment of Joyce's philosophy: "years dreams return."[375]

It is not necessary to trace the Homeric echoes in meticulous detail here, as this has already been done by Stuart Gilbert. The major parallels can be quickly mentioned. Ulysses, man of many devices, finds his modern parody in Leopold Bloom, practical man of affairs. The son Telemachus is the bewildered intellectual, Stephen Dedalus. The figures that these characters meet recall those of the fabulous episodes of the Ulysses legend with mock-heroic effect, as the aged and wise Nestor is seen in a garrulous schoolmaster; the Cyclops in a chauvinistic bar-fly; the dainty maiden, Nausicaä, in the vulgar shopgirl, Gerty MacDowell; and the chaste Penelope in the adulterous Molly Bloom.

Joyce has handled the framework of the *Odyssey* with great freedom. The major change is the elaboration of the wanderings of Ulysses and the consequent minimizing of the account of the return. Homer told of the adventures of Ulysses in only one-third of the work, and most of them are recounted in indirect discourse; the homecoming occupies half of the ancient epic. Joyce expands the peregrinations of Bloom to about three-quarters of his novel, all narrated with direct immediacy, and the homecoming chapters comprise only one-sixth of the work. The emphasis is thus placed upon the homelessness of modern man, and the final return is eloquently undramatic and anti-climactic.

It is apparent that the casual looseness of stream-of-consciousness fiction is unified in many ways. The adaptation of Homeric episodes is foremost; the time-scheme is equally apparent. The tonal pattern, the emotional and stylistic rendition of the time-scheme, has, strangely enough, never before been pointed out. Nor has the geographical coverage of the city of Dublin. Finally, there is the intricate scholastic catalogue of symbolic references to arts, colors, and organs of the body. Like the *Divine Comedy*, which Dante explained could be read on four levels, *Ulysses* can be read on the classical (Homeric), medieval (symbolic), naturalistic (time and place), and poetic (tonal) levels.

A word should be said about the geographical locale, before turning to more esoteric and symbolic problems. On the naturalistic plane, *Ulysses* is a fictional Baedeker of Dublin. The heart of the city, an area of approximately two square miles, is encircled by the canal and divided neatly into quarters. The River Liffey, running from west to east, cuts through the middle of the city, and Sackville Street runs north and south and crosses the Liffey at O'Connell Bridge. The northeast quarter contains the slum and dock areas ("Circe"; "Eumaeus"). Southeast, the reader can follow Bloom's walk to the baths ("Lotus Eaters") from the quay down Westland Row and past Trinity College. Southwest, the business district centering around the castle is dealt with in the "Wandering Rocks." Northwest, the Ormond Hotel and Kiernan's saloon are described in the "Cyclops" and

PLAN OF *ULYSSES*

I. THE TELEMACHIAD

1. "Telemachus." 8:00 A.M. Stephen's breakfast	Martello Tower, southeast of city	Stephen—Telemachus
		Friends—suitors *Theology*
2. "Nestor." 10:00 A.M. Stephen teaching	Dalkey, on Dublin Bay	Mr. Deasy—Nestor *History*
3. "Proteus." 11:00 A.M. Stephen on beach	Sandymount beach, southeast of city	*Philology* (why not metaphysics?)

II. BLOOM'S ADVENTURES

4. "Calypso." 8:00 A.M. Bloom's breakfast	7 Eccles St., northwest	Molly—Calypso (?) *Economics* (?)
5. "Lotus Eaters." 10:00 A.M. To the baths	Southeast from river to Trinity College	*Botany—chemistry*
6. "Hades." 11:00 A.M. To the funeral	From southeast, through center of city to northwest suburb	Dignam—Elpenor Caretaker—Pluto *Religion*
7. "Aeolus." Noon. To newspaper office	At Nelson's Pillar, center of city	*Rhetoric*
8. "Lestrygonians." 1:00 P.M. To lunch	South from river to college district	*Architecture* (?)
9. "Scylla and Charybdis." 2:00 P.M. In library	Kildare Street	*Literature*
10. "Wandering Rocks." 3:00 P.M. Ensemble in streets	Mostly southwest	*Mechanics*
11. "Sirens." 4:00 P.M. Ormond Hotel	North bank of river, west of main bridge	Barmaids—Sirens *Music*
12. "Cyclops." 5:00 P.M. Saloon	North of Ormond quay	Citizen—Cyclops *Politics*
13. "Nausicaä." 8:00 P.M. On the beach	Sandymount beach	Gerty—Nausicaä *Painting* (?)
14. "Oxen of Sun." 10:00 P.M. At hospital	Holles St., southeast, near Merrion Square	*Medicine*
15. "Circe." Midnight. At brothel	Slum area behind Customs House, east	Bella—Circe *Magic*

III. THE HOMECOMING

16. "Eumaeus." 1:00 A.M. Cab-shelter	River bank near Customs House	*Navigation* (?)
17. "Ithaca." 2:00 A.M. Bloom's kitchen	7 Eccles St.	*Science*
18. "Penelope." 2:45 A.M. Bloom's bedroom	7 Eccles St.	Molly—Penelope

"Sirens" episodes. The center of town, from Nelson's Pillar down Sackville Street, across O'Connell Bridge, and through the shopping district, can be traced almost step by step as Bloom makes his way to lunch ("Lestrygonians"). A sweep across town from the southeast, through the center of the city to the northern outskirts, is described from the funeral carriage ("Hades").

In Stephen's breakfast scene the young poet is subjected to humiliation and ridicule by his companions, as was Telemachus by the suitors. The conflict lies between Stephen's introverted skepticism and Mulligan's hearty paganism. To Mulligan the sea is "our great sweet mother"; to Stephen the curving lines of the bay serve only to recall the bowl of green bile at his dying mother's bedside. He broods over his defection from the church, thinks of the heretics of the past. Hence theology may be said to be the dominant art here, though similar speculations continue to trouble his mind throughout the day. In this episode an interesting visual symbol is utilized—the bowl. There is the shaving bowl, blasphemously likened by Buck to the chalice at Mass, the bowl of bay, and the bowl at the mother's sickbed.

As Stephen teaches school, problems of history occupy his mind. The recitation is on Roman history; the young poet speculates on the "infinite possibilities"[26] of the past. The past is "an old pilgrim's hoard, dead treasure, hollow shells,"[30] like the shells and coins which the schoolmaster, Mr. Deasy, collects. Mr. Deasy's age, his love of giving advice, his interest in horses, recall Nestor.

Stephen's walk on the beach is one of the most esoteric chapters of the novel. There is an elaborate interweaving of the doctrines of Buddhists, mystics, and
Platonists in the young skeptic's meditation. Stuart
Gilbert provides an excellent commentary here. Suffice it to say that the earlier speculations on theology
and history here reach the ultimate level of metaphysics—the problems of existence, causation, and change.
These are symbolized by the "seawrack, the nearing
tide, that rusty boot."[38] Stephen's concern with the
"form of forms"[45] is closely allied to his reverence for
language. He is to "read," he feels, "signatures of all
things"[38] in the detritus of the shore, for "these heavy
sands are language tide and wind have silted here."[45]
The pertinence of the mythical man of the sea, Proteus, spirit of change and of magic, is apparent.

In reviewing the Telemachiad, we note the slight
resemblances to Telemachus, Nestor, and Proteus.
The arts of theology, history, and metaphysics permeate the respective episodes. Of the symbols elucidated by Gilbert—heir, horse, and tide—one can say
that it would be equally plausible to select the bowl,
shells, and seawrack. The association of the colors—
first, white and gold; second, brown; and third, green
—appears to be arbitrary, for, as a matter of fact,
gold appears only once in the breakfast scene, and
then in describing the fillings of Mulligan's teeth![5]
Scarcely an important symbol, especially as green occurs eight times in the same chapter. On the other
hand, gold appears no less than nineteen times in the
"Sirens" episode and fifteen in "Circe," for neither of
which a color symbol is given.

The chapters on Bloom's morning adventures are of

varying relevance to Homer. The house on Eccles Street might seem a far cry from Calypso's enchanted isle, but Gilbert would have us believe that the place of Molly's birth (Gibraltar), her maiden name (Tweedy), her morning serving of cream, are not accidental. If so, the significance will hardly be noticed by the reader.

The "Lotus Eaters" chapter has a more effective use of themes. There is a marked predominance, during Bloom's walk to the baths, of references to perfumes, flowers, and other symbols of escape (geographical, suggested by the tea company's window; marital, in Martha's letter; religious, in the church; physical, in the relaxation of the bath).

The parallels between the funeral and the descent to Hades are ingenious, though perhaps less defensible artistically. With the use of elaborate character parallels and geographical accidents, it seems that Joyce at times protests too much in his delight in analogy.

In keeping with the diverse interests of Bloom— erotic, musical, scientific, political, literary, personal —the chapters in which he carries on his morning activities have a less obvious principle of unity than those of the Telemachiad. To associate with the breakfast scene the organ of the kidney, the art of economics, the color orange, and the symbol of the nymph is to select four aspects of a multifaceted chapter. The kidney which Bloom purchases and fries is scarcely a symbol of great artistic validity; as for the art of economics, such thoughts are not limited to this chapter but, throughout the day, rub elbows with thoughts of science, the exotic appeal of the East, politics, music, cheap literature, and the philosophy of metempsychosis. The color orange is not even mentioned. The symbol of the nymph is introduced by way of a chromo in the bedroom. It suggests eroticism and metempsychosis, but the cat figures more prominently in the episode—a symbol of sensuality as well as a means of evoking Bloom's pity and curiosity.

Gilbert's chapter-by-chapter analysis fails to take account of the fact that Joyce's themes are never limited to single chapters but must be followed through the entire novel. It is the major purpose of this study to undertake such a task on a scale more complete than has hitherto been done in Joyce criticism.

The Homeric correspondences in these three sections are ingenious, though scarcely necessary for a comprehension of the basic problem—the characterization of Leopold Bloom. He is indeed a wanderer, caught in the toils of Calypso, thinking nostalgically in the manner of the Lotus Eaters, and reflecting upon death as he rides to the cemetery. The arts—economics, botany, chemistry, and religion—may be more reasonably associated with these episodes than may the organs of the body—kidney, genitals, heart—or the symbols—nymph, Eucharist, caretaker.

To think of the newspaper office as a cave of the winds is amusing, but the emotional effect of this blatant chapter is more significant than the ingenious Homeric parallels—the brazen walls of the palace of Aeolus likened to the tramlines; the many winds, drafts, and opening doors; the instances of frustration and interruption. The color is supposed to be red, the organ may reasonably be the lungs, but why select the editor as a symbol instead of the giant presses, which drown out the human voice as did the waterfall, the voice of nature, in *The Magic Mountain?*

In Bloom's walk to lunch the dominant metaphors are dietary; the art of architecture is scarcely recognizable, and the constables, supposedly the symbol, are mentioned only in passing. The organ is certainly the stomach.

The library interlude bears only a shadowy resemblance to the tale of Scylla and Charybdis; the organ, the brain, is more plausible, as the chapter is dominated by intellectual discussion; the art is, of course, literature.

The counterpoint chapter of the streets of Dublin, with the constant motion and cross-currents of humanity, is metaphorically parallel to the Wandering Rocks, which were mentioned only casually in Homer. Gilbert has identified many instances of motion and of mechanics, the technology of motion. One might expect the limbs, the organs of motion, to be selected, but we discover to our surprise that it is the blood! Here, as in the "Aeolus" section, the technique is far more interesting in its own right for its originality and appropriateness to the subject matter.

In the late-afternoon sections of *Ulysses* Joyce seems to be turning away from his model to an increasing degree and to be expanding his own technical experimentation and criticism of life. The Sirens are the barmaids in the Ormond Hotel, though Bloom is not lured by them. The environment is musical, and the style is singularly suggestive of musical forms. The ear is the appropriate organ.

The dark cave of the Cyclops, presided over by the savage cannibal, is next recalled by the dingy interior of the saloon, with the Citizen, patriot and anti-Semite, and a mangy dog as the principal denizens. Examples of brute force abound—hanging, prize fighting, flogging in the navy—climaxed by the brawl which concludes the episode. There are also frequent references to the eye. Anonymity (an echo of the "noman" trick of Ulysses) is prevalent. The narrator, a debt-collector, is unnamed, as is the Citizen. But it is in the parodies that the satiric effect lies. To translate the mean prejudices of the average man into heroic terms is to exploit the crass quality of chauvinism, anti-Semitism, and anti-intellectualism.

The chaste Nausicaä is reduced to absurdity in the cheap sentimentality of Gerty MacDowell, who sees the sad-looking stranger on the beach. The organs of eye and nose, the color blue, the art of painting, and the symbol of the virgin, may possibly be found by the diligent reader. Far more significant are the implications of the rocket display, symbolic of orgasm; the snickering toll of the cuckoo clock; and the deepening twilight, evocative of Bloom's loneliness and frustration.

The gigantic anthology of parodies in the hospital scene immediately strikes the attention; indeed, it is so dominant that the reader runs the risk of overlooking the story, not to speak of esoteric correspondences. The talk of the medical students is sexual, which provides the necessary art and organ; beyond this it is scarcely profitable to go. The Oxen of the Sun were symbols of fertility; their impious slaughter has only the slight parallel of a passing reference to birth control.

Circe's transformation of men into swine is more

clearly exemplified in the brothel scene. But Joyce has colored the Homeric fable with the overtones of medievalism. The setting is closer to *Faust* than to the *Odyssey*. Without question, magic is the art; but one might think that the Freudian id, or subconscious, would be a more fitting bodily emblem than the locomotor apparatus.

In the cabman's shelter the social implications are far more significant than Homeric correspondences. It is not of great importance that there are many references to the mariner's return, the hypothetical return of Parnell from the grave, or Rip Van Winkle and Enoch Arden. Navigation may well be the art, and nerves (or nervous fatigue) the organic detail; but to choose the sailors as symbol is less convincing than the deserted streets of the city, so relevant to the spirit of isolation evoked.

Even further from Homer is the kitchen scene. No slaying of the suitors, no triumphal return, no reunion, is possible for Bloom. The art here is certainly science, but the choice of the skeleton is more figurative. The stars are an eloquent symbol of the cosmic pettiness of man.

In Molly Bloom's long soliloquy, Homer is entirely forgotten. Gilbert finds here flesh as the organ, the earth as a symbol. In fact, the three homecoming chapters seem almost completely modern rather than Homeric, with contemporary society viewed sociologically in the shelter (the talk turns to unemployment, travel, prostitution, crime, and politics), scientifically and cosmically in the kitchen, and psychoanalytically in the bed.

In reviewing the symbolic interpretation of *Ulysses*, certain conclusions may be reached. The framework is undoubtedly Homeric, but of varying degrees of pertinence. The most successful adaptations seem to be "Proteus" (Stephen on the beach), the "Lotus Eaters" (Bloom's walk to the baths), the "Cyclops" (the saloon), "Nausicaä" (Gerty on the beach), and "Circe" (the brothel). Joyce also appears to grow increasingly independent of his classical source as the story goes on. Possibly its social and philosophical implications became more interesting to him than were adventitious recollections of his model.

In regard to the arts of the episodes, it may be said that too often this type of analysis makes the reading of *Ulysses* a chapter-by-chapter matter rather than a unified aesthetic experience. Most of the arts are evoked in more than one chapter, such as Stephen's favorite topics—philosophy, history, theology, and literature—or Bloom's preoccupations with economics, politics, and science. And the style of the entire book could be said to exemplify the art of music.

In the selection of symbols, too, the choice often seems arbitrary. *Ulysses* is a giant symbolist poem, each chapter having a host of symbols. The organs of the body are more carefully limited to their respective chapters, yet they seem even less important.

In general, it may be said that most of the symbolic details are examples of artifice rather than of art. They are unnecessary for the narrative tone, and even more irrelevant to the understanding of the social and philosophical meaning. To study them too exclusively is to fall into the danger of missing the major direction of the narrative, much as a listener, preoccupied with the ingenious variations of the bass in the finale of Brahms's *Fourth Symphony*, may miss the rich music that overlies it. Joyce's understanding of the plight of modern society and his pity for humanity are far more important than his technical virtuosity, great as that may be.

Harry Levin has reached a conclusion that will appeal to all but Joyce idolators. He notes that we are pleased with the parallels we can recognize but that, "if the symbols are more extrinsic, we are less pleased; and if they are entirely out of sight, we seldom miss them."[75] One cannot quite agree with Levin's next statement that they are merely examples of intricate technique, not of esoteric philosophy. Evidences of intricate technique they certainly are. But they are part and parcel of Joyce's scholastic mentality, disciplined by years of Jesuit schooling. Joyce shares the medieval love of minute decorative detail. And, more than that, their inclusion is part of an effort to make of one day in the life of modern man a microcosm of human experience, just as the adventures of Ulysses were, for Joyce, representative of human nature in all ages.

Edmund Wilson, in his excellent analysis in *Axel's Castle*, found it difficult "not to conclude that Joyce elaborated 'Ulysses' too much—that he tried to put too many things into it."[214] But time will undoubtedly place these devices in their proper perspective. To be puzzled or annoyed by them is to risk losing the unquestioned values of the novel—the vigor and rhythm of its style, the amazing vividness of its setting, its rich humor and pathos, its understanding of human character, its analysis of the dilemmas of modern civilization.

IV

WHEELS WITHIN WHEELS:
INTEGRATING THEMES

wheels within wheels[160]

IN *ULYSSES* Joyce has combined with surprising art two complementary principles—the mutation and the continuity of experience. That life persists and yet that living things constantly change has been a problem of metaphysics since the school of Elea in pre-Socratic Greece. Is change real or only apparent? With the stream-of-consciousness technique, novelists have at last been given an art form that enables them to detect and to record the infinitesimal, moment-by-moment changes in human character. Yet the stubborn fact of continuity is not so easily achieved by this technique.

Readers of the "Wandering Rocks" episode will recall the artful use of recurring characters and situations to capture the feeling of change and continuity in a cross-section of Dublin. What is done there in miniature by means of characters is done in the novel as a whole by a more elaborate utilization of integrating themes.

Most striking is the frequent intimation of the time of day. The device is tastefully used by Virginia Woolf in *Mrs. Dalloway*. There the time is indicated no less than nine places in the course of the 296 pages of the story, in each case by the striking of Big Ben. *Mrs. Dalloway* shows many instances of indebtedness to *Ulysses;* in this instance as in all others, it is in the direction of simplifying and refining into delicate lyricism the innovations of her model.

The time of day is given by Joyce in many ways. As Stephen gazes out to sea from the Martello tower, a cloud drifts across the sun, shading the bay.[11] An echo of the phrasing informs us that it is the same shadow which depresses Bloom as he hurries home from the butcher.[61] We learn later that this is shortly before 8:45, for Bloom hears the tolling of the bells of St. George's church as he starts his day.[69] The time of the funeral is a second landmark. Molly asks about it as she eats breakfast,[63] Bloom plans to check it in the paper[69] and thinks as he walks to the bath that he will have plenty of time, for it is scheduled for 11:00 A.M.[70] After lingering at the post office and the church, he notes that it is only a quarter past[82] (that is, 10:15) and he will be able to buy the soap. The funeral procession passes through the heart of the city at 11:20.[92]

The visit to the *Freeman's Journal* office follows. The Racing Special is put into circulation,[142] presumably the noon edition. Bloom walks to lunch at 1:00,[152] and, finishing before 2:00,[170] ducks into the portals of the museum to escape meeting Boylan. It is then "after two."[180] Father Conmee consults his watch before starting on his afternoon walk in the "Wandering Rocks" episode; it reads five minutes of three.[216] Fifteen pages later it is after three o'clock.[230] At the Ormond bar the clock strikes four,[261] and the willing Lydia Douce snaps her garter to sound the time.[262] Four-fifteen is the time of Boylan's appointment with Lenehan,[226] 4:30 that of his assignation with Molly;[278] but we cannot verify it until Bloom notes on the beach that his watch had stopped then[363] and

later speculates on the coincidence.[367] We are told at
Kiernan's that Doran is thoroughly intoxicated at
five o'clock.[308] The twilight of the beach episode is
enough to set the time, but one also has references to
the glowworm, the "nine o'clock postman."[372] Bloom
guesses it is nearly 9:00,[375] and the episode concludes
with the ironical chiming of the cuckoo clock.[376]

The thunderstorm that interrupts the conversation
at the hospital is at 10:00,[390] and the roisterers leave
early enough to get into a bar before closing time,[419]
which is 11:00.[420] The scene at Bella Cohen's is well
advanced before the midnight chimes are heard.[469]
The vision of Elijah announces that it is 12:25,[497] and
it is "getting on for one" as Bloom thinks of inviting
Stephen to come home with him from the cab-shelter.[641] The bells of St. George's toll 1:30 or 1:45 as
they retire;[688] the final peal of 2:00 A.M. interrupts
Molly's soliloquy.[757]

Joyce's indications of time constitute a most careful, ingenious, and varied set of landmarks in the
progress of Bloom's day. Characteristic of the author's impressionism is the indirect notification of the
date. It is Thursday, for Bloom thinks it a bad day to
buy mutton kidney;[56] that the month is June we may
learn from his mental calculation of the time before
Molly's birthday, "Junejuly augseptember";[166] and
that it is the sixteenth we note from his observation
on the announcement of a bazaar.[180] Finally, the full
date is typed on a business letter by Boylan's secretary.[226]

We are frequently informed about the weather. It
is very warm[70] and humid.[73] Later it clears, "cricket

weather";[85] but on the way to the cemetery a slight shower falls.[89] Clouds continue to threaten,[162] but it turns fair in the afternoon.[220] The twilight sky is heavy,[373] and there is a thunderstorm at ten o'clock.[390] The atmosphere is refreshingly cool and clear,[598] and early in the morning the stars shine through a humid haze, bringing a cosmic perspective to the end of the day.[683]

The events of June 16 appear frequently as integrating themes. The liner "General Slocum," which burned in New York Harbor with considerable loss of life, is often mentioned. It is suggested to Bloom by his pity for the blind piano-tuner as another instance of the injustice of life.[180] To Father Conmee's sanctimonious mind it suggests thoughts of contrition when he sees it announced on the news hoardings.[218] Tom Kernan, in more practical vein, wonders about the corruption of the inspection system.[236] It is noted by Bloom in the evening paper that he reads in the cabman's shelter.[631]

The Ascot Gold Cup race is the major topic of conversation during the day. Bantam Lyons interrupts Bloom on his way to the bath, eager to find out about Maximum II. He interprets Bloom's remark about the newspaper—"I was just going to throw it away"—as a tip on Throwaway and dashes off—"God speed scut."[84] The racing edition of the *Freeman* appears at noon, and Lenehan picks Sceptre.[126] Nosey Flynn studies the form sheet at lunch; Bloom decides not to give him Lenehan's choice,[171] whereupon Lyons enters, giving evasive hints on his hunch.[176] We next see Lenehan in the "Wandering Rocks," ducking into a bookie's to see Sceptre's starting price,[229] and there meeting Lyons, backing his choice.[230] Lenehan's faith in his horse is increased by a drink with Boylan at the Ormond,[261] but he reports at Kiernan's that Throwaway has won.[320] Bloom was apparently the only man in Dublin to win, as Lenehan had dissuaded Lyons from betting on his supposed tip. The idea of Bloom's getting a hundred to five infuriates the debt-collector at the bar and precipitates a fight.

At the hospital the call of newsboys is heard, announcing the racing results in the *Evening Telegraph*.[372] A little later Lenehan enters and tells of how Throwaway ran, sportingly complimenting the winning jockey.[408] A prostitute in the brothel damns her luck in not picking the winner;[522] Corny Kelleher, rescuing Bloom, is sure that his friend has been successful.[588] The race results appear in the evening paper that Bloom reads,[631] and the form sheet is accurately given.[632] Finally, in the kitchen scene, one of Bloom's many money-making schemes mentioned is that of a private telegraph system which would enable him to bet on races before the results are known in Dublin.[702] More commendable is his mood at not winning—"He had not risked, he did not expect, he had not been disappointed, he was satisfied."[660]

J. Alexander Dowie, the evangelist, is announced in the pamphlet *Elijah*. The path of this throwaway is traced from the time Bloom receives it when walking to lunch,[149] then tosses it into the Liffey,[150] until it floats past the Customs House,[224] John Rogerson's Quay,[236] and out to the schooner "Rosevean" in the bay[246]—a visual symbol of the constant flux of movement which pervades *Ulysses*. *Elijah* and Dowie continue in Bloom's subconscious, emerging at the Ormond,[275] forming a mock-heroic accompaniment to his humiliating exit from Kiernan's,[339] suggesting the final parody of the hospital chapter,[420] being incarnated in the "Circe" dreams as Dowie[482] and Elijah,[496] and echoing in his recollections of early lovemaking.[537] The throwaway later appears as one of the tips that Bloom might have had on the race[660] and Dowie as an exemplar of one of Bloom's possible careers.[674]

Among theatrical attractions afforded to dear, dirty Dublin are the music-hall performance of Marie Kendall (spelled "Kendal" in the newspaper) and the performance of *Leah* by Mrs. Bandman Palmer. Posters advertising the first are noticed by Miss Dunne, Boylan's secretary,[226] by Lenehan,[229] and by Dignam's son;[247] her face smiles unseeingly upon the cavalcade.[249] Similarly, a poster announcing the comedian, Eugene Stratton, is noted by Bloom;[90] Conmee sees one in the cavalcade scene,[219] and it recurs in Bloom's thoughts in the brothel.[436] And Mrs. Palmer's performance catches Bloom's eye as he goes to the baths[75] and as he rides to the cemetery.[90] He thinks of going, but it is too late.[373] However, he uses the pretense of having attended as an excuse in the dream sequence.[439] And among the disappointments of the day is listed his failure to go;[714] he also uses the play as an excuse to his wife.[720] The *Lily of Killarney* is showing,[91] but Bloom does not attend.[373] On the morrow the Gordon Bennett motor race is to be held in Germany; it is mentioned in the funeral carriage[96] and in the evening paper.[631]

Even such a trivial detail as the arrival of a schooner is used as an aid to integration. It is described in consciously poetic style as Stephen sees it from the beach:

Moving through the air high spars of a threemaster, her sails brailed up on the crosstrees, homing, upstream, silently moving, a silent ship.[51]

The evangelistic pamphlet finally floats out to it, anchored in the harbor,[246] and one of the crew regales Stephen and Bloom with traveler's tales in the shelter.[609]

It was Arnold Bennett who coined the penetrating phrase, "the dailiest day possible," to describe June 16, 1904. In commenting on the choice of that day he remarks that Joyce is "evidently of a sardonic temper, and I expect that he found malicious pleasure in picking up the first common day that came to hand." What might Bennett have said had he known, as we learn (J. S. Atherton, *N & Q*, 1949), that allusions to Boucicault's *Nora of the Kiss* slyly hint that this day was the one on which he met his future wife, Nora Barnacle!

Joyce's handling of the newspapers of the day is as clever as might be expected. The morning *Freeman*, the noon Racing Special, and the *Evening Telegraph* play large roles in the story. Bloom plans to check the time of the funeral in the morning paper;[69] he takes the folded sheet from his pocket and taps his legs nonchalantly as he goes to the post office to get Martha's letter;[71] bored with M'Coy's conversation, he glances at it, noticing the advertisement for Plumtree's potted meat.[73] He folds Martha's letter within it, so as to read surreptitiously her note;[76] it provides Lyons with his tip on Throwaway.[84] In the funeral carriage he glances at the obituaries, recalling again Martha's letter.[90] In the two inventories which he makes of his belongings, we learn that he has it as he enters the museum,[181] but not in night-town.[430] His discarding the paper is further confirmed in the catechism chapter.[660] The Plumtree advertisement and the list of deceased, "Callan, Coleman, Dignam," linger in his thoughts throughout the day.

One of the main concerns of provincial Dublin at the time is the prevalence of the hoof-and-mouth disease among Irish cattle. It is on this subject that Mr. Deasy writes his importunate letter, ludicrously abridged by Joyce.[33] We learn that there is to be a meeting of the cattle-traders' association in the afternoon at the City Arms Hotel[36] (where Bloom had once resided). Joe Hynes comes from this meeting to Kiernan's[309] and informs the group that the M.P.'s, Field and Nannetti, are going over to London to inquire about it in Parliament,[310] a disappointment to Bloom, who was hoping to ask Nannetti about Keyes's advertisement.

Lenehan enters the hospital to remark upon the appearance of Deasy's letter in the evening paper.[391] A conversation about the problem ensues. Rumor has it that the Irish cattle are to be slaughtered because of the epidemic; Bloom expresses concern,[392] but Stephen assures the group that a veterinary surgeon, "the best quoted cowcatcher in all Muscovy," is to come and "take the bull by the horns,"[393] and the conversation degenerates into a punning bee.

Joyce's documentary naturalism is nowhere so clearly shown as in his actual use of the day's newspapers, the morning *Freeman's Journal* and the *Eve-*

ning Telegraph. No commentator has yet consulted these papers, despite their extensive treatment in the novel. Through the courtesy of Joseph Hanna, assistant librarian at Trinity College, microfilms of these papers have been secured. From the morning paper Joyce has taken little. The performance of *Hamlet* is there reviewed, and the two vessels, the "Eblana" (seen by the wanderers at the Customs House Quay in the early morning[603]) and the " 'Rosevean,' from Bridgwater with brick" (compare the wording in *Ulysses*[246]) are mentioned in the shipping lists. But Joyce's description of the evening paper is a fascinating amalgam of actual detail and imaginative construction.

Bloom picks up the late pink edition of the *Evening Telegraph*, the sporting extra, and reads it casually in the shelter at 1:00 A.M. The "tell a graphic lie" has been lying on the counter. Bloom glances at the captions. "First he got a bit of a start but it turned out to be only something about somebody named H. du Boyes, agent for typewriters"—his start, of course, being due to his obsession about Boylan. The respective notices follow:

Great battle Tokio. Lovemaking in Irish £200 damages. Gordon Bennett. Emigration swindle. Letter from His Grace William ✠. Ascot *Throwaway* recalls Derby of '92 when Captain Marshall's dark horse, *Sir Hugo*, captured the blue riband at long odds. New York disaster, thousand lives lost. Foot and Mouth. Funeral of the late Mr Patrick Dignam.[631]

The *Evening Telegraph* is a four-page, nine-column sheet. Its contents reflect the same balance of interests in modern society as is found in *Ulysses*. Of its 36 columns, the distribution is: advertisements, 9;

sport, 6; markets, 4; miscellaneous items from court and Parliament, 4; short features, 3, ranging from a reprinting of Tennyson's "Flower in the Crannied Wall" to notes on the number of M.P.'s named John and the news coverage given Theodore Roosevelt's daughter on her visit to the St. Louis exposition.

The feature story of the day is "GAELIC LEAGUE AND LOVE AFFAIRS, AMUSING CORRESPONDENCE, VERDICT FOR £200," three columns devoted to a breach-of-promise suit brought by a Miss Maggie Delany, singer and Gaelic enthusiast, against Frank P. Burke, secretary of the Gaelic Society of Kilkenny, who sponsored her vocal lessons and acted as stage manager for her. The press comments that this "was a busy part, but the defendant found time for abstraction, as lovers will." The story proceeds with the reading of love letters in Irish, the plaintiff's desiring to find out "the reason why he was taking such an interest in her," and asserting that "I took your word, and I believed you were a gentleman." Since Joyce quotes so much of the rest of the paper verbatim, it is surprising that this story made no more appeal to his sense of the ludicrous. Or perhaps Frank P. Burke, concert manager, is the model for Boylan?

The first page consists of eight columns of business notices, only the right-hand margin devoted to brief items of interest, "GLEANED FROM ALL SOURCES." Among the amusements listed, we read of *Leah*, playing at the Gaiety, of the "Tremendous Success" of the Elster-Grimes Grand Opera Company in *The Lily of Killarney* at the Queens. The Empire Palace Theatre of Gaieties features Marie Kendal, and the Theatre Royal boasts "The World Renowned Comedian"

Eugene Stratton, and the forthcoming *Fun at the
Bristol*. The role which these attractions play in
Ulysses has been noted.

Page 2 has a margin of advertisements (including
Plasto the hatter), then the masthead with a leader on
"THE AMERICAN HORROR," the "Slocum" disaster. A
double-column spread describes the forthcoming Gordon Bennett motor race in Germany, mentioned by
Cunningham in the funeral carriage.[96] A map of the
course and three pen sketches are printed. The last
column, "THE WAR," is subtitled "Big Battle at Telis-
sa," the third line reading "Russian Defeat."

The facing page features the breach-of-promise suit,
with crude cuts of the principals, and another item
on the motor race, subheaded "Racing Cars in Danger from Blazing Petrol." A story of a "Bogus Emigration Agent" appears. Under "SPORTING" we read:

ASCOT MEETING

THE GOLD CUP

THE OUTSIDER WINS

From a weather point of view the Cup day was the most en-
joyable of the three, the sun shone forth with great power and a
refreshing wind swept across the Heath. . . . .

The Ascot Gold Cup . . . . was, of course, the principal attraction of the afternoon. . . . . The four runners to-day was a
fair average for the race, and these included last year's winner,
Maximum II.

Maximum II is the French horse that Bantam Lyons
looked up so eagerly in the newspaper which Bloom
was about to throw away at 10:30 in the morning.[84]
The journal finds it not surprising that Zinfandel was
the favorite "after his display in the Coronation Cup

at Epsom," the race that Lenehan referred to at lunch in Byrne's ordinary.[171] The account continues:

However the despised one created a great surprise, as with the exception of being once headed by Sceptre, he made all the racing, and won in the style of a thorough stayer. . . . .

3—The Gold Cup, values 1000 sovs., with 3000 sovs. in specie in addition, out of which the second shall receive 700 sovs., and the third 300 sovs., added to a sweepstakes of 20 sovs. each, h. ft., for entire colts and fillies. Two miles and a half.

Mr. F. Alexander's THROWAWAY, by Rightaway-Theale
5 yrs. 9 st 4 lb. . . . . .W. Lane 1
Lord Howard de Walden's ZINFANDEL, 4 yrs. 9 st. . . . .
M. Cannon 2
Mr. W. Bass's SCEPTRE, 5 yrs. 9 st 4 lb. . . . . .O. Madden 3
Mr. J. de Bremond's MAXIMUM II, 5 yrs. 9 st 4 lb.. . .G. Stern 0

(Winner trained by Braime)

Race started at 3.5.
Betting 5 to 4 on Zinfandel, 7 to 4 agst Sceptre.
10 to 1 agst Maximum II, 20 to 1 agst Throwaway (off).

The transcript given by Joyce is almost word for word (the names of the mare Theale and the trainer Braime being misspelled), with the additional facetious remark about Lyons' horse, "not in yet but expected any minute."[632] It is interesting to note, too, the accuracy of Lenehan's statement in the hospital about Lane's bringing in three winners during the day[408]—in the Gold Cup at 3:00, the New Stakes at 3:30, and the St. James Palace Stakes at 4:30. Joyce fans may enjoy comparing Lenehan's version of the race at the hospital with the news account:

THE RACE

Throwaway set a fair pace to Sceptre, with Maximum II last, till fairly in the line for home, when Sceptre slightly headed Throwaway, and Zinfandel took close order with him. Throw-

away, however, stayed on, and won cleverly at the finish by a
length; three parts of a length divided second and third.

Time—4 mins, 33 2-5 secs.

In the column adjoining the racing form we read of
"Dublin University Bicycle Sports," the announcement of which annoyed Bloom.[95] "The weather, after
a fine morning, broke down at the time of the meeting, but afterwards the atmospheric conditions tem-
pered." The band of the Second Seaforth Highlanders
was present. Joyce introduces the band in the "Wandering Rocks" episode: The band prevents Artifoni
from catching his tram,[225] and later its blaring rendition of "My Girl's a Yorkshire Girl" provides an accompaniment to the cavalcade.[250]

In the account of the events at College Park we
read of the exploits of W. E. Wylie, the brother of
Gerty MacDowell's beau ideal, Reggy.[343] Wylie won
the second heat of the half-mile bicycle handicap in
1 minute, 17 seconds; was second in the finals; second
also in the two-mile handicap; but failed to place in
the one-mile club championship. It was a busy day
for W. E.

In *Ulysses*, while the cavalcade passes, Joyce notes
that "the quartermile flat handicappers, M. C. Green
['Greene' in the *Telegraph*], H. Thrift, T. M. Patey, C.
Scaife, J. B. Jeffs ['Jones'], G. N. Morphy [*sic*], F. Ste-
venson, C. Adderly, and W. C. Huggard [not in the *Telegraph*] started in pursuit."[250] This is the same order in
which the identical characters are mentioned by the
sports editor in the account of the fourth event of the
meet!

Among the political notes there is a reference to a
parliamentary discussion of the British ban on native

Irish sports, one of the conversational topics parodied in the scene at Kiernan's.[310]

The last page of the paper contains full market reports, including American securities, such as Chesapeake and Ohio, Erie ordinary, and U.S. Steel (at 9 and a fraction); a large box advertises Grape Nuts! Half a column is devoted to the APPALLING AMERICAN DISASTER, with subheads, EXCURSION STEAMER ON FIRE and 485 BODIES RECOVERED.

Of the items noticed by Bloom in the paper, all can be found save the announcement of H. du Boyes, the letter of His Grace William, Archbishop, and the reference to the dark horse that won the Derby. The rest are there—*Leah; The Lily of Killarney;* Marie Kendal; Eugene Stratton; the "Slocum"; the Gordon Bennett, Ascot, bicycle, and relay races; the Highland band; lovemaking in Irish; the Russian defeat! Into this matrix of fact are interwoven the narrative additions; the foot-and-mouth essay by Mr. Deasy, placed by Stephen;[36] and the clever account of Dignam's funeral, with its amusing errors. Upon four pages of newsprint Joyce has erected the foundations of his fictional world!

As an aid to verisimilitude, many prominent public personages are introduced. We hear much of Charles Stewart Parnell, of course, for the shadow of his failure colors the entire book. Then there are many references to the leaders of the Irish revival. A. E. actually appears for a moment, "beard and bicycle," chatting with a bohemian young woman disciple.[163] Mary Anderson is mentioned,[91] as is John McCormack.[92] The lunatic, Cashel Boyle O'Connor Fitzmaurice Tisdall Farrell, provides an eccentric in this swarming cast of characters; that he was a noted Dublin personage is indicated by his reappearance in Gogarty's *As I Was Walking down Sackville Street*, the memoirs of the model for Mulligan. Gogarty characterizes Farrell whimsically in his rambling observations of Dublin.

Most humorous of all the minor incidents of Bloom's day are the activities of the five sandwich men, H, E, L, Y, and 'S. They circulate through the streets of Dublin, advertising a sale, oblivious of their destiny as a ludicrous center of gravity in the modern epic. Bloom sees them on his way to lunch, Y lagging behind, munching bread;[152] they pass the florists as Boylan purchases fruit for Molly;[224] they continue dutifully on their rounds[226] and halt for the viceregal procession.[250] Bloom's impression of them merges with that of Breen's excitement over an anonymous postcard; in the brothel he envisions Breen bearing sandwich boards with the insulting message.[438]

Even more extensive are the themes associated with Bloom's own experiences during the day. Such a trifling detail as his failure to carry his house-key is touched upon. He realizes that he has failed to put it in his suit[56] but forgets to pick it up when he returns for breakfast[82] and has to climb in through the basement window when he arrives with Stephen early in the morning.[652]

The funeral of Paddy Dignam in Glasnevin Cemetery is one of the principal events of Bloom's day and pervades the narrative. Bloom thinks of mentioning it to the tradesman O'Rourke, as he goes off for kidneys;[58] as she is eating breakfast, Molly asks the time of the service,[63] which her husband verifies in the paper.[70] Bloom is dressed for the occasion, in a dark suit[57] that he is afraid of soiling.[68]

On the way to the baths he reflects that Corny probably got the job for the undertaker, O'Neill, and thinks of asking Kernan for tea when he sees him.[70] M'Coy, who is unable to attend, meets him and arranges to have his name registered.[74] Bloom's mood is dulled, he thinks the funeral a bore but charitably adds: "O well, poor fellow, it's not his fault."[82] He looks forward to the bath because of the glumness of the affair.[83]

At the funeral Bloom duly gives M'Coy's name, but his attention is attracted by a man in a brown mackintosh, who mysteriously joins the party at the grave, making the thirteenth. The reporter Hynes hastily takes down the names of those present, identifying the stranger as Macintosh.[110] This man of mystery sees the cavalcade in the afternoon.[251] He haunts Bloom's mind;[285] he is remembered when Bloom sees a stranger on the beach;[369] and the question of his identity was, we are told, one of the problems of the day.[714] A rat seen in the cemetery is equally unforgettable;[112] it lingers in his consciousness as a symbol of decay.

After the funeral Bloom goes to the newspaper office, where he sees Hynes, probably with the account of the service.[117] Again he feels that a funeral upsets a man's day.[123] On the way to lunch he discusses the funeral with Mrs. Breen. In answer to her solicitation he feels that he "may as well get her sympathy" and pretends that Dignam was a close friend.[154] Nosey Flynn, stupid as ever, fails to notice the mourning band while lunching with Bloom.[174]

We also hear of Simon Dedalus' attendance at the funeral, for he explains to his daughter that he has had to have a shave before going and has thus further depleted the family finances.[235] At the Ormond bar, too, Simon mentions meeting Bloom at the funeral.[284] The fund collected by Cunningham for the widow recurs throughout,[242] as do the negotiations for insurance, which so annoy the debt-collector at Kiernan's.[308] It is at Kiernan's that Alf Bergan expresses surprise at hearing of Dignam's death, insisting that he had seen Paddy only a moment before;[295] there, too, Bob Doran, in a maudlin state of intoxication, asks Bloom to express his sympathy.[308] Even Gerty MacDowell is connected with the event, for she explains that her father was kept home by gout.

At the brothel Dignam's spirit arises;[464] the man in the mackintosh is also seen,[475] as is the rat.[465] In one of his several incarnations, Bloom's father is dressed in that unforgettable brown mackintosh.[500] The newspaper account of the event, which was seen by Molly in the afternoon paper that Boylan brought her,[758] is read with great interest by Bloom in the cabman's shelter, where, with characteristically journalistic inaccuracy, there is a line of erratic type and a reference to "L. Boom"; the names of Stephen and M'Coy (who were absent) and the mystery man, now M'Intosh appear.[632] Bloom believes that the nonsense line probably slipped the proofreader when Bloom interrupted him about the Keyes advertisement.[120]

As Bloom retires, he thinks of the activities of the day,[713] as he had on the beach,[373] and a question directs our attention to the fact that the funeral party are all at rest.[689] No wonder that Molly, lying awake in bed, reflects that her husband was upset by the funeral,[727] though her thoughts come down to earth with a remark about the danger he incurred of tearing his trousers as he leapt into the areaway.[753] And, after all, she continues, the whole crowd attending the service were a pretty bad lot, and the funeral itself couldn't have been anything to match the romantic glamour of military burial.[759]

In keeping with the purpose of this part of the analysis, only the superficial references to the event are here noted. Bloom's musings on death naturally drift into channels of religious speculation, which may better be considered with kindred thoughts in the chapters on the philosophy of the novel.

The advertisement for Alexander Keyes's liquor store is Bloom's major business concern. It is in his mind at the cemetery, where the caretaker's keys suggest it;[106] immediately after the funeral he gets the copy from Red Murray,[115] takes it to the newspaper office, and explains the design—crossed keys in a circle, a reminder of the symbol of the Manx Parliament and hence an innuendo for Irish home rule.[119] It is necessary for him to negotiate with Keyes for a renewal. He telephones in vain,[126] then walks out to Dillon's auction-rooms to meet him.[128] Returning to the news office with the promise of a two months' renewal, he asks for a little extra puff from the editor.[144] His request is rudely snubbed,[145] nettling him for the rest of the day.

He plans to go to the National Library to check on the advertisement in a provincial paper;[159] he is led to the files by the obsequious Quaker librarian.[198]

Meanwhile, his mind is busied with the thought of his commission, with which he can buy a silk petticoat for his wife.[177] He also thinks of calling on Keyes but reconsiders, afraid of wearing out his welcome.[180] Later, his concern over the editor's snub mingles with the thought of the petticoat, which, in turn, is associated with the pulp romanticism of the book, *Sweets of Sin*, that he has just rented for Molly:

Must see him about Keyes's par. . . . For Raoul. Eat. If I net five guineas with those ads. The violet silk petticoats. Not yet. The sweets of sin.[256]

At Kiernan's he asks Hynes to help influence the editor,[318] and the phrase "that ad I must"[365] is a brief indication of his constant preoccupation with the problem of placing it. At twilight he recalls that he must nail the advertisement by working Hynes and Crawford, a thought suggested by his reflections on lingerie.[374] Alexander Keyes appears in the "Circe" visions, asking the glorified statesman Bloom, "When will we have our own house of keys?"[480] The Keyes theme also occurs briefly when the evening paper is read, [632] also as a type of an ideal advertisement in the catalogue of Bloom's life in the kitchen scene,[667] as one of the rites of the day,[713] and, finally, as one more sign of Molly's annoyance with her husband:

itll be a change the Lord knows to have an intelligent person to talk to about yourself not always listening to him and Billy Prescotts ad and Keyess ad and Tom the Devils ad then if anything goes wrong in their business we have to suffer . . . .[760]

Ironical conclusion of the odyssey of an advertisement! What starts as a mere matter of business routine becomes another source of Bloom's frustration, then merges into dreams of sexual satisfaction and generosity, only to be repudiated by Molly as she thinks of an ideal lover.

Three minor themes connected with Bloom's activities remain to be mentioned—the lemon-scented soap he purchases for Molly, the correspondence he is carrying on with Martha Clifford, and the volume, *Sweets of Sin*. Molly, who has finished the gothic romance, *Ruby: The Pride of the Ring*, with the contemptuous remark, "There's nothing smutty in it,"[64] has asked her husband to get another. He goes to the bookstall in mid-afternoon, turning the pages of the *Sweets of Sin*, and, much affected by what he reads, takes it. The phrases which haunt his mind through the day are a perfect parody of such pulp fiction:

> —*All the dollarbills her husband gave her were spent in the stores on wondrous gowns and costliest frillies. For him! For Raoul!*[232]

The bookseller recommends it—"That's a good one"[233]—and Bloom walks off with his pornographic treasure.

Henceforth it colors his erotic dreams. He goes to the Ormond bar, "bearing in his breast the sweets of sin," "bearing sweet sinful words."[254] His thoughts of spending his money from Keyes's advertisement for a silk petticoat echo the "Raoul" and "sin" phrases;[256] and a poster in the bar, picturing mermaids with hair streaming, suggests "For Raoul."[259] The "heaving embon" of the heroine of this romance comes to his mind as he hears the singing,[281] and the recall continues as he leaves the bar:

> Up the quay went Lionelleopold, naughty Henry with letter for Mady, with sweets of sin with frillies for Raoul . . . . [283]

His thoughts linger on "embon," "Raoul," and "frillies" while he walks on the beach in the twilight;[375] when he witnesses the vision of Boylan's assignation in the "Circe" scene, Bloom hears Molly address her lover as "Raoul."[551] His proud display of Molly's picture to Stephen at the shelter is colored by thoughts of his wife's *embonpoint*.[637] It is on a blank page of the *Sweets of Sin* that Stephen draws the Irish alphabet while they are conversing in the kitchen.[672] Upon retiring, Bloom mentions the new novel to Molly,[720] who later ruminates on what kind of book it may be.[750]

No less pervasive is the occurrence of the soap which Bloom carries in his pocket throughout the day. We are told of its purchase at the chemist's,[84] of its lodging in Bloom's hip-pocket in the funeral carriage,[86] of its hasty transfer to a coat-pocket at the cemetery,[99] of its retransfer to the hip-pocket in the news office,[122] of Bloom's fear of losing it as he dodges into the museum,[181] of its becoming sticky in his trousers,[282] of its penetrating odor,[369] of Bloom's patting it as he touches his pockets before entering Cohen's.[430] Confronted by the vision of Molly, he mentions his visit to the chemist, and the soap arises in the east, a new sun, singing.[433] Bloom washes his hands with it in the kitchen of his house, at which time its history is parenthetically recalled.[656]

Leopold's principal transgression, the writing of clandestine letters to Martha Clifford, is revealed through several key words—Plasto's, the hat-label which hides the card he uses at the post office to identify himself; Flower, his pseudonym; and perfume, for

Martha asks in her letter what kind of perfume Molly uses. Characteristically, the first reference to this phase of the hero's life is ambiguous, merely a statement that Bloom checks to see that a slip of paper is inside his hat.[56] The card is transferred to his pocket,[70] being no further identified until he presents it at the post office.[71] The letter is read and the card replaced behind the hatband.[78]

The letter itself represents a plausible intimation of the cast of Martha's mind; it is a speaking likeness of confessional letters everywhere: "Are you not happy in your home you poor little naughty boy?"[76] she inquires. And continuing alternately to scold and to beg to meet her correspondent, she pleads that he grant her request "before my patience are exhausted." In a typically incoherent sentence she concludes: "I have such a bad headache today and write *by return*." Her postscript inquires about Molly's perfume.[77]

This question about perfume lingers in Bloom's mind like a half-remembered phrase of music. He recollects it as he purchases the soap,[83] as he replaces the soap in his hip-pocket;[122] as he passes the *Irish Times*, in which he had advertised for a secretary;[157] as he hears the aria from *Martha* at the Ormond.[271]

While walking to the Ormond, he thinks of answering her letter,[257] buys paper en route,[259] and sits down to write as the aria from *Martha* is sung.[270] In his answer he pours out his loneliness,[275] the dominant theme of the chapter. On the beach he wonders whether he has mislaid her letter;[361] and at the brothel he is accused under his alias, Henry Flower,[447] whereupon Martha appears, crying "thou lost one," a recall of the *Martha* aria.[448] We are told, in the catalogue of his belongings, that three letters from her are already safely hidden,[705] to which is added the fourth.[707] He naturally omits mentioning Martha in his account of the day to his wife.[720]

Joyce's use of theme is ingeniously elaborate. More than a hundred key thematic words can be identified, most of them appearing several times. *Ulysses* is a book of many strands; its motifs are stated, developed, interwoven, modulated, and recapitulated in the manner of music. It is interesting to note that Dujardin, first exploiter of the stream-of-consciousness technique, acknowledged his indebtedness to Wagner's musical use of the leitmotiv. Concurrent with Joyce's work, Thomas Mann and Marcel Proust, each in his distinctive manner, used symbolic objects, words, scenes, and situations to develop their interpretations of life.

It remains to note several places in the narrative where Joyce recapitulates the themes of his epic. At twilight Bloom walks along the beach, tracing his activities:

Long day I've had. Martha, the bath, funeral, house of keys, museum with those goddesses, Dedalus' song. Then that bawler in Barney Kiernan's.[373]

Here the preceding chapters dealing with Bloom are reviewed in a natural fashion—Martha (the walk to the post office); the funeral; house of keys ("Aeolus"); museum (the conclusion of the lunch episode); Dedalus' song (the "Sirens"); Kiernan's (the "Cyclops").

A second recall occurs in the De Quincey parody. It is at the hospital; Bloom dreams of the past:

The voices blend and fuse in clouded silence: silence that is the infinite of space: and swiftly, silently the soul is wafted over regions of cycles of cycles of generations that have lived. A region where grey twilight ever descends, never falls on wide sagegreen pasturefields, shedding her dusk, scattering a perennial dew of stars.[407]

And in this setting of cosmic space and mystery, Bloom's meditations turn to the dreamland of the East, Agendath Netaim; to thoughts of metempsychosis and parallax; to Martha.[407] While the earlier summary is conscious and intellectual, this is pervaded with a dreamlike emotion.

The "Circe" hallucinations are themselves elaborate visions of the preoccupations and frustrations of the day. To elaborate these would be to re-write the chapter, the longest in the novel. At one point the daughters of Erin, summoned to Bloom's mind by a phrase on his lips, chant together a litany, each phrase echoing one of the day's episodes. The exit from the brothel is imagined as a rout pursuing Bloom, the "hue and cry zigzag gallops in hot pursuit."[571] Here we find most of the characters of the book, practically all of whom have snubbed or insulted Bloom during the day.

As Bloom retires, we are given two more résumés of his day. The major events are summarized as holy rites[713] and as a digest of his conversation with Molly before falling asleep.[720]

In such fashion does Joyce demonstrate the role of sensation and experience in the consciousness of man. *Ulysses* is a medley of the permanence and change in life, showing that memory (voice of the past) and desire (hope for the future) mingle and intertwine in the psychological present.

V

BLOOM ALONE: *THE ISOLATION OF THE INDIVIDUAL*

Under the sandwichbell lay on a bier of bread one last, one lonely, last sardine of summer. Bloom alone.[284]

ULYSSES is one of the loneliest of books. The constant burden of Thomas Wolfe, "O lost, and by the wind grieved," is here set forth in comprehensive and objective terms. What in Wolfe seems the tragic cry of an individual soul is here a pervasive condition of modern civilization. Trams may circulate through the city at their scheduled times, individuals pass and repass each other on the streets, but of genuine community there can be none. If religion, politics, even marriage, are devoid of soul-satisfying significance, the chill emptiness of Bloom's day is to be expected.

Leopold Bloom, the most completely characterized figure in modern fiction, occupies himself with trivial tasks and futile hopes. Filled with yearning for his deceased son and carrying in his memory the recollection of his father's pathetic suicide, he makes frequent halfhearted attempts at social intercourse, only to be slighted. A gradual crescendo of interest in the character of Stephen Dedalus leads to a final meeting, in which Bloom envisions his lost son Rudy. But when he walks home with Stephen in the chill hours after midnight, the very style echoes the impersonality of the encounter. Inspired to renewed busyness by his new-found acquaintance, he attempts desperately to pierce to the level of intimacy; Stephen, walking by his side, preoccupied with his own isolation, replies in the most offhand and noncommittal fashion. As they converse over cocoa in the kitchen on Eccles Street, Bloom's thoughts turn to the inevitable loneliness of modern metropolitan existence. In the coldness of question-and-answer technique Joyce states that Bloom "reflected that the progressive extension of the field of individual development and experience was regressively accompanied by a restriction of the converse domain of interindividual relations."[65]

In this modern inferno—better, limbo—that is the twentieth-century city, each of the characters is haunted by a sense of loneliness. Stephen, of course, and Bloom; but also Gerty MacDowell and the voluptuous Molly. Even the extroverts of the story, one feels, fail to conceal the emptiness in their souls or to escape the yearning for companionship.

Thoughts of his lost son are seldom far from Bloom's consciousness. Opening the letter from Milly, his daughter, now visiting in Mullingar, he recalls that Rudy would now be eleven, and, we are told, "his vacant face stared pitying at the postscript."[66] In the funeral carriage he is a trifle annoyed at Simon Dedalus' concern over his son but immediately reflects:

He is right. Something to hand on. If little Rudy had lived. See him grow up. Hear his voice in the house. Walking beside Molly in an Eton suit. My son. Me in his eyes. Strange feeling it would be.[88]

He thinks of Rudy's little grave-plot and sensitively turns his face as the clods of earth are hurled upon Dignam's coffin.[109]

Indeed, the loss of his son has affected his own participation in marital relationships.[165] Consequently, much of his eroticism, so offensive to some readers, is directly traceable to his strong sense of human isolation. Passing a lingerie shop on his way to lunch, physical desire is clearly associated with loneliness:

High voices. Sunwarm silk. Jingling harnesses. All for a woman, home and houses, silk webs, silver, rich fruits, spicy from Jaffa. Agendath Netaim. Wealth of the world.

A warm human plumpness settled down on his brain. His brain yielded. Perfume of embraces all him assailed. With hungered flesh obscurely, he mutely craved to adore.[166]

Rapt in similar meditations, Bloom sups at the Ormond Hotel. From the bar come the strains of "When First I Saw That Form Endearing," sung by Simon Dedalus. Bloom signals the waiter to open the door to the bar, and the music stirs his soul:

Good, good to hear: sorrow from them each seemed to from both depart when first they heard.[269]

His thoughts drift to his first meeting with Molly,[271] and he reflects on the essential pathos of life, that love increases the sense of loss:

Cruel it seems. Let people get fond of each other: lure them on. Then tear asunder. Death.[273]

And inevitably his memory of Rudy arises—"No son. Rudy. Too late now."[280]

The birth of Mina Purefoy's son at the hospital in the evening brings to his mind the pitiful body of the infant Rudy, wrapped in a "fair corselet of lamb's wool" that he be not entirely exposed.[384] Again he thinks that "there is none now to be for Leopold, what Leopold was for Rudolph."[407]

The climax of the day, the rescue of Stephen from

his offensive companions, which had been in his mind at the hospital,[384] comes as they leave Bella Cohen's, early in the morning. The silent, unseeing figure of a child of eleven, dressed in an Eton suit with fantastic accouterments, appears before his eyes. To Bloom's ejaculation of happiness, the fairy boy does not respond, continuing his reading.[593]

No less does the memory of his father's suicide haunt his mind.[75] At the funeral he recalls the parting message, "Be good to Athos," and thinks of the death of the faithful dog soon after.[89] The custom of driving a stake through the heart of a suicide appalls him, "as if it wasn't broken already."[95] The father, Rudolph Virag, stern, but kindly, plays a large part in the drunken visions in the "Circe" scene, and in the early morning hours a topic of conversation—writing— turns Bloom's thoughts to the suicide note, penned in a lonely hotel lobby eighteen years before.[669] The observation of the vigil a year ago had, we learn, prevented his attendance at the funeral of Stephen's mother[680] and will keep him from accompanying Molly on her concert tour.[100] The suicide note itself reposes in his drawer.[708] We learn in strictly impersonal detail the pathetic last days of this aged man, grief-stricken over the death of his wife, suffering from acute neuralgia[708] and progressive senescence.[709]

One might expect that the presence of his daughter Milly would alleviate Bloom's brooding loneliness. But Milly is too closely associated in his mind with his unfaithful wife, and he feels the distance between father and daughter acutely. He recollects her early flirtatiousness,[63] thinks of her vanity with "troubled affection,"[66] concludes that mother and daughter are alike, "same thing watered down."[88] He thinks of visiting her,[67] as a surprise,[98] but is afraid of the possible intrusion—"Who knows? Ways of the world."[365] She is, after all, a flirt like her mother[362] and bears many resemblances to the lascivious cat in the kitchen![678] Bloom's distrust of his wife is transferred to his daughter. She can never take the place of his son Rudy, though he treasures the drinking cup she gave him[661] and has many happy memories of her childhood.

Bloom's most pathetic reminiscences are those of his early love for his voluptuous wife. He is proud of her dark Mediterranean beauty, despite the jealousy he feels so acutely. At the chemist's he reflects that the wax of the lotion he is ordering "brings out the darkness of her eyes."[83] Walking to lunch, he thinks of her smooth-fitting gray dress of ten years before, and adds: "Happy. Happier then."[153] Dreaming of those past days, he remembers her concert with D'Arcy, the wind blowing her skirts on her way home, the soft plop of her stays on the bed.[154] He can feel "the thrill in the air" when she sings in concert.[81] The old Harp Theatre again turns his mind to earlier days, and he puzzles over the passing of time:

I was happier then. Or was that I? Or am I now I? Twenty-eight I was. She was twenty-three when we left Lombard street west something changed. Could never like it again after Rudy. Can't bring back time. Like holding water in your hand. Would you go back to then?[165]

The warmth of the Burgundy on his tongue at lunch brings a total recall of his flirtation with Molly on the

Hill of Howth years ago. Sensing again her cool caress, her lips, her figure, he concludes his meditation with a pathetic anticlimax:

She kissed me. I was kissed. All yielding she tossed my hair. Kissed, she kissed me.

Me. And me now.[173]

Though he carry on a clandestine correspondence with Martha Clifford and notice with avid interest all females he chances to meet, it is to the memory of his bride Molly that his thoughts return. Even as he sits in the Ormond dining-room to pen his reply to Martha, he dreams of his first meeting with Molly and of the yellow-and-black costume she wore.[271] A melancholy note in the music echoes his sadness:

The voice of dark age, of unlove, earth's fatigue made grave approach, and painful, come from afar, from hoary mountains, called on good men and true.[278]

A concert that he attended with Molly comes to mind, and he visualizes her low-cut crocus dress.[280] He concludes his letter with the pathetic postscript, "I feel so sad . . . . so lonely";[275] loneliness is the dominant mood of the Ormond episode, nine of the sixteen uses of the word and its derivatives being found within these pages.

The settling twilight on the beach is another occasion for Bloom's memories of Molly. He thinks of her physical radiance,[368] the scene on Howth again comes to mind,[370] her Moorish eyes are remembered.[371] But, like Rip Van Winkle—"All changed. Forgotten. The young are old"[371]—he knows that the past can never return. Even Howth, he feels, is old, too:

Far out over the sands the coming surf crept, grey. Howth settled for slumber tired of long days, of yumyum rhododendrons (he was old) and felt gladly the night breeze lift, ruffle his fell of ferns.[372]

At the cab-shelter he displays to Stephen with obvious pride a faded and crumpled old photograph of his wife[636] and thinks with panic, "suppose she was gone," when he returns home.[637] It is with this background of his longing that we can understand more clearly his sexual ambitions, so coldly set forth in the catechism chapter[707] and possibly excuse the intimacy of his homecoming.[719]

Closely related to his longing for his wife is his timid embarrassment in regard to her lover. As with such tender subjects, Boylan's name recurs frequently, and Bloom's distraction is equally evident. He is seen by Jack Power from the funeral carriage, "airing his quiff," and Bloom studies his nails.[91] Nosey Flynn mentions him at lunch, and Bloom "raised his eyes and met the stare of a bilious clock."[170] Bloom's first encounter with his rival at the door of the museum is rendered in dramatic fashion:

Straw hat in sunlight. Tan shoes. Turnedup trousers. It is. It is.
His heart quopped softly.[180]

After a hasty and nervous search for the cake of soap, he ducks into the portals of the museum. He next sights Boylan entering the Ormond. With a repetition of the fatal "it is," he forgets to pay the store clerk,[259] then discreetly enters the dining-room instead of the bar.[261] Seeing Boylan leave and realizing that his shame is to be consummated, he wishes for more music, "Keep my mind off,"[276] and laughs self-consciously at his own jokes. The subject of Boylan

comes up again at Kiernan's (Boylan is the sort whom
everyone knows), and Bloom steers the conversation
back to tennis.[312] In the brothel the act of writing idly
on the tablecloth recalls the Ormond Hotel and his
letter to Martha;[549] the image of Boylan appears to
re-enact the assignation. A final reference to the gay
blade of Dublin brings the usual self-conscious distraction; as Corley suggests to Stephen that Boylan
arrange to get him a job, Bloom gazes intently at a
dredger anchored in the river.[603]

Just as Boylan is everywhere the center of attention, so Bloom suffers ridicule wherever he goes.
Truly a wandering Jew, he is at the mercy of the gibes
of friends and strangers alike. At the funeral, Menton
asks Lambert about him and exclaims at Molly's ever
marrying him.[105] He is snubbed by Menton as he calls
attention to the dent in his hat,[114] pursued by urchins
as he leaves the news office,[128] insulted by Crawford in
regard to the Keyes ad.[145] Mulligan exclaims "sheeny"
as he appears at the library;[198] Bloom tiptoes self-consciously past the group when he leaves.[215] Lenehan
tells a joke about his shame with great relish.[231] The
drinkers at Kiernan's enjoy ridiculing him,[297] especially the two loafers, the Citizen and the debt-collector. The apotheosis of his shame is the exit from
Bella Cohen's. Having charitably thrown money on
the table to pay for the chandelier broken by Stephen,
he is pursued, we are told in a stage direction, by the
phantoms of practically the entire dramatis personae
of the book.[571]

The fact that Bloom is a Jew adds to his sense of isolation. Mr. Deasy jokes that Ireland had never persecuted the Jews only because she never let them in.[37]

Actually, only 3,898 Jews registered in the census of
1901, or eight in ten thousand of the population. The
selection of a Jew as the central figure of *Ulysses* has
puzzled some critics. Is it not because the Jew, like
the Irishman, has been homeless for centuries? And
because the Jew is the prototype of modern commercial existence? Also because his native shrewdness
makes him a perceptive commentator?

Mr. Deasy delivers himself of an anti-Semitic
speech to Stephen as he pays him. It is the old story—
"England is in the hands of the jews .... And they
are the signs of a nation's decay."[34] Cunningham
gibes at Bloom behind his back in the funeral carriage,
in ridiculing a passing Jew.[92] The anti-Semitism of the
Citizen in Kiernan's leads to violence, but Bloom has
the courage to retort

—Mendelssohn was a jew and Karl Marx and Mercadante
and Spinoza. And the Saviour was a jew and his father was a
jew.[336]

Pathetically, Bloom fears to let Martha see him in
profile;[363] and he makes an effort to convince Stephen
of the injustice of prejudice in his conversation in the
shelter:

—Jews, he softly imparted in an aside in Stephen's ear, are
accused of ruining. Not a vestige of truth in it, I can safely
say.[628]

He receives the recital of an anti-Semitic song by
Stephen in hurt silence.[676]

It is this estrangement from family and acquaintances that Bloom hopes to escape. He is fascinated by
the East, largely because to his imagination it represents asylum. It is first suggested to him by the

thought of the sunrise. Before his romantic mind arise scenes of the Orient—turbaned men, crowded noisy streets, the shadows of the mosques at twilight.[57] At the butcher's he picks up a brochure describing a colonizing scheme in the Near East. Orange and olive groves fill his busy mind as he notes the title, *Agendath Netaim*.[60] But a shadow passes over the sun, and a gray mood descends upon him. Reverting to his habitual loneliness and disillusion, he reflects:

> No, not like that. A barren land, bare waste. Volcanic lake, the dead sea: no fish, weedless, sunk deep in the earth. No wind would lift those waves, grey metal, poisonous foggy waters. Brimstone they called it raining down: the cities of the plain: Sodom, Gomorrah, Edom. All dead names. A dead sea in a dead land, grey and old.[61]

And the hereditary curse of Judaism comes to mind, how these forgotten people "wandered far away over all the earth, captivity to captivity."[61]

Yet after breakfast he still thinks of "Agenda,"[68] and throughout the day visions of ideal happiness will be associated in his mind with the original home of his people. His dreams are aroused further at the Oriental Tea Company windows by the advertisement of Ceylon tea:

> The far east. Lovely spot it must be: the garden of the world, big lazy leaves to float about on, cactuses, flowery meads, snaky lianas they call them. . . . . Lethargy. Flowers of idleness.[70]

Passing the lingerie windows, later in the morning, his visions of fair women suggest silk, spices, and "Agendath Netaim. Wealth of the world."[166] At lunch his reflections on food turn to the orange groves of the project;[172] as he dodges into the museum, we discover that he has kept the folder.[181] With ironic undertone

Joyce shows us Boylan dashing impatiently to his assignation, past the porkshop which first suggested romantic love to the deceived husband.[275]

That Bloom's association with the East is one of personal fulfilment and absence of sexual rivalry is shown by his pathetic ruminations at twilight on the beach. Perfume, Raoul, embon, Molly's eyes merge into one thought, with the wistful note "Agendath."[375] The haunting sense of loneliness arises again at the hospital, when Bloom thinks of his lost Rudy; and his meditations, translated into the style of De Quincey, show the passing of his dreamland:

all is gone. Agendath is a waste land, a home of screechowls and the sandblind upupa. Netaim, the golden, is no more.[407]

As he lights the incense in his kitchen from the taper formed by the carefully saved brochure, we realize that, in truth, Netaim is no more.[691]

But, meanwhile, its place in his affections has been taken by Stephen. Indeed, it is toward the meeting of Stephen and Bloom that the entire movement of the novel seems to point. We remember Bloom's melancholy over his son's death and his ever growing attraction to young Dedalus. The two almost meet at the newspaper office, but Bloom steps out to see Keyes about the advertisement[128] just before Stephen enters.[130] At the library their paths cross for an instant.[215] A third time they almost meet, as Bloom leaves the bookstall with the *Sweets of Sin*,[233] shortly before Dedalus arrives.[238] When at last they do meet at the hospital, the elder is "loth to leave" and joins in the conversation.[382] They immediately find in common an aversion to the ribald disrespect shown by their companions.[383] Bloom worries about Stephen's irresponsible acquaintances;[384] but the talk flows on in the same channels, for such "seemed the only bond of union among tempers so divergent"[403] (another commentary on the lack of community today). It is when the stupefied Stephen is rescued from the brothel that their intimacy begins, at which time Bloom, we recall, sees the vision of his dead son Rudy.[593]

Yet this meeting cannot be so propitious as the lonely Bloom hopes it to be. Their divergence is noted as they walk homeward. Passing Beresford Place, Stephen thinks of Ibsen (one recalls similar literary associations in the *Portrait*[204]); the advertising solicitor's mind resounds with a jingle about a near-by bakery:

O tell me where is fancy bread? At Rourke's the baker's, it is said.[598]

With forced eagerness, Bloom pursues the conversation. He warns Stephen about his companions,[598] speaks favorably about Simon Dedalus,[604] but to no avail. Stephen walks on in silence or vents a few contemptuous remarks, such as the dampening of Bloom's enthusiasm over the Italian they hear spoken —"They were haggling over money."[606] Likewise, Bloom's solicitude for the plight of prostitutes is met with scornful indictment of Ireland at large:

—In this country people sell much more than she ever had and do a roaring trade.[617]

Bloom turns the conversation to religion and receives a weary and evasive reply,[618] whereupon he urges Stephen to partake of what was called coffee at the shelter where they lingered.[619] A rude remark on his table manners passes unnoticed. No wonder that, after the lurid tales of the seaman had been ended, interest "was starting to flag somewhat all round."[622]

Bloom enjoys no more favorable response from his discussions of anti-Semitism or patriotism, being answered with the curt "We can't change the country. Let us change the subject."[629] Nevertheless, he continues to think of the advantages of intellectual stimulation that he might receive from cultivating Stephen's acquaintance and, with his never failing ingenuity, imagines that perhaps it would help him to one of his cherished goals, that of writing pulp fiction![631] His paternal instincts are aroused by the thought of Stephen's loss of his job, his separation from his father,[603] his inadequate diet.[640] So, though the stranger seemed "a bit standoffish and not over effusive," Bloom timidly proffers hospitality for the night.[641] An almost saintly pity is shown as the younger man is led out of the shelter:

—It will (the air) do you good, Bloom said, meaning also the walk, in a moment. The only thing is to walk then you'll feel a different man. It's not far. Lean on me.[644]

A little upset that Stephen does not share his taste for light opera,[645] Bloom nevertheless conjures up dreams of a happy friendship as they walk along in silence. Stephen might study music and perhaps reach the height of giving a grand concert on King Street! He could dabble with his writing in the meantime![648] Perhaps a good-natured family joke, this, for Elliot Paul recalls that Nora Joyce was always a little dubious about her husband's profession—only a writer, she said to Paul, he who had once sung with John McCormack.

Reaching home, Bloom makes cocoa for his guest, giving him his favorite cup and even using some of Molly's morning ration of cream.[661] These gestures pass unnoticed. Despite the cruel distance between them, Bloom even goes on to dream of Stephen's marrying Milly and giving Molly Italian lessons.[679] With the reluctance of Stephen to respond to any of these overtures, it is no wonder that Bloom ends his day with contemplations of the ultimate in loneliness, "the cold of interstellar space."[689]

So carefully integrated are the details of the fact-crammed chronicle of Bloom, that one can reconstruct his past from his numerous recollections. Born in 1866, as we know from his memories of his father's suicide,[75] as well as from the factual chapter,[663] he is now thirty-eight. He attended a school conducted by a Mrs. Ellis[697] and remembers his high-school teacher, Vance, who taught the law of Archimedes[71] and the colors of the spectrum,[370] cracking his knuckles as he lectured. His first verse was written at the age of eleven;[661] he finished high school in 1880.[687] His father's suicide occurred in 1886.[669]

In 1887, an *annus mirabilis* in this tale, he met Molly. It was at Mat Dillon's, and the couple were paired off in a game of musical chairs.[271] Menton recalls being attracted to her,[105] and Bloom remembers the solicitor's irritation at the courtship—"hate at first sight."[113] He was an agent for the stationery firm of Hely's at the time, Menton remembers,[105] a job he got the year he married.[153]

Their love was consummated on the Hill of Howth.[173] They were married in 1888, on October 8, Bloom being twenty-two, Molly eighteen.[720] A valentine of that year is recalled, an acrostic on his nickname.[662] Milly was born on June 15, 1889, as we first learn from Bloom's reflection on his daughter's letter[66] and later from the catechism chapter.[677] They lived on Lombard Street until 1893;[651] in 1894 Rudy died,[165] eleven days old.[721] These, we recall, were the happiest years of their marriage. Then they resided at the City Arms Hotel, where Leopold acted the Samaritan for Mrs. Riordan.[664] The job at Hely's had been followed by one at the cattle market, from which Bloom still recalls with distress the pathetic lament of the victims led to slaughter.[168]

A residence at Ontario Terrace in 1895[677] is chiefly remembered as the scene of an unfortunate affair with the servant girl, Mary Driscoll, whose apparition accuses him in the brothel[452] and who is regarded by Molly as a common thief.[724] Temporary lodgings in Raymond Terrace,[88] about 1893, and Holles Street,[757] about 1897,[677] cannot be exactly dated, or the jobs at Thom's, the printer's,[336] which followed Hely's,[153] and at Drimmie's, insurance agents,[754] neither of which Bloom was able to hold.[757] At the lowest ebb of the family fortunes Bloom had been unemployed, and Molly had earned some money by playing the piano in a coffee shelter.[264]

Here is a true diary of a commonplace man. Leopold Blooms crowd the streets of all cities, for the most part ignored and forgotten. Burdened by domestic and financial cares, they pass like Bloom from job to job, never achieving success, security, or, what is even more serious, never coming any closer to the will-o'-the-wisp of personal fulfilment. Yet upon their hearts there lies the weight of buried dreams.

The story of Leopold Bloom is a dramatic exemplification of the corruption of innate decency by an alien environment. How pertinent are the words of Stephen Hero, protesting against the deadening stupor of Ireland! Though ostensibly a diatribe against the church, the tenor of the remarks is singularly appropriate:

Exultation of the mind before joyful beauty, exultation of the body in free confederate labours, every natural impulse towards health and wisdom and happiness had been corroded. . . . .[194]

Leopold Bloom is completely and concisely characterized in the words of Émile Gebhart's description of Homer's Ulysses. This statement is quoted by Valéry Larbaud, in his pioneer discussion of Joyce's novel on December 7, 1921, reprinted in *Criterion*, October, 1922: "A man, loving his country, his wife, his father and his friends, noted for sympathy and benevolence, not free of human frailty."

VI CURSED JESUIT: *THE INTELLEC-TUAL IN MODERN SOCIETY*

you have the cursed jesuit strain in you, only it's injected the wrong way.[10]

IF THE little man Leopold Bloom is condemned to an irrepressible loneliness and isolation throughout the day, his plight is magnified and given an intellectual, as well as an emotional, basis in the character of Stephen. Sensitive to the point of neurasthenia, possessing a literary gift which is doomed to neglect in a land which extols political oratory, prize titbits, and sentimental song, Stephen is a man without family, church, or calling. His very qualities contribute to his plight. Pride, which leads him to consider himself a man apart and one destined to contribute a prophetic message to mankind, merely stands in the way of his making any satisfying human contacts. He has turned from the church, refusing to be its slave. His superiority to his family isolates him from them, and his sensitivity makes Mulligan and his other associates repellent. He is incapable of love and of friendship and, in contrast to the sociable Bloom, even unable to enjoy passing acquaintanceships.

To protect himself against the rebuffs of the world Stephen assumes a mask of cynical materialism. In answer to Haines's eager interest in his sayings and his expressed intention of making a collection of them, Stephen asks coldly whether he would make money by it,[17] an attitude repeated in the library scene, when

Best encourages him to write an article on his theory of *Hamlet*.[211] Yet he is constantly imposed upon, lending money to Mulligan,[12] running errands for his schoolmaster, Deasy.[36] He feels Haines to be a usurper[24] and his wealthy charges at the school to be in position to take advantage of him.[25] Like Hamlet—indeed, like Ireland—he feels himself regarded as a social inferior, tolerated rather than respected:

A jester at the court of his master, indulged and disesteemed, winning a clement master's praise.[26]

Yet, as Professor MacHugh pointedly remarks in the news office, it is difficult to know whether he is more bitter against others than against himself.[147] He is sensitive about the lack of appreciation of his literary gifts, but even more sensitive about his own failure to produce anything deserving praise.[43] He justifies himself in renouncing his mother's plea to pray for her on the grounds of his own independence, yet this refusal costs him many a bitter memory.

Like Hamlet, who knew not "seems," Stephen is utterly uncompromising. To Haines's question as to whether he was a believer "in the narrow sense of the word," he answers that "there's only one sense of the word."[21] His intransigence at his mother's deathbed puzzles Mulligan. His downright sincerity has cost him so much in the past that he can well say, "I fear those big words . . . . which make us so unhappy,"[32] for unhappiness is all that his own stubborn integrity has brought him. He detests action,[573] feeling himself an unwilling participant in the struggle of life:

I am among them, among their battling bodies in a medley, the joust of life. . . . . Jousts. Time shocked rebounds, shock by shock. Jousts, slush and uproar of battles, the frozen deathspew of the slain, a shout of spear spikes baited with men's bloodied guts.[33]

Thus Stephen is a far more isolated figure than the extrovert Bloom. Haunted throughout the day by the memory of his dying mother and his recalcitrant refusal to pray at her bedside, he is an image of lonely pride. The odor of rosewood and ashes lingers in his thoughts, at breakfast,[7] at school as he helps tutor a boy in algebra,[28] as he walks on the beach;[39] his mother's corpse haunts him in night-town.[565] The phrase *Liliata rutilantium*, from the prayer he refused to utter, likewise sounds as a knell to his spirits. As he dresses, he recalls the scene;[12] when he walks off to school, it accompanies his paces;[24] it interrupts his meditations on Hamlet in the library,[188] appears again in the "Circe" scene,[564] and still resounds as he hears the bells of St. George's clock tolling the hour of 2:00 A.M.[688] The medieval phrase *Agenbite of Inwit*, "prick of conscience," title of a fourteenth-century religious treatise, is also linked with his sense of guilt, occurring in every scene in which Stephen appears.

Nine days before this, a man had drowned, we are informed by a boatman whom Stephen meets after breakfast.[23] The image will not leave his mind. It is immediately associated with thoughts of his mother. As he walks along the beach, he reflects:

His human eyes scream to me out of horror of his death. I . . . With him together down. . . I could not save her.[46]

It also suggests the lines from the *Tempest*, "full fathom five" and from "Lycidas," "Sunk though he be.''[50] The association recurs as he meets his sister at the bookstalls in the afternoon,[240] for Stephen feels responsible for his mother's death; Mulligan's taunts fail to disperse the feeling of guilt:

In a dream, silently, she had come to him, her wasted body within its loose graveclothes giving off an odour of wax and rosewood, her breath bent over him with mute secret words, a faint odour of wetted ashes.

Her glazing eyes, staring out of death, to shake and bend my soul. On me alone. The ghostcandle to light her agony. Ghostly light on the tortured face. Her hoarse loud breath rattling in horror, while all prayed on their knees. Her eyes on me to strike me down. *Liliata rutilantium te confessorum turma circumdet: iubilantium te virginum chorus excipiat.*

Ghoul! Chewer of corpses!

No, mother. Let me be and let me live.[12]

From this passage it can easily be seen that the stream-of-consciousness style in Joyce's hands is capable of reaching emotional depths yet untouched by conventional fiction, that it forms a striking parallel to Shakespeare's use of the soliloquy.

Stephen's brooding spirit colors his meditations on history. Man delights not him, and the achievements of man in the past are mere weavings of the irresponsible wind of events—"The void awaits surely all them that weave the wind."[22] "Weave, weaver of the wind," recurs as a refrain through his meditations, whether in the schoolroom[26] or in the library, where it forms a metaphor of the artistic process;[192] with it is linked the problem of the possibilities of the past. His sympathy goes out to the long line of heretics,[22] to the soldiers under Pyrrhus,[25] to the forgotten masters of Arabian mathematics.[29] The destiny of lost causes fascinates him and seems to echo his own defeatism:

Had Pyrrhus not fallen by a beldam's hand in Argos or Julius Caesar not been knifed to death. They are not to be thought away. Time has branded them and fettered they are lodged in the room of the infinite possibilities they have ousted. But can those have been possible seeing that they never were?[26]

History thus reveals the rough injustice of fate: "History, Stephen said, is a nightmare from which I am trying to awake."[35] In the bleak mood of rebellious adolescence God, too, is but a shout in the street. This sentiment ruffles the paternal schoolmaster, Deasy, when it is uttered in his presence;[35] it is ironically repeated in the brothel scene as a comment on the blatant playing of evangelistic hymns on a nearby phonograph.[494]

Stephen is sensitive to the ill destiny of being Irish. He feels himself the servant of two masters, equally tyrannical, priest and king.[22] The Irish inhabit "houses of decay";[40] in such an environment he will not serve.[567] He must kill both priest and king,[574] a grandiloquent statement which, amusingly enough, is taken literally by the intoxicated privates who overhear it. To him his country is far less important than himself—"let my country die for me."[576] Bloom registers bewilderment at the expression of such a sentiment:

I suspect, Stephen interrupted, that Ireland must be important because it belongs to me.

—What belongs? queried Mr Bloom, bending, fancying he was perhaps under some misapprehension. Excuse me. Unfortunately I didn't catch the latter portion.[629]

Aware of the decay of the modern world, especially apparent in subservient Ireland, Stephen recalls the words of Blake:

The harlot's cry from street to street
Shall weave old England's winding sheet.[34]

The lines are most appropriately remembered in the brothel scene.[582] Akin in mood are the phrases which seem to describe so perfectly the spirit of *Ulysses* and its place in modern cultural history:

I hear the ruin of all space, shattered glass and toppling mason-ry, and time one livid final flame.[25]

Stephen's recollections of the home-rule conspirators in Paris echo the phrase;[44] it colors his conversation in the hospital;[385] and it accompanies the dramatic gesture of smashing the chandelier in the brothel.[567]

Uncompromising and intransigent, Stephen explains that an accession to his mother's dying wish would have been an offense to himself. His contempt for his father, "All too Irish,"[607] is in striking contrast to Bloom's admiration for Simon.[604] He fears the conspiracy of the world of respectability, the nets which the earlier Stephen of the *Portrait* hoped to escape. His mind is truly in bondage.[209] To Mulligan this attitude is sinister.[7] He traces it rightly to a cursed Jesuit strain, injected the wrong way,[10] and feels that his friend suffers from "g.p.i.," the general paralysis of the insane. Stephen admits that he detests action[573] and, like Hamlet, contemplates suicide:

Open your eyes. No. Jesus! If I fell over a cliff that beetles o'er his base, fell through the *nebeneinander* ineluctably. . . . . Am I walking into eternity along Sandymount strand?[38]

In Hamlet mood he plays with the word, "dogsbody," hurled at him by Mulligan.[7] It occurs as he gazes into the mirror while dressing,[8] is ironically symbolized by

a dead dog on the beach,[47] and is reiterated by the
vision of Mulligan in "Circe."[565] His wild and whirling
words also play upon the fable of the fox who buried
its grandmother under a holly bush. He springs it on
his class at school, much to their bewilderment.[28] It
comes to mind as he sees the dog's carcass on the
beach;[47] it recurs in his conversation at the brothel,[545]
and the fox itself appears immediately thereafter.[557]

The shadow of *Hamlet* falls over the pages of *Ulysses*, and echoes of the verse of Shakespeare provide a
ground bass to the modern rhythms of both Stephen's
and Bloom's thoughts. Certainly, as important as the
much-heralded resemblances to the *Odyssey* is the
identification of these two isolated individuals with
the dilemma of the noble Dane. Hamlet is, in fact, one
of the major characters of the modern epic; the word
in its various forms occurs forty-seven times and is the
two hundred and seventy-fifth word in order of frequency.

The parallels between Hamlet and Stephen are
striking. Both feel a conscious duty to perform, yet
are incapable of action; both sense the injustice and
the indifference of an alien world. Both are deprived
of normal family relationships. It is no wonder that
Stephen feels drawn to his prototype and that his interpretation of the enigma of Hamlet's character is
the laughingstock of his associates.[17] Mulligan caricatures it as they go for a swim:

He proves by algebra that Hamlet's grandson is Shakespeare's
grandfather and that he himself is the ghost of his own father.[19]

When Haines shows interest in the theory, Mulligan cries out in protest, "I'm not equal to Thomas

Aquinas and the fifty-five reasons he has made to prop it up," and pleads that they wait until he has a few pints in him.[19]

Postponing for a moment Stephen's interpretation, given at length in the library scene, it is well to call attention to the numerous *Hamlet* references in the text. The Martello Tower reminds Haines of the beetling cliffs at Elsinore,[20] a thought that twice recurs[38] to Stephen, walking alone on the beach.[45] Stephen echoes the phrase "very like a whale" during this same meditation[41] and thinks of his Hamlet hat.[48] But more important than such obvious parallels is Stephen's pervasive mood. Alienated from his family, he is no more at home among his companions than Hamlet was in the court of Claudius. Mr. Deasy might as well be a modern Polonius as a re-creation of Nestor, and Stephen's mockery of him is akin to Hamlet's ridicule of the aged councilor. The sensitivity, discursiveness, and melancholy of Hamlet's soliloquies are to be found in Stephen's stream-of-consciousness, especially as he walks on the beach.

Even Bloom, surprising though it seem, feels a kinship with Hamlet. He reflects on Ophelia's suicide and on his father's;[75] at the cemetery he recalls the gravediggers and thinks of Shakespeare's "profound knowledge of the human heart."[107] The words of the ghost come to mind as he walks to lunch.[150] He echoes phrases from the play as he thinks of the secret service[160] and as he walks in the twilight.[366] Even the Shakespeare-Bacon controversy arouses his curiosity.[618]

After such a complete identification of the Hamlet problem with Stephen's state of mind, the remarks of the mild-mannered librarian about the universality of the play are unconsciously ironic:

URBANE, TO COMFORT THEM, THE QUAKER LIBRARIAN PURRED:
—And we have, have we not, those priceless pages of *Wilhelm Meister?* A great poet on a great brother poet. A hesitating soul taking arms against a sea of troubles, torn by conflicting doubts, as one sees in real life.[182]

With this direct challenge to comparison with one of the *loci classici* of *Hamlet* criticism, Joyce opens the library scene and creates an interpretation of the play that will stand with its predecessors in intuitive insight and originality.

The *Hamlet* of Stephen's interpretation is a myth of paternity. Shakespeare, according to the interpretation of the young intellectual, is troubled by the same problem that besets Dedalus—How can one know his own spiritual father? At the outset the contrast between sophisticated London and provincial Stratford is equated with that between Paris and Dublin.[186] The ghost's message to the young prince is perhaps a veiled allusion to the unhappy domestic life of the playwright.[187] Shakespeare had been seduced by the older Ann Hathaway,[189] and the burden of the temptations of the flesh lies henceforth upon his uneasy conscience.[194] Stephen's own unhappy sexual experiences may be recalled from the *Portrait*. To continue the identification, Stephen assumes that Ann had become a religious fanatic (an indirect portrait of May Dedalus), atoning for her sins.

The climax of the discussion, where one can see Stephen's own problem of allegiance most perfectly expressed, is his notion of the distance between physical and spiritual fatherhood. Paternity "is a mystical estate, an apostolic succession"[204]—clearly a rationalization of Stephen's strained relations with his own family and his search for a loyalty more meaningful to him, for, as Stephen says, quoting Maeterlinck, *"If Socrates leave his house today he will find the sage seated on his doorsteps."*[210] The Hamlet of the library episode is obviously the Hamlet of Stephen's struggle within his own soul. Then, as if fearing that he had revealed too much of himself, he resumes the antic disposition. In answer to Eglinton's question as to whether he believes his own theory, he promptly responds, "No."[211] He will not publish his interpretation unless there is money to be gained by it—another refuge from the loneliness that eats his heart.

Stephen thus represents the barrenness of a skeptical intellectualism. Believing in nothing, lacking any positive faith in a world that has retained only the shreds and husks of outworn beliefs, he can contribute nothing to society. His pride and arrogance bar him from any true sense of community with the fellow-sufferers about him. His cold critical eye can see naught in the pathetic Bloom. Hardened by cynicism, he is incapable of anything but self-pity; giving nothing, he receives nothing and, in turn, has nothing to give. Never in modern literature has the dilemma of the intellectual been so clearly analyzed. Art for art's sake soon becomes art for my sake. The mask of silence, exile, and cunning which Stephen chose for himself in the *Portrait* can easily become an escape from responsibility and, what is worse, an escape from social action.

VII

—You know Simon Dedalus? he asked at length.

—I've heard of him, Stephen said. . . . .

—He's Irish, the seaman boldly affirmed, staring still in much the same way and nodding. All Irish.

—All too Irish, Stephen rejoined.[607]

IF THE depiction of Leopold Bloom and Stephen Dedalus shows that Joyce is keenly sensitive to human emotions, the minor characters reveal a lusty humor and ingratiating charm. No coldly indifferent nihilist, contemptuous of human life, isolated behind the barriers of intellectualism, could have portrayed Buck Mulligan, Blazes Boylan, and Molly Bloom with such Chaucerian gusto. Just as Shakespeare alleviates the tragic tension of his masterpieces with bawdy humor, so Joyce sets off Stephen's lofty pride and Bloom's pathetic loneliness with these character types, seen in their habits as they lived. The contrast serves both to relieve and to heighten the poignancy of the major theme.

Too little attention has been given to this rich background of Dublin characters. There is a full-blooded zest for life in the depiction of these habitués of race track, tavern, and brothel. We see the carefree humor, the Irish love of music, the easy contact with people characteristic of the Dubliner. To meet them again and again gives to the story considerable verisimilitude. And not only that, they are interesting characters in their own right. Once we have met them, we anticipate their later appearances, and seeing them again and again gives cheer and humor to the day which we pass in their midst.

The creator of these characters is more akin in spirit to Buck Mulligan than to the self-conscious aesthete who wrote *Stephen Hero* and the *Portrait*. The adolescent Joyce had felt nothing but disdain for the vulgarity of the man in the street. Far from the hearty relish of *Ulysses*, the early works had been caustic and humorless. Where the later Joyce would have drawn closer to catch the nuances of personality, Stephen Hero had been revolted by the spectacle of three billiard players:

—If I had remained another minute I think I would have begun to cry.
—Yes, it is bloody awful, said Cranly.
—O, hopeless! hopeless! said Stephen clenching his fists.[218]

Even *Dubliners*, which displays far more sympathy and in which many of the minor characters of *Ulysses* make their first appearance, is far less robust. Joyce's early works were pervaded either by astringent bitterness or by sentimental sympathy. Looking back upon his country now, his perspective mellowed by reminiscence, he creates an Irish background that is amusing and tender as well as sordid.

Foremost among these characters are Molly Bloom, Buck Mulligan, Simon Dedalus, and Blazes Boylan. Those who are eager to make a moralist of Joyce interpret Molly as an abandoned woman, a horrible example of the sins of the flesh. Voluptuous she is, to be sure, and self-centered, and, above all, well experienced in what are euphemistically known as the "facts of life." She lies abed late in the mornings,[74] she feeds her carnal imagination with lurid stories,[64] and her thoughts turn always toward clothing and sensual gratification. Yet there is such a downrightness about her and her portrait is painted with such gusto that it is difficult to see in her merely a savage caricature. There is no doubt that Joyce had a lot of fun portraying her.

Bloom appreciates her coarse straightforwardness. He recalls with pleasure her characterization of Dollard as a "base barreltone"[152] and agrees in part with her contempt for philosophy. The phrase "O, rocks," uttered by her after his halting definition of "metempsychosis," lingers in his mind with approval.[152] Her intelligence is rudimentary and untrained. We are told that she "understood little of political complications," that she added with her fingers, that she constantly misinterpreted foreign words "phonetically or by false analogy or by both: metempsychosis (met him pike hoses)."[670] Nor were Bloom's efforts at her mental improvement successful, despite their persistence. In response to his teachings, she

gave attention with interest, comprehended with surprise, with care repeated, with greater difficulty remembered, forgot with ease, with misgiving rerembered, rerepeated with error.[671]

Molly is a masterpiece of comic portrayal; comparison with Chaucer's Wife of Bath is inevitable. Both have a hearty animal-like acceptance of life in all its aspects. She shows no acquaintance with her literary predecessor, though it is probable that she would waste no love on her fifteenth-century rival, for her opinion of Defoe's Moll "from Flanders" is unflattering.[741]

The spirit of comedy is closely related to that of common sense. Molly's judgments of personality are shrewd and clear-eyed, if a bit severe. She sees through people with uncanny insight, whether they be her lovers or the women she has known. Boylan is a brute,[726] Lenehan a sponger, and Val Dillon a heathen.[735] But consistency is not one of her mental traits. Virag must have been "a bit foolish in the head" to commit suicide as he did, though she supposes that he must have felt lost without his wife.[752] In a vein of glorification of her sex she argues that the world would be much better ruled by women,[763] yet a moment later she admits that "we are a dreadful lot of bitches."[764] Such inconsistency can be traced to a constant struggle within her mind between her practical outlook and her inherent higher aspirations. Creature of flesh though she is, she is not content with life lived on the sensual level.

Thus Mrs. Riordan, whom Bloom had befriended, is just an "old faggot" who "never left us a farthing"; yet, on second thought, "I like that in him polite to old women."[723] So, too, the wool garment knitted for Rudy is at one moment merely "that woollen thing"[725] and a bit later "that little woolly jacket I knitted crying."[763] And though her youth in Gibraltar as the daughter of Major Tweedy has left its mark—"I love to see a regiment passing in review"—she is clear-eyed enough to realize the pathos of war:

they could have made their peace in the beginning or old oom Paul and the rest of the old Krugers go and fight it out between them instead of dragging on for years killing any finelooking men there were.[734]

Though men are cowards,[723] deceitful,[724] and lascivious,[727] and her husband is no exception, Molly still has respect for Bloom's knowledge,[728] his fastidiousness,[729] and his romantic idealism.[732] Bloom is, of course, shiftless, with his endless changes of jobs,[737] and he is an old fool, writing letters to Martha[724] and getting in at four in the morning.[749] He is full of harebrained plans,[750] and political notions.[756] She thinks of the absurdity of his character—"if I only could remember the one half of the things and write a book out of it"[739] (*Ulysses* might have had a feminine author!)—yet springs instinctively to her husband's defense. She will protect him against his ungrateful friends: "theyre not going to get my husband again into their clutches if I can help it making fun of him then behind his back."[758] Molly's heart is, after all, in the right place. And her greatest virtue is honesty: "I hate that pretending of all things."[736]

A final word needs to be said in her defense. Her heart responds to sympathy and beauty. Though she is ready to use her husband without qualms, thinking that he can just as well get breakfast for Stephen and herself,[765] and, despite her contempt for men in general and her ridicule of the little man she married, she concludes that "Id rather die 20 times over than marry another of their sex," adding hurriedly in self-defense, "of course hed never find another woman like me to put up with him the way I do."[729] Her long soliloquy indicates a fervid love of nature:

I love flowers Id love to have the whole place swimming in roses God of heaven theres nothing like nature the wild mountains

then the sea and the waves rushing then the beautiful country
with fields of oats and wheat and all kinds of things and all the
fine cattle going about that would do your heart good to see
. . . .[766]

And in answer to those who deny the existence of
God, "I wouldnt give a snap of my two fingers for all
their learning."[767]

Her acceptance of sex is wholehearted and unashamed: "it didnt make me blush why should it either
its only nature."[762] Her meditations conclude with a
magnificent coda in which the themes of sex, beauty,
nature, and love of life reach a climax:

Gibraltar as a girl where I was a Flower of the mountain yes
when I put the rose in my hair like the Andalusian girls used or
shall I wear a red yes and how he kissed me under the Moorish
wall and I thought well as well him as another and then I asked
him with my eyes to ask again yes and then he asked me would
I yes to say yes my mountain flower and first I put my arms
around him yes and drew him down to me so he could feel my
breasts all perfume yes and his heart was going like mad and
yes I said yes I will Yes.[768]

Buck Mulligan, medical student and roomer at
Martello Tower, is introduced in the first sentence of
the novel. Genial and blasphemous, his plump figure
"recalled a prelate, patron of arts in the middle ages."[5]
He is a dilettante, a wit who can turn all the resources
of his insight to the purpose of mockery:

—God, he said quietly. Isn't the sea what Algy calls it: a grey
sweet mother? The snotgreen sea. The scrotumtightening sea.
Epi oinopa ponton. Ah, Dedalus, the Greeks. I must teach you.[7]

He indulges in genial ridicule of Haines's interest in
folklore:

Five lines of text and ten pages of notes about the folk and the
fishgods of Dundrum. Printed by the weird sisters in the year of
the big wind.[14]

Yet his outspoken language conveys a hearty love of
life. A true pagan, he has nothing but contempt for
the strained involutions of Stephen's conscience. Like
Hofrat Behrens of *The Magic Mountain*, he is willing
to accept life and death with equanimity. He sees
Stephen's mother as "beastly dead,"[10] and that's that.
He finds nothing but an absurd point of honor in
Stephen's former refusal to follow his mother's wishes:
"Humour her till it's over."[10] When the young idealist
replies that he is not so much concerned with the offense
to his mother as that to himself, Mulligan exclaims,
"O, an impossible person!"[10] His philosophy is best
expressed in his own words as they go down the steps
to bathe:

—Look at the sea. What does it care about offences? Chuck
Loyola, Kinch, and come on down.[11]

Commanding a wide range of anecdote, versed in
questionable story, limerick, and witty comeback, he
is a born conversationalist. He is equally at home with
the peasant milkwoman at the tower,[16] the waitress at
the restaurant,[245] the intellectuals at the library,[195]
and the convivial medicos at the hospital.[395] Though
censors may frown at his speech, even his blasphemy
is pardonable, for, as the English folklore student,
Haines, says, "his gaiety takes the harm out of it
somehow, doesn't it?"[21]

At the library we hear that Mulligan is going to a
party at George Moore's,[190] from which he comes to
the hospital.[390] But in the meantime he has arrived at

the library, where he mocks the adulation of Shakespeare:

—Shakespeare? he said. I seem to know the name.
A flying sunny smile rayed in his loose features.
—To be sure, he said, remembering brightly. The chap that
writes like Synge.[195]

And Dowden's Victorian evasion of the problems of
Shakespeare's moral life is good for a laugh:

He lifted his hands and said: *All we can say is that life ran very
high in those days.* Lovely![202]

During the discussion, Bloom enters, to be contemptuously termed "sheeny."[198] Mulligan's opinion of the
Irish revival is no less outspoken. Like Joyce, he could
see it only as a self-consciously aesthetic futility:

We went over to their playbox, Haines and I, the plumbers' hall.
Our players are creating a new art for Europe like the Greeks or
M. Maeterlinck. Abbey theatre! I smell the public sweat of
monks.[213]

In the "Wandering Rocks" episode we see him at
the D.B.C. (tearoom of the Dublin Bakery Company,
nicknamed the "Damn Bad Cakes") with Haines, un-
loading the tray for the waitress and eating hungrily
as they discuss Stephen's *idée fixé*.[245] Appearing at the
hospital in the evening, Mulligan, as ever the center
of attention, passes out printed cards advertising his
sexual services.[395] He meets Bloom and humiliates
him by offering himself to Bloom's wife if necessary.[397]
No wonder that to Bloom the apparition of Mulligan
appears in the "Circe" episode as a sex specialist, who
pronounces him sexually abnormal.[483]

We see Mulligan, too, as he affects others. Simon
Dedalus, who is not, in fact, so different but in spirit

more conventional, worries about his son's association with the "contaminated bloody doubledyed ruffian."[87] And Bloom likewise feels it necessary to warn Stephen as they walk home together:

I wouldn't personally repose much trust in that boon companion of yours who contributes the humorous element, Dr Mulligan, as a guide, philosopher, and friend, if I were in your shoes. He knows which side his bread is buttered on.[604]

Simon Dedalus, Stephen's father, who has been contemptuously characterized in the *Portrait* as "a medical student, an oarsman, a tenor, an amateur actor, a shouting politician, a small landlord, ... a drinker, a good fellow, a storyteller, somebody's secretary, something in a distillery, a taxgatherer, a bankrupt and at present a praiser of his own past,"[284] is nonetheless a colorful character.

Lover of anecdote, true Irishman as he is, his personality contributes to the rich loam of Irish humor in the book, for in Dublin even the caretaker at the cemetery can linger over a tale of two drunks looking at night for the tomb of a friend, though he may do it only, as Cunningham says, "to cheer a fellow up. . . . It's pure goodheartedness: damn the thing else."[106]

There is a considerable amount of pure goodheartedness in Simon's character. We first meet him in the funeral carriage, where he remarks that the sky is "as uncertain as a child's bottom"[89] and gives the dryly humorous climactic line to the tale of the reward of a florin given by Reuben J. Dodd upon the rescue of his son: "One and eightpence too much."[93] The convivial spirit of an Irish wake pervades the conversation of the group in the carriage, though Simon remarks that "poor little Paddy wouldn't grudge us a laugh. Many a good one he told himself."[94] And his fundamental tenderness of heart comes out as he views his wife's grave:

—Her grave is over there, Jack, Mr Dedalus said. I'll soon be stretched beside her. Let Him take me whenever He likes.[103]

Simon is known for his genial habit of taking off his friends. Bloom recalls his mimicry of the squint of the grocer O'Rourke;[58] his ability to tell a story;[150] his remark about Braydon, "all his brains are in the nape of his neck";[116] his taunt about Sheehy becoming an M.P.—that Parnell would rise from the grave to lead him out of the House of Commons.[163] It is natural, then, to see him settling down in the newspaper office to ridicule the pomposity of Dan Dawson's political oratory[122] and to laugh at the clothes of Ben Dollard.[240] In the "Sirens" episode he teases the waitress[257] and, after repeated urgings, plays the piano and sings.[263] He gossips with Ben Dollard about Molly Bloom,[265] and we learn later that he was one of Molly's many lovers.[716] No wonder that to Bloom in "Circe" he appears on the jury which is judging the misdemeanors of Bloom's past.[461]

Our final impression is that given in Molly's long soliloquy. He is "such a criticiser with his glasses up with his tall hat on him at the cricket match"[753] and, though he was always turning up half-drunk and "was always on for flirtyfying too," nevertheless "he had a delicious glorious voice."[759]

Blazes Boylan is the essence of the debonair. A dandy and *bon vivant*, he is characterized by the words "jingle" and "jaunty." He appears principally as Molly's lover, but such a vivid personality as his impresses itself upon everyone he sees. Milly mentions him in her letter from Westmeath.[62] Nosey Flynn,[170] Rochford,[229] Alf Bergan,[312] even the drunken bum Corley,[603] know of him.

His companion is Lenehan, the humorist. Their meeting in the Ormond bar is a neat bit of Irish genre painting:

> Miss Douce reached high to take a flagon, stretching her satin arm, her bust, that all but burst, so high.
> —O! O! jerked Lenehan, gasping at each stretch. O!
> But easily she seized her prey and led it low in triumph.
> —Why don't you grow? asked Blazes Boylan. . . . .
> —Here's fortune, Blazes said.
> He pitched a broad coin down. Coin rang.
> —Hold on, said Lenehan, till I . . .
> —Fortune, he wished, lifting his bubbled ale.
> —Sceptre will win in a canter, he said.[261]

His carefree insouciance is apparent in his contacts with the blond clerk in Thornton's florist shop. He views her physical charms with apparent satisfaction, the stalk of a carnation between his teeth.[225] Master Dignam sees, later, "a red flower in a toff's mouth and a swell pair of kicks on him,"[247] as he walks to the Ormond bar. There Miss Kennedy and Miss Douce outdo one another in responding to his greeting.[260] The bronzeheaded Douce is especially impressed—"sparkling bronze azure eyed Blazure's skyblue bow and eyes."[262]

Boylan strides through life with relish. On his way to his assignation with Molly he is described:

By Bachelor's walk jogjaunty jingled Blazes Boylan, bachelor, in sun, in heat, mare's glossy rump atrot, with flick of whip, on bounding tyres: sprawled, warmseated, Boylan impatience, ardentbold.[265]

No wonder Molly reflects upon her conquest of this most eligible of Dublin's wealthy bachelors and defies those who feel superior to her, "Miss This Miss That Miss Theother."[747] To all such she would say:

let them get a husband first thats fit to be looked at and a daughter like mine or see if they can excite a swell with money that can pick and choose whoever he wants like Boylan[748]

Lenehan is one of the most colorful of the minor characters. Since he is a tip-sheet editor, his major interest during the day is in the Ascot Cup. His humor is contagious. It is verbal, and its proper place is the *Freeman* office, where he first appears. He hears "feetstoops"; complains of his knee, "the accumulation of the *anno Domini*";[127] gives the riddle of the opera like a railway line—*Rose of Castille*;[133] recites a limerick,[132] a palindrome;[135] comments on catching a cold in the park because the gate was open;[133] says of Moses that he died "with a great future behind him."[141] He has a good story on Bloom, which he tells in the "Wandering Rocks" episode.[231]

As he appears at the Ormond bar, he makes overtures to Mina Kennedy, the barmaid,[258] calling her Rose of Castille,[260] opening his eyes as she stretches to take a flagon from a shelf,[261] and finally urging her to snap her garter.[262]

His horse for the Ascot was Sceptre;[126] he thought it would win in a canter[261] but accepts his loss stoically at Kiernan's:

Such is life in an outhouse. . . . . Frailty, thy name is *Sceptre*.[320]

At the hospital he pours the ale with gusto,[383] engages wholeheartedly in the discussion of sex,[386] and shows his sportsmanship by his admiration of the riding of the winning jockey.[408]

Familiar with Boylan, he is another whom Bloom distrusts, and he consequently appears on the jury in the "Circe" episode[461] and demonstrates Boylan's guilt before Bloom's horrified eyes.[550] We learn that he, too, had been a lover of Molly's.[716]

Lenehan is one of the many minor characters who appeared earlier in *Dubliners*. There we discover that he was considered a leech; that he was "a sporting vagrant armed with a vast stock of stories, limericks and riddles"; that his name was "vaguely associated with racing tissues."[59]

Martin Cunningham, though betraying embarrassing anti-Semitic prejudices in the funeral carriage,[92] is yet more sensitive than his companions. He feels deeply Power's *faux pas* in referring to suicide.[95] Bloom thinks him intelligent and sympathetic, with a face like Shakespeare's.[95] His thoughts are on the plight of Dignam's family, and, even before leaving the cemetery, he is discussing it with the solicitor, Menton.[113] On this matter he writes to Father Conmee.[216]

We see him in the "Wandering Rocks," taking up the collection for the widow,[242] and in Kiernan's, arranging for the insurance,[307] in which Bloom undertakes to help. He appears as Shakespeare in the "Circe" episode,[554] and Bloom thinks later of getting a pass through him for a vacation.[610]

He had been portrayed in this very role in "Grace,"

the story of the rather reluctant conversion of Tom
Kernan in *Dubliners*. It is interesting to compare the
direct and conventional characterization here with
the impressionism of *Ulysses*. We are told that he was
the very man to effect the conversion; that his domestic life was not happy; that he was "a thoroughly
sensible man, influential and intelligent,"[199] with a
face like Shakespeare's.

A comic counterpart to the generous spirit of Cunningham is the unctuous Father Conmee. Joyce describes the character with superb irony in the "Wandering Rocks" episode:

THE SUPERIOR, THE VERY REVEREND JOHN CONMEE, S.J. RESET
HIS smooth watch in his interior pocket.[216]

As he starts on his walk, he thinks of Cunningham's
letter. His reaction to it is in striking contrast to the
spirit that prompted its writing. Conmee is anxious to
oblige, for Cunningham is a "good practical Catholic:
useful at mission time"[216]—a perfect depiction of the
contrast between genuine and professional Christianity.

Conmee is a born church careerist. He thinks, "but
not for long," of victims of war; he is most gracious
to Mrs. Sheehy, for, after all, her husband is an M.P.
He smiles confidently, vain about his freshly cleaned
teeth, and smiles again, even more complacently, as he
thinks of Father Vaughan's cockney evangelism and
of the "invincible ignorance" of the dissenting minister, Greene.[217] Benign to all, with a benignity born of
self-satisfaction, he proceeds on his walk. Of his relation to the schoolboys at Clongowes Wood College

(which Joyce himself attended), it is said: "He was their rector: his reign was mild."[221]

Three characters deserve special mention, not only because of their intrinsic interest, but also on account of the novel way in which Joyce presents them to us. First in appearance is the anonymous narrator of the "Cyclops" episode. His outlook on life is rendered by his own comments on characters and situations. A broad, racy, vernacular style, it embodies the characteristic prejudices of the lower-class, semiliterate citizen. Except for an ingrained anti-Semitism, he is non-political. A discussion of the Russo-Japanese War is merely "bloody codding";[290] the Citizen's conversation on Irish freedom is met with contempt: "Talking about new Ireland he ought to go and get a new dog so he ought."[300] When Bloom enters the discussion with a humane and tolerant view of modern society, it is mentioned as "Bloom trying to back him up moderation and botheration and their colonies and their civilisation."[319]

As could be surmised, he has no higher respect for Bloom's curiosity. Scientific explanation is described as "his jawbreakers about phenomenon and science and this phenomenon and the other phenomenon."[299] Bloom's sympathetic interest in Mrs. Dignam's legal affairs is no less bitterly ridiculed:

Then he starts all confused mucking it up about the mortgagor under the act like the lord chancellor . . . . till he near had the head of me addled.[307]

Yet there is a stratum of horse sense in this vulgar mind. Inconsistent with his anti-Semitism though it is, his disgust at the newspaper account of a lynching is wholesome: "Gob, they ought to drown him in the sea after and electrocute and crucify him to make sure of their job."[323] But his major interest remains drink, and on that subject he waxes eloquent. "I was blue mouldy for the want of that pint," he exclaims, after the first.[293] The second is accepted with a "Could a swim duck?"[307] The third is almost interrupted by Molloy's discussion of the technicalities of law, but the bibulous debt-collector sagely asks: "Who wants your opinion? Let us drink our pints in peace."[316] With the fourth comes a blessing to Joe Hynes, the generous provider: "May your shadow never grow less."[325]

By this time the narrator is willing to believe anything. His latent anti-Semitism, aroused by Bloom's gentility, curiosity, and humane wisdom, is inflamed by the suspicion that the Jew had won 100 to 5 on the dark horse, Throwaway. He witnesses with enthusiasm the anger of the Citizen, former champion shot-putter and now barroom loafer, the very incarnation of brute force. The flying biscuit-tin receives his benediction[339] as he fades from the scene, anonymous, worthless, but unforgettable, an all too Irish pub-crawler.

Gerty MacDowell, ingénue, filled with adolescent romanticism bred from cheap fiction, is revealed in a different manner. She does not narrate the next, the "Nausicaä" episode, but it is told in a style of senti-mental cliché appropriate to her thoughts. Here is stream-of-consciousness rendered by indirect (and ironic) discourse.

We are told of her beauty, her "innate refinement,"[342] "that haunting expression" about her eyes (thanks to eyebrowleine), her "crowning glory"[343] of wavy brown hair. She was dressed "with the instinctive taste of a votary of Dame Fashion."[344] She feels "that dull aching void"[343] for Reggy Wylie, though he is not her "beau ideal."[345] Her dreams pass on to domesticity;[346] a sentimental religious romanticism is aroused by the anthem of a vespers service near by.[348] Bloom arrives, and she realizes that "here was that of which she had so often dreamed."[351] The twilight recalls to her the girlish treasures she has kept in her toilet-table drawer; she feels that "she too could write poetry if she could only express herself" like the poem, "*Art thou real, my ideal*," she had copied from the newspaper[357] (a poem which appears in *Stephen Hero* as the epitome of vulgar sentimentality[83]).

And so for eighteen uproarious pages, fifty clichés to a page, we see the romantic soul of Gerty MacDowell probed with astringent wit.

Redbearded W. B. Murphy, ablebodied seaman, met in the cabman's shelter at 1:00 A.M., is another unforgettable figure. We see him largely through Bloom's eyes. Suspicious of him from the first, Bloom tries in vain to warn Stephen not to give his name,[607] for he feels that "it required no violent stretch of the imagination to associate such a weirdlooking specimen with the oakum and treadmill fraternity."[620] Stephen is indifferent to both advances and warnings, but the good man continues undaunted. He demonstrates with apparent relish (and with appropriate sound effects) Simon Dedalus' circus act: "I seen him shoot two eggs off two bottles at fifty yards."[607] His tongue loosened, he regales the strangers with his travels:

I seen Russia. *Gospodi pomilooy*. That's how the Russians prays.

—You seen queer sights, don't be talking, put in a jarvey.

—Why, the sailor said, shifting his partially chewed plug, I seen queer things too, ups and downs. I seen a crocodile bite the fluke of an anchor same as I chew that quid.

He took out of his mouth the pulpy quid and, lodging it between his teeth, bit ferociously.[609]

He tells of Chinese paper flowers; then: "Cooks rats in your soup, he appetisingly added, the Chinese does."[612] Going on to recall a knifing, he produces the weapon to demonstrate, appreciatively adding, "That's a good bit of steel."[613] Proud of the tattoo marks on his chest, he exhibits them gladly, proffering information about the artist: "He's gone too. Ate by sharks after. Ay, ay."[616] Yet he confesses boredom with his job. "I'm tired of all them rocks in the sea," he says, squelching Bloom's sentimental query about Gibraltar, Molly's home. Far from glamorizing ships, he dismisses them contemptuously as "salt junk, all the time."[614] Finally he relieves himself of a bawdy sea song, and sinks into the evening paper, an appropriate exit.[624]

Though these characters, as well as a hundred others, appear throughout the book, the "Wandering Rocks" remains their main habitat. For a moment the odyssey of Bloom is interrupted, and we see the streets and environs of Dublin. Some fifty characters pass one another, each bent on his own activity, often oblivious of the presence of his fellow-men. Coming midway among the scenes of the book, this novel in miniature is an excellent example of Joyce's counterpoint technique. It contains eighteen sections, as does the novel, and concludes with a most effective ensemble scene in which each of the characters is seen viewing the royal cavalcade.

Father Conmee's afternoon walk opens the chapter. He passes a one-legged sailor, blessing him profusely, for, as Joyce slyly notes, he realizes that his purse holds only one silver crown. Mr. Denis J. Maginni, dancing teacher, deferentially steps aside as he passes Lady Maxwell. Father Conmee sees Corny Kelleher at the undertaking establishment, then takes the tram to Howth Road. Walking in the country later, he surprises two lovers in a field.

The second section focuses on Corny Kelleher totting up figures on the Dignam funeral, and the third brings the one-legged sailor past the Dedalus sisters to Bloom's house, where a woman's hand tosses out a coin. In these two brief episodes we are reminded of Conmee's walk and are introduced to J. J. O'Molloy, who is told to meet Lambert at the warehouse.

Next we are taken to the Dedalus kitchen and discover that Dilly is at the auction-rooms. We again hear of Father Conmee's walk in the country, and the brief scene concludes with a description of the evangelistic handbill, which Bloom had discarded at lunchtime,[150] floating down the Liffey.

In the fifth scene Boylan orders fruit for Molly. He sees five sandwich men, H, E, L, Y,' S, advertising a store in which Bloom once worked.[738] A dark figure, scanning books at a stall, is also mentioned here. Boylan telephones his office and leaves the florist's.

A glimpse is given of Stephen, conversing in Italian at Trinity College with Artifoni, who fails to catch his tram because it is filled with the members of a Highland band (later to be heard from College Green as the parade passes).

The seventh scene depicts Miss Dunne, Boylan's secretary, answering his phone call. We are told that a disk numbered 6 slides into place, but for the present are puzzled as to its significance. Meanwhile, H, E, L, Y, and 'S still parade the streets.

The eighth scene covers the meeting of O'Molloy with Lenehan at the warehouse. Another provocative hint is given—a glimpse of a bearded man bending over a chessboard. Lenehan has been showing the warehouse, formerly an abbey, to a curious sightseer, the Reverend Love. There is also a recall here of the lovers whom Father Conmee disturbed on his stroll. The same sentence is repeated, implying that the action in this entire chapter is almost instantaneous.

In the ninth part the number 6 is explained. Tom Rochford, the jockey, is demonstrating a number machine to Lenehan and Flynn. Lenehan leaves to meet his appointment with Boylan at the Ormond. Ritchie Goulding, carrying his inevitable cost-bag, notices an elderly lady at the courts of chancery; the viceregal cavalcade then starts from Phoenix Park; Molly Bloom replaces the sign in the window, which was dislodged as she tossed the coin to the begging sailor.

Bloom, the dark figure at the bookstall in the fifth scene, now picks up *Sweets of Sin* for his wife. Maginni crosses O'Connell Bridge; an elderly female leaves the building of the courts of chancery (a recall of the preceding episode).

The eleventh scene takes place at the auction-rooms, where Dilly Dedalus meets her father. Kernan, tea merchant, walks along James Street; the cavalcade passes out of Parkgate.

Kernan continues his walk in the next scene, thinking of the explosion of the "General Slocum" in New York Harbor. Father Cowley meets Simon Dedalus; the cavalcade reaches Pembroke quay: the evangelistic broadside floats on.

Stephen arrives at the bookseller's in the thirteenth scene. Conmee, we are reminded, continues his walk.

The meeting of Dedalus and Father Cowley is now brought into focus. The Reverend Love walks away from the abbey which he had admired; the demented Farrell strolls down Kildare Street.

Next, Cunningham and Power discuss the fund for the Widow Dignam; Boylan walks on toward the Ormond; the cavalcade comes within earshot; the barmaids at the Ormond look out.

At last, in the sixteenth scene, the chess game is explained. Parnell's old brother makes a move in the restaurant D.B.C., where Mulligan and Haines chat. The begging sailor continues his rounds; the crumpled broadside reaches a schooner at the wharf.

A brief scene shows Artifoni walking past Holles Street, preceding the insane Farrell, who bumps the blind piano-tuner, whom Bloom had aided earlier in the day. The last section finds Dignam's orphan son, carrying home pork steaks, passing Boylan on the way.

The technique of this chapter resembles that of the moving picture. Episodes may be interrupted at will with brief glimpses of preceding or following scenes. Occasionally, we have the literary equivalent of the closeup, when incidents previously mentioned in passing are brought within range for extended treatment. The use of the sandwich men, H, E, L, Y, 'S, the floating handbill, and the cavalcade resembles the adoption of visual symbols to set the mood and establish the continuity of the film.

The finale defies paraphrase. In a style appropriate to everyone of the thirty-two characters mentioned, each is seen gazing in awe, mockery, or indifference at the imperial procession which makes its way through the heart of Dublin. Miss Kennedy and Miss Douce, at the window of the Ormond bar, "watched and admired"; it is they, of course, who strike the opening note of the magnificent overture to the "Sirens" scene. Gerty MacDowell "knew by the style it was the lord";[249] Mulligan gazed gaily (fortunately his thoughts are not revealed); Parnell's brother "looked intently" at his chessboard. The political criticism clearly illustrates the skill with which Joyce uses his chosen weapons of silence and cunning.

H, E, L, Y, 'S stop; the handicap racers take to the wall; the young Dignam raises his cap with greasy fingers; the blind stripling is passed, as is the mysterious man in the brown mackintosh.

The essential spirit of Ireland, however, is represented by Blazes Boylan's attitude. With a zest that reveals the Joyce who wrote *Ulysses* as quite different from the contemptuous Stephen, Boylan is described not as "all too Irish," but as the incarnation of Irish blandness, geniality, and vivacity:

By the provost's wall came jauntily Blazes Boylan, stepping in tan shoes and socks with skyblue clocks to the refrain of *My girl's a Yorkshire girl*.

Blazes Boylan presented to the leaders' skyblue frontlets and high action a skyblue tie, a widebrimmed straw hat at a rakish angle and a suit of indigo serge. His hands in his jacket pockets forgot to salute but he offered to the three ladies the bold admiration of his eyes and the red flower between his lips.[250]

VIII

. . . . Weary?
He rests. He has travelled.[122]

THE much-traveled Ulysses covered most of the Mediterranean Sea during his ten-year voyaging. His modern counterpart, Leopold Bloom, though he limits his activities to the environs of Dublin during the day, nonetheless is a voyager among men. The streets of the Irish metropolis are traversed and retraversed. It is an easy task to trace the wanderings of Bloom on a map of Dublin.

The young Joyce was a peripatetic observer and philosopher. Stephen Hero, on his way to the university, used to get off the tram at Amiens Street Station instead of riding through to Nelson's Pillar, so that he could walk through the streets and "partake in the morning life of the city," his ears and eyes "ever prompt to receive impressions." Words, which were the young poet's treasure, he found not only in Skeat's *Etymological Dictionary* but also "in the shops, on advertisements, in the mouths of the plodding public."[30] The nature of these impressions is given more fully in the *Portrait*. As might be expected, they resemble the literary-philosophical musings of Stephen Dedalus far more than the earthy reactions of Bloom:

His morning walk across the city had begun; and he foreknew that as he passed the sloblands of Fairview he would think of the

cloistral silverveined prose of Newman; that as he walked along
the North Strand Road, glancing idly at the windows of the
provision shops, he would recall the dark humour of Guido Caval-
canti and smile; that as he went by Baird's stone cutting works
in Talbot Place the spirit of Ibsen would blow through him like
a keen wind. . . . .[204]

Such philosophical daydreams seem far removed
from the spirit in which Joyce re-creates Dublin in
Ulysses. An astounding degree of concreteness characterizes the setting. Bakeries, schools, auction-rooms,
antique-shops, confectioners', hotels, public buildings, stonecutters' yards, the gas works, statues of
prominent Dubliners, above all, pubs—here is the
confusion of a modern city. Nearly two hundred es-
tablishments are mentioned. And in describing them,
Joyce almost always creates a sense of movement.
Trams pass, pigeons fly, smoke drifts upward, sounds
are constantly heard, the reek of lunch pervades the
air, the sunlight brings out the glossy sheen of silk in
a show window. Here is the sensateness of modern
materialistic civilization, the world of Leopold Bloom,
quite different from the abstract meditations of the
medieval-minded Stephen.

Joyce undoubtedly built his setting upon the foundations of Thom's *Dublin Directory.* Of the many
characters in *Ulysses* supposedly living in Dublin in
1904, some thirty can be found in the directory. Naturally, the major characters are fictitious, but Thom's
tells us of Fathers Coffey, Conmee, Conroy, and
O'Hanlon; of Denis Breen and Davy Byrne; of Reuben J. Dodd and Ritchie Goulding; of Quaker Lyster,
the obsequious librarian; and of the innocuous Rich-

ard Best, his assistant, a folklore and philology scholar. Also listed are the caretaker at the cemetery, the
dancing master Maginni, J. H. Menton, and even
Larry O'Rourke, goodnatured pub-keeper.

At one point Bloom's meditations sound as though
they were inspired as much by a city directory as by
the sights in the streets. He remarks upon the valua-
tion of No. 80 (Upper Dorset Street) and upon the
fact that it is still unlet, both of which details, together with the names of the real estate agents, Tow-
ers, Battersby, North, and MacArthur, would be
listed in Thom's.[61] Of course, Bloom had a job with
the company in 1894,[153] and a directory, of the year
1886, heads the catalogue of his meager library.[693]
But one suspects that the voice is the voice of Bloom,
but the hands are the hands of Joyce.

The detailed locale serves many ingenious artistic
purposes. It enables Joyce to extend his commentary
on modern life to an enormous range by the simple
expedient of having the citizen Bloom, ever alert and
sharp-witted, albeit often muddle-headed, wander
through the streets observing and reflecting upon
what he sees. It gives a remarkable illustration of the
way in which the human mind receives sense-impressions. Like a recording machine, the mind is subjected
to a continuous flow of sights and sounds. And no
better dramatization of modern confusion, restlessness, and lack of direction has yet been written.

An examination of the geography of *Ulysses* provides another instance of Joyce's meticulous methods
of composition.

Bloom resides at 7 Eccles Street, which, we learn
from Thom's *Dublin Directory* for 1904, was actually

vacant at the time. Eccles Street is about two blocks
south of the North Circular Road, and No. 7 is close
to the intersection with Upper Dorset Street. A few
yards past Dorset Street is St. George's Church,
whose bells are heard in the morning[69] and evening.[688]

The little man steps around the corner of Dorset
Street to purchase the kidney for breakfast. The sun
stands near the steeple of the church. Avoiding the
loose cellarflap of No. 75 (Eccles Street), he next approaches the grocery shop of the affable Larry
O'Rourke (No. 72 Dorset) who, he thinks, has a better
location than M'Auley[57] (82 Dorset). He passes St.
Joseph's National School (Nos. 81–84) on his way to
the butcher Dlugacz (not in Thom's). He thinks of the
maid next door at Woods' (an R. Woods is listed as
living at 8 Eccles) and hurries homeward, hoping to
catch a glimpse of her swaying hips. A hag crosses
from Cassidy's (No. 71). The sunlight comes in from
Berkeley Road "swiftly, in slim sandals."[61]

On his way to the baths, Bloom is first seen on Sir
John Rogerson's Quay, half a mile east of O'Connell
Bridge. He walks past Windmill Lane, Leask's the
linseed dealer (Nos. 14, 15, and 19), the postal telegraph office (No. 18), and the sailors' home (No. 19).
On Lime Street, he passes Brady's Cottages (No. 5);
he crosses Townsend Street and passes Nichols' undertaking establishment (26 Lombard). The Belfast
and Oriental Tea Company (6 Westland Row) next attracts his attention and sets him dreaming of the romantic East.[70] He stops at the postal substation on
Westland Row (Nos. 49–50) to get Martha's letter
but is interrupted by M'Coy across from the Grosvenor Hotel (No. 5) before he has a chance to read

it.[72] At the corner of Great Brunswick Street he pauses
to look at the hoardings before turning to the right;[75]
then another right turn brings him into Cumberland
Street, past Meade's lumberyards, which face on
Brunswick (No. 159).[76] At last he reads the letter,
tearing up the envelope as he goes under the railroad
bridge behind the Westland Row Station; "an incom-
ing train clanked heavily above his head." He enters
the rear door of All Hallows' Church (46 Westland
Row).[78] Leaving the church, he walks south to the
establishment of F. W. Sweny, dispensing chemists (1
Lincoln Place),[82] where he purchases the soap. Bantam Lyons runs into him as he leaves the shop, rushing off with his tip to Conway's corner (31–32 Westland), and Bloom passes the time of day with the
porter of Trinity College on his way to the baths on
Leinster Street.

The funeral procession goes along Tritonville Road
on its way from the southeast section of the city
diagonally across town to the cemetery north of
Bloom's home. It passes Wallace's bottleworks on
Ringsend Road (No. 3A) and crosses Dodder
Bridge.[87] A conversation distracts Bloom's attention
for a moment, but he notices the halt at the Grand
Canal. The gas works are passed;[89] Bloom glances at
the paper, then notices the sights on Great Brunswick
Street, the Queen's Theatre (No. 209), Meade's lumberyards again (No. 159), the National School (Nos.
121–14), the Antient Concert Rooms (No. 42), St.
Mark's (No. 40),[90] and Plasto's (No. 1),[91] where he
had purchased his hat, in which he has hidden his card
with the pseudonym "Henry Flower." At the Cramp-
ton Memorial Fountain (end of College Street) they

glimpse Boylan, "airing his quiff." Past the statue by
Farrell (of Smith O'Brien, at Westmoreland and D'Ol-
ier) and those of O'Connell (O'Connell Bridge)[92] and
Gray (Sackville Street) they go.[93] Passing Nelson's
Pillar, they continue up Sackville Street. Bloom notices how dead his side of the street is, with the temperance hotel (No. 56), Falconer's railway guide (No.
53), Maguire's civil service college (No. 51), Gill's
bookselling establishment (No. 50), the Catholic
Club (No. 42), and the foundation for the industrious
blind (No. 41). Passing the foundation stone for Parnell, the carriage reaches the Rotunda[94] and Rutland
Square.[95] Going diagonally northwest along Frederick
Street and entering Blessington and Berkeley streets,
they are close to Bloom's home. The Ward for Incurables of the Mater Misericordiae (34–38 Eccles) is noticed.[96] A drove of cattle halts them, but they soon
proceed to Dunphy's corner (a lane two blocks north
of Circular Road), then along Phibsborough Road to
the Royal Canal.[97] Past the Brian Boroimhe house,
they are close to the cemetery, seeing the statues of
Dennany (Prospect Avenue, Glasnevin).[98]

The newspaper scene takes place near the General
Post Office at Nelson's Pillar. Mail-vans, trams, and
brewery trucks are depicted in one of Joyce's most
successful evocations of city traffic. Bloom goes from
Ruttledge's office to the press of the *Evening Telegraph* (4–8 Prince's Street).[115] He ducks around the
corner to Dillon's auction-rooms on Bachelor's Walk
(No. 25) to try to see Keyes[128] but soon returns.[144]

As he walks to lunch, he passes the confectionery
display of Lemon and Company (49 Sackville Street).
He pauses at the river, glancing from the corner of

Butler's music warehouse (34 Bachelor's Walk) toward Dillon's.[149] Crossing the Liffey on O'Connell Bridge, he pauses to feed the gulls and to throw away the evangelistic pamphlet, whose journey is later traced as it floats down the river.[150] He enters Westmoreland Street, meeting the sandwich men, noticing the Rover cycle-shop (No. 23),[153] and stopping to chat with Mrs. Breen outside of Harrison's (No. 29).[155] The office of the *Irish Times* (No. 31), where he had advertised for a secretary,[157] and Bolton's restaurant (Nos. 35-36) are passed on the way to the House of Parliament,[159] the Dublin Bakery (33 Dame),[161] and the "surly front" of Trinity College.[162] Entering Grafton Street, near Sexton's silver display (No. 118), he glimpses Parnell's brother.[162] The luxury of Grafton Street—the Bond Street of Dublin—is symbolized by the windows of lush silk at Brown Thomas (Nos. 15-17),[165] which send Bloom into exotic daydreams. Turning into Duke Street, he finds Burton's Hotel (No. 18) too nauseating for his lunch and compromises on the establishment of David Byrne, wine and spirit merchant (No. 21).[169] He walks toward Dawson Street[176] on Duke, passing the plumbing shop of Miller (No. 17)[177] and Gray's confectioners (13 Dawson). The blind piano-tuner is met in Dawson Street and helped across the traffic to Molesworth.[178] Bloom passes the post office (No. 4) and Doran's pub (No. 10),[179] sees Sir Frederick Falkiner entering the freemason's hall (Nos. 17-18), reaches Kildare Street, and dodges into the museum to escape meeting Boylan.[180] His peregrinations have brought him through a great circle directly south of O'Connell Bridge, as his earlier walk to the baths had covered the area just east of this. And in his travels he, like Ulysses, has seen much of the customs and commerce of man.

The National Library (6 Kildare, T. W. Lyster, librarian) is the scene of Stephen's discussion on *Hamlet*, and the foot-weary sightseer may rest for a moment. But an even more extensive geographical exploration of Dublin awaits him. In the "Wandering Rocks" episode we are introduced to no less than fifteen separate areas of town. Father Conmee starts from the vicinity of Mountjoy Square (north) on his afternoon walk to Artane while Corny Kelleher sits in O'Neill's undertaking establishment at Newcomen Bridge; the begging sailor enters Eccles Street; the girl at Thornton's (63 Grafton Street) sells a red carnation to Boylan; Artifoni talks to Stephen at Trinity College; Lambert shows to the Reverend Love the groined ceiling of St. Mary's Abbey (west of Nelson's Pillar, behind Capel Street); Lenehan and his friends saunter in the neighborhood between Trinity and the Castle; Bloom rents the *Sweets of Sin* (at the stall of Francis Fitzgerald, near the metal bridge, west of O'Connell Bridge); the Dedalus family meet at Dillon's auction-rooms; Kernan walks along the business section north of the river; Father Cowley and Simon Dedalus chat in the neighborhood of the metal bridge; the mad Farrell bumps his way along Merrion Square (southwest); in the Grafton Street district the orphan son of Dignam brings pork steaks home.

Almost the entire central area of Dublin is covered. To the north, Conmee, the begging sailor, Corny; riverward, Lambert, Bloom, the Dedaluses, Kernan, Cowley; south, Boylan, Artifoni, Lenehan, Dignam. These scenes are so intertwined and the streets, shops, and landmarks so extensive that it would require a full chapter to identify them. And, throughout, the paths of the ignoble pamphlet *Elijah* and the splendid regal parade provide an ironic-heroic counterpoint. The pamphlet floats unnoticed down the Liffey into the bay. The procession goes from Phoenix Park along the river to the center of town, thence southwest past Merrion Square to Haddington Road and Ballsbridge. The royal representatives are on their way to open a charity bazaar. The curious reader may enjoy tracing the progress on a map, as the place indications are clearly given.

The bustle of the city is less pronounced throughout the late afternoon and evening. Bloom walks along Ormond quay to the hotel (Nos. 41 and 42), passing displays of pipes, antiques, and religious art; he purchases stationery en route. On leaving the hotel he gazes vacantly at a melodeon in Mark's antique shop (No. 16).

Bernard Kiernan and Company, wholesale grocers, wine and brandy shippers (8, 9, 10 Little Britain Street), is the scene of the political dispute with the Citizen. Kiernan's is about three blocks north of Ormond quay, just off Capel Street. The twilight scene takes place on the same beach where Stephen walked in the morning, and the hospital scene is at Horne's National Maternity Hospital (29–31 Holles Street, north of Merrion Square). Shortly before midnight Bloom stumbles through the slum area north of the Customs House, purchasing a sheep's trotter at Olhousen's (72 Talbot Street). The brothel is Mrs.

Cohen's, 82 Lower Tyrone Street (about a quarter of a mile west of the Amiens Street Station, and the same distance north of the Customs House).

Bloom and Stephen wander together by way of the Customs House, Stephen thinking of Ibsen at Baird's stoneyard as he had in the *Portrait*.[204] They linger in the cabman's shelter of Skin-the-Goat Fitzharris, in the dock area.

Their path homeward is cited as the answer to the first question in the homecoming chapter. Passing through Gardiner Street, Temple Street, and crossing the circus before St. George's Church, they finally reach 7 Eccles Street; and the long day's journey is over.

In addition to the resemblances between *Ulysses* and Homer and the echoes of *Hamlet* which can be noticed, the influence of Dante is apparent. Such careful geographical documentation reminds one of the accuracy with which the Inferno, Purgatory, and Paradise of the medieval epic were traced, and the many maps of Dante's dreamworld which zealous scholars have drawn. Bloom is a wanderer in an inferno only too real and worldly. In each area, characteristic of the theme of the given chapter, he meets personages, observing them and conversing with them. Like Dante, Joyce does not scruple to use living individuals to people his scene. The symbolic significance of the episodes is typically medieval; so, too, the deliberate attempt to include all phases of civilization within the scope of a single story. A minor resemblance is that of the theme of reunion in both works—

the meeting of Dante and Beatrice having its profane counterpart in the acquaintance of Bloom and Stephen. Above all else, *Ulysses* becomes a microcosm of modern civilization, as the *Divine Comedy* represents the summation of medieval culture in its harmonious union of science, art, politics, poetry, and religion.

It is worthy of note that Blake, Defoe, and *Hamlet* were the subjects of lectures given by an obscure teacher at the Commercial Academy of Trieste in 1913 and that this teacher, as Gorman points out,[220] finished the *Portrait* and began *Ulysses* the same year. Defoe and Blake represent the poles of Dante's art as well as those of Joyce's—objective detail and metaphysical speculation.

IX THE STREAM OF LIFE: *PSYCHO-LOGICAL ASSOCIATIONISM*

Always passing, the stream of life, which in the stream of life we trace.[85]

ONE of the striking features of Joyce's style is the unusual fluidity with which it turns from the outer to the inner world. It is a style capable of rendering sense-impressions directly as they fall upon the mind and of showing how these impressions give rise to a chain of association within the mind. The ease and clarity with which these two facets of reality are depicted is amazing. The stark words descriptive of the sights and sounds of contemporary Dublin are contrasted with the elliptical syntax, the broken and incomplete phrases, the lack of logic, the fragmentary or distorted words, by which Joyce suggests thought in the process of becoming. Direct interpretation by the novelist is eliminated; indeed, no indication is made of the shift from outer to inner. The stream of life is rendered as it flows. In contrast to Marcel Proust, engaged on much the same quest, Joyce does not linger over the discoveries he makes regarding the action of the mind, weaving a tapestry of rumination about his theme and its implications; all is direct, immediate.

Most common of the mental laws which Joyce demonstrates is that of association. The reference in Milly's letter to a popular song about the seaside

girls calls to Bloom's mind an early seaside vacation
with his wife;[66] McCoy's question about the concert
tour—"Who's getting it up?"—suggests getting up
in the morning, and Bloom thinks of his wife still lying
in bed, telling fortunes by cards.[74] A longer train of
association is seen in the announcement of Mrs. Palmer's performance of *Leah*. It recalls her playing
Hamlet the night before, which, in turn, prompts
thoughts of his father's admiration for the play, of
Ophelia's and his father's suicides.[75] We see Bloom
reckoning dates,[153] attempting to estimate mentally
the profits in porter, the figures fading from his mind
by lapse of attention[58] or the calculation being interrupted by the roar of a train on an overhead bridge.[78]

He tries to recall the names of people, Peter Carey
coming to mind because of St. Peter Claver (actually
James Carey).[80] He tries vainly to place Peake, one of
the deceased listed in the morning paper;[90] Father
Coffey, who preaches at the grave, has a name that
reminds him of coffin,[102] just as earlier the thought of
the fruit citron leads him to recollections of a former
neighbor of that name.[60] The grave of Robert Emery
brings to mind the Irish patriot, Robert Emmet,[112]
whose dying words linger on his lips as he leaves the
Ormond Hotel late in the afternoon.[286] Thought trans-
fers also occur in the case of the mixing of Mrs. Purefoy, who is in childbirth at the hospital, with Beaufoy, the successful author of *Titbits*.[156] Frequently the
mental processes of Bloom are difficult to recognize,
as the thought remains suspended, sometimes for
hours, during the day. The names of the deceased in
the morning paper, "Callan, Coleman,"[90] come to
mind as he writes to Martha at four in the afternoon[275]

and are given as references by the drunken Bloom undergoing trial in a vision at midnight.[456] The law of floating bodies, suggested to him at ten in the morning,[71] is finally associated with Archimedes at twilight.[371] "Pen . . . ?"[153] becomes Penrose an hour later.[179]

The adoption of disguises or *personae*, as an individual creates a mask in meeting someone, is demonstrated in Bloom's greeting of his neighbor O'Rourke,[58] as he practices a nonchalant air before asking for his letter at the post office,[71] and as he converses with Mrs. Breen.[154] Interesting illustrations of Freud's theory that a slip of the tongue may reveal a hidden inhibition are to be found. Bloom substitutes "managerer" for "manager" as he speaks in the brothel of the concert tour, the dubious relation that exists between Boylan and his wife being responsible for the slip.[433] His shame at the sexual excitement of seeing Gerty MacDowell on the beach causes him to think of Milly's voluptuousness, "handed down from father to mother to daughter, I mean."[365] Molly's unfaithfulness also leaves its mark upon the conversation at Kiernan's, where Bloom, discussing Mrs. Dignam's insurance, amusingly substitutes "admirers" for "advisers":

So the wife comes out top dog, what?
  —Well, that's a point, says Bloom, for the wife's admirers.
  —Whose admirers? says Joe.
  —The wife's advisers, I mean, says Bloom.[307]

The slip is recalled in the "Circe" visions, indicating that it rested uneasily in Bloom's subconscious.[441]

It is the range of the associations and the variety of Bloom's interests that make *Ulysses* so comprehensive a picture of modern civilization. The eager intelligence and keenness of perception of this alert little man allow no observation to pass unnoticed. In the "Lotus Eaters" chapter, where the only action is Bloom's stroll to the baths, this facet of the novel can best be demonstrated. The Homeric motif of this chapter (oblivion) is quite pertinent.

Bloom walks along the quay. Passing a post office, he recalls Martha's letter; a small boy smoking gives rise to paternal instincts. He thinks of the time of the funeral, then of Corny, the undertaker's assistant. A tea advertisement starts him dreaming of the oblivion of the East, then of the force of gravity (suggested by the notion of floating in the Dead Sea), and of his high-school teacher of physics. The inexactness of his recollection of scientific law is an oblique commentary upon mass education. He recalls the provocative swagger of the hips of the girl he met at the butcher's. As he asks for his letter at the branch post office, a recruiting poster turns his thoughts to army discipline, imperialism, and home rule. The soldiers look hypnotized (another instance of oblivion). His opening of the letter is interrupted by a meeting with M'Coy, who talks about the funeral. Bloom listens halfheartedly, more interested in the letter than in the conversation.

His attention is further distracted by a glimpse of a handsome woman about to step into a carriage. He forms a scornful opinion of society women, but his eagerly awaited glimpse of her ankles (this is 1904) is interrupted by a passing tram. He remembers seeing a

girl adjusting her garters; he glances at an advertisement in the paper; meanwhile, the conversation takes
its desultory course. He speaks of Molly's tour, recalls her slovenly habits of rising late. A theater announcement suggests his father's literary interests and
his suicide. M'Coy goes, and he considers him with
contempt. A pair of geldings munching oats again leads
to the oblivion theme.

Passing a cab-shelter, he displays his ever present
sympathy for the unfortunate as he thinks of the
difficult occupation of cabbies. He hums one of his
wife's songs. A child playing marbles beside a blinking
cat (oblivion) recalls his school days. The letter is read
and reflected on. The inclosure, a flower, turns his
thoughts to the language of flowers. The pin suggests
a vulgar song about Mairy's drawers, sung long ago
by two sluts in the slums. Martha's name brings to
mind a religious picture of Mary and Martha, and we
are afforded a glimpse of his sentimental taste in
painting. As he tears up the envelope, he thinks of
tearing up checks, of wealthy men, of profits in distilling.

A church attracts his attention, and, stepping inside, Bloom sees a poster on missions, which again
brings up the East (oblivion). He criticizes the sacra-
ments somewhat rationalistically, toys with the idea
of meeting Martha in church, then turns to the mur-
derer Carey, who received communion. A glance at
the choir leads to music and to the monastic life.

As he leaves the church, he notices his unbuttoned
waistcoat, with reflections on sex attraction. He checks
the time, remembers his wife's prescription. While he
is walking to the chemist's, his forgotten house-key

and the funeral come to mind. The chemist's shop brings to mind drugs (oblivion) and cosmetics. Leaving, soap in hand, he meets Lyons, eager about the Gold Cup race, and gives him the newspaper and the unconscious tip. Gambling next occupies his thoughts, and Fleming's escape to America after embezzling (oblivion). A poster advertising bicycle races is scrutinized with professional acumen. The weather suggests cricket, and he anticipates the oblivion of the bath as he passes from sight.

With such trivial and fleeting thoughts is Bloom's mind completely revealed to us. So, too, are science, politics, sex, childhood, business, religion, chemistry, and sports touched upon, as well as Bloom's relationship with his entire circle of acquaintances and relatives—Molly, Boylan, his father, M'Coy, and Martha. No wonder that, to the casual reader or to one conventionally minded in literary taste, *Ulysses* seems merely a grab-bag of miscellaneousness. Even less remarkable is it that the student of modern literature finds it one of the most carefully integrated and technically brilliant achievements of fiction, a work that in its comprehensiveness remains the masterpiece, not only of Dublin, but of modern civilization.

One must always beware of taking *Ulysses* too seriously. A psychological document of some importance it assuredly is, but frequently one suspects that Joyce's intention is as much comic as profound; for is not this little man, Leopold Bloom, with his rambling and inconsequential mind, as ludicrous in his way as his earlier forebears, Uncle Toby and his brother, father of Tristram Shandy? Like Sterne, Joyce seems often to feel that the most unpredictable, and hence the most comic, thing in creation is the human mind. Unruly, illogical, often ribald, its vagaries are preposterous to the point of unbelief.

The supreme achievement of psychological insight is reached in the "Circe" scene, where the night-side of the mind, the subconscious, is effectively dramatized. Taking place in the slums, the sinister figures only half-apprehended by the intoxicated Bloom, the setting is most appropriate to the theme—the rendition of the animal impulses of the id. The stagnant backwaters of urban life are described—dilapidated houses, tram tracks, squabbling men and women, danger signals, a deaf-mute idiot, a pigmy woman, a sprawled figure against a dustbin, a crone with a smoky lamp. The atmosphere is lurid:

Snakes of river fog creep slowly. From drains, clefts, cesspools, middens arise on all sides stagnant fumes.[426]

A fire blazes on the horizon. Stephen and Lynch enter the brothel, followed by the panting Bloom, who is almost struck by a sandstrewer of the tram company.[428] A mangy dog (perhaps suggestive of Athos) brings before Bloom's mind the vision of his father,[430] the voice of Bloom's own guilty conscience.

With the grating voice of a bawd, Bloom comes back to reality and approaches the house.[434] An eight-page interlude of reproving visions apparently occurs almost instantaneously, Gerty MacDowell and Mrs. Breen embarrassing him with their questions. Bloom *"walks on towards hellsgates"*[422] to the accompanying jeers of loiterers.

Associations of the day's experiences pile upon one another in bewildering profusion. As in a nightmare, the memories of experience merge and entangle. Wreaths of smoke become the *Sweets of Sin;*[444] the mangy dog begins to resemble Garryowen, the hound at Kiernan's;[445] Bloom's thought of kindness to animals suggests the circus, and the sadistic Maffei[446] of Molly's morning reading.[64] The uniform of a watchman brings to mind Martha,[448] whose letter he got at the post office while gazing at the recruiting poster.[71] In attempting to justify himself before the personifications of his guilt, Bloom engages in wishful thinking, identifying himself as an author-journalist.[449] Beaufoy, author of "Matcham's Masterstroke,"[68] now accuses him of plagiarism,[450] and a trial ensues (perhaps suggested by the discussion of famous trials in the newspaper office at noon[137]). J. J. O'Molloy defends him against numerous accusers before a jury comprised of acquaintances of the day. The vision recedes, and it is discovered that the imagined sound of kisses arises from the sequins on the dress of the prostitute Zoe.[466]

From the time Bloom leaped to the curb to avoid the street-cleaner (on p. 428) until he is greeted by Zoe at Bella Cohen's (p. 466) not more than a few seconds must have elapsed; yet in this time Bloom has lived through a nightmare of experience. His father and mother, the druggist, Molly, Gerty, Mrs. Breen, Alf Bergan, Richie Goulding, Pat, the waiter at the Ormond, Garryowen, the gulls, Bob Doran, Maffei, Beaufoy, Martha, Myles Crawford, the ghost of Dignam, and the entire court scene have passed before his mind.

A vulgar conversation with Zoe follows, and the

contemptuous suggestion that Bloom make a speech leads to the second long apparition. This time it is a delusion of grandeur, the apotheosis of the little man's many ingenious commercial and political schemes.[469] We realize that this extended vision is also the product of only a split second's reflection, for the words of the prostitute about making a speech are followed, twenty pages later, by "Talk away till you're black in the face,"[488] which is apparently the conclusion of her former assertion.

In a burst of applause from representatives of the public Bloom becomes Lord Mayor and proclaims his municipal and national reform program, ridiculously distorted in an alcoholic vision. But the reproving voice of the evangelist Dowie is heard[482] (from the *Elijah* brochure of the morning).[149] The evidence of Mulligan and the medical students of Holles Street Hospital is added;[483] the crowd turns against him, and he imagines himself burned to death[488] (an echo of the fire brigade, heard rushing to south Dublin at eleven).[420]

Bloom enters and follows Zoe into the music-room to hear the pianola.[491] A man passes with *"apes's gait."* The room is crowded, Stephen standing by the machine, Lynch seated on the floor beating time. The point of view now shifts to Stephen, whose philosophical conversation is mocked by Lynch's cap.[493] The characters of the prostitutes merge, the visions of Bloom and Stephen coalesce. Elijah appears, as do the participants in the library discussion; a grotesque Virag (Bloom's father) wears the brown mackintosh,[500] which had puzzled Bloom at the cemetery.[108] Reality once again intrudes; the silver-foil chocolate wrapper[514] and Bella Cohen's fan impinge upon the consciousness.[516]

The depth of Bloom's shame is reached in ensuing visions. He is transformed into a woman;[526] the most nauseating humiliations are inflicted upon him. For a moment he is Rip Van Winkle, turning his senile memory to the joys of his first married days;[530] again, he witnesses Boylan's seduction of Molly.[551] Reduced to the point of maudlin tears, he admits his sins and cries for forgiveness.

Meanwhile, Stephen's visions continue. His schoolmaster, his father, the corpse of his mother, and Mulligan emerge. The pianola blares forth the tune "My Girl's a Yorkshire Girl."[561] A mad dance ensues; to Bloom it is the dance of the hours,[561] suggested by his morning memory of a bazaar dance with Molly;[69] to Stephen it is the "noise in the street"[559] by which he had defined God to Mr. Deasy at school.[35] The dance reaches its climax:

The couples fall aside. Stephen whirls giddily. Room whirls back. Eyes closed, he totters. Red rails fly spacewards. Stars all around suns turn roundabout.[564]

In the dizzy motion so deftly described in this stage-direction, Stephen's mother makes her last plea to him. He refuses thrice, finally smashing the chandelier with his cane. The room is plunged into darkness, depicted in the phrase of Stephen's morning meditation:

Time's livid final flame leaps and, in the following darkness, ruin of all space, shattered glass and toppling masonry.[567]

Shouts fill the room. Bella threatens to call the police. Bloom pays for the damage and hurries into the street after his protégé, followed in imagination by the spirits of all his casual acquaintances.[571] On the street, Stephen's intoxication leads him to utter anti-British sentiments. Two privates are about to challenge him. The excitement of this altercation merges with the din of the slums and the distant flare of the fire to create a true *Götterdämmerung*—a symbolic picture of the chaos that *Ulysses* portrays:

Brimstone fires spring up. Dense clouds roll past. Heavy Gatling guns boom. Pandemonium. Troops deploy. . . . . Shrieks of dying. Pikes clash on cuirasses. Thieves rob the slain. Birds of prey, winging from the sea, rising from marshlands, swooping from eyries, hover screaming . . . . The midnight sun is darkened. The earth trembles. The dead of Dublin from Prospect and Mount Jerome in white sheepskin overcoats and black goatfell cloaks arise and appear to many. A chasm opens with a noiseless yawn. . . . . It rains dragon's teeth.[582]

As the fight in the street gains in momentum, Bloom's friend, Corny Kelleher, arrives to rescue them. The young intellectual, collapsing in the street, appears to the paternal Bloom as his beloved Rudy, dressed in an Eton suit, holding a book in his hand, a white lambkin peeping from his pocket.[593]

No paraphrase or analysis can do justice to the significance of the "Circe" episode. Practically every character met during the day, all ideas, experiences, and impressions, culminate in intoxicated dream. On the naturalistic plane a description of the underside of urban existence, it is allegorically a prophecy of the doom of a world without God. Psychologically, it is one of the most ambitious attempts in literature to render the world of the subconscious, the seething mass of memory, desire, and frustration elucidated by Freud.

X   MUSIC EVERYWHERE: *THE WORLD OF SOUND*

Sea, wind, leaves, thunder, waters, cows lowing, the cattle market, cocks, hens don't crow, snakes hissss. There's music everywhere.[277]

THOUGH Joyce has been universally hailed as one of the most accomplished stylists in English literature, no commentator has attempted to define his linguistic mastery. It is no wonder; to describe poetic qualities is the despair of the critic. Like music, the finest stylistic achievements defy analysis. One can only point to particular passages and say "Si monumentum requiris, circumspice." Technical features—alliteration, rhythm, repetition, cadence—can be noted, but the final effect must be grasped intuitively.

If artistic achievement is to be gauged by the harmony of matter and manner, *Ulysses* represents the peak of Joyce's art. The *Portrait* is more limited in scope and often self-consciously literary in the vein of Walter Pater; the stories in *Dubliners* are exquisitely rendered, but in a minor key; *Finnegans Wake* is a tour de force which lacks the astonishing variety of *Ulysses*. Here one sees such a brilliant display of style, so many passages of amazing virtuosity, that it seems impossible to select among them. Of the hundreds of quotations cited in this study it may be said that any of them can be re-read with increasing perception of the harmony of meaning and expression, be it sensuous, satiric, or philosophical.

The structure of *Ulysses* is itself musical. Ezra Pound has likened the work to the sonata, with the two major themes, those of Stephen and Bloom, introduced, developed, combined, and recapitulated. The earlier chapter on the "Dance of the Hours" shows an even more striking resemblance to the orchestral suite, with the important changes of style determined by the tonal intention of the various episodes. Readers will recall that the book is far from being a series of finger exercises in technique but that one could almost label the episodes symbolically, in the manner of Milton's companion poems on the happy and the contemplative man. We are shown the outer and inner life of the intellectual, the life of the man of business, life in industrial and urban society, life as seen from the perspectives of poetic yearning, subconscious desire, and cosmic mystery.

It is a world of sound that *Ulysses* describes. The major characters think in terms of music or poetry. To Stephen recur the prayer, *Liliata rutilantium*, which he failed to utter for his mother,[12] a song from Yeats's *Countess Cathleen*, lines from "Lycidas,"[26] Blake,[34] the seventeenth-century lyric "White thy fambles,"[48] and, above all, phrases from *Hamlet*. Buck Mulligan's taste is hardly on this level. He sings ditties about coronation day,[12] Mary Ann "hising up her petticoats,"[15] the ballad of Joking Jesus,[21] and a limerick when the occasion arises.

Bloom's consciousness buzzes with the phrases of his wife's songs. She is to render "Lá ci darem" and "Love's Old Sweet Song" in her next recital;[63] throughout the day he recalls Boylan's tune about the seaside

girls, mentioned in Milly's letter;[66] he remembers two
sluts in the Coombe singing about Mairy's drawers,[77]
and the drunken song of Mrs. Cunningham, "The
Geisha of Asia."[95] A silly rhyme echoes in his consciousness as he tells Mrs. Breen about the funeral;[155] he
catches himself singing at the grave.[103] Lines on "the
hungry famished gull" come to mind as he throws
crumbs into the Liffey, and he speculates on the nature of poetry.[150] Warmed by Burgundy at lunch, he
hums a passage from *Don Giovanni*.[177]

Bloom confides his love of music to Stephen as they
walk home, but his preferences—Moody and Sankey
hymns, Rossini, *Don Giovanni*, and *Martha*—are
scarcely such as to interest his companion, who admires the Elizabethan lutanists and the seventeenth-
century Dutch composer Sweelinck.[645]

To trace the recurrences of these thematic songs
would reveal how large a part music plays in the consciousness of the two characters. Music is one of the
most potent of subconscious recalls; it rises unexpect-
edly to mind and, in turn, leads to appropriate moods
and associations. Such constant psychological interplay defies detailed analysis; an index of themes will
serve to indicate the multitude of musical references
in the text, but the careful reader will take pleasure in
discovering for himself Joyce's revelation of how extensive a part sound plays in the operation of the
mind—a fact never so completely demonstrated in
literature as by *Ulysses*.

The noises of city life provide a running accompaniment to the narrative of the day. Stephen at school
hears the clatter of hockey-sticks in the hallway,[28] the

cries of the boys on the field,[29] the referee's whistle,[33] and the "shout in the street" which provides him with a skeptical definition of God.[35] During his walk on the beach the crunch of his footsteps on the sand is noted;[38] the ceaseless roar of the waves forms the accompaniment of his meditation.

Turning to Eccles Street, we hear the plaintive whine of the cat[55] and the jingle of the loose metal quoits on Molly's bed.[56] A "creak and a dark whirr" in the air introduces the first tolling of the bells of St. George's Church.[69] A clanging tramcar intercepts Bloom's anticipated glimpse of a woman's ankles as he walks to the bath,[73] a train rumbling overhead distracts him from some calculations.[78] We are aware of the rattle of the funeral carriage over the cobblestones;[86] we hear the angry shouts of the cattle-drover,[96] the cries of peddlers at Nelson's Pillar,[94] the thud of the damp clay on the coffin,[109] and the stirring pebbles which attract Bloom's attention to the rat.[112]

The newspaper scene opens with the bawling of the tram starter and the clangor of city traffic. The din of the presses forces Bloom to use sign language to explain his advertisement to the compositor.[119] Emerging from the office, he again hears the traffic of the city. There are street-cries,[150] overheard conversations,[151] the trams again,[153] the heavy accents of gorging diners at the lunch-joint.[167] In the "Wandering Rocks" episode the noise of the cavalcade and the blaring music of the Highland band rise to a crescendo, a magnificent fanfare, immediately followed by the melodies of the "Sirens" scene. Here music is of the essence—content, mood, and style form a brilliant study in rhythmic and melodic variation.

Of the remaining episodes, only the "Circe" scene uses sound to any extent. It is as though, in keeping with the spirit and narrative tone of the saloon and hospital scenes, the confined indoor atmosphere precludes normal tones, as the sound technician of radio or screen muffles the accompaniment when a door is shut. The bleak and cold impersonality of the homecoming is noted only by the tolling of St. George's clock.

In "Circe" there are the street cries, the unintelligible mutter of the idiot, bawdy songs, the rattling bells of the cyclists, and the gong of the tram. Among remembered sounds are those of the cuckoo clock and the bed quoits,[461] the chimes of St. George's,[463] the bell of Dillon's auction-rooms,[527] the sound of a waterfall,[536] the bleat of a goat on Howth Hill,[537] the song of the sluts.[539] We hear the rustling of sequins on Zoe's dress,[466] the blare of a gramophone,[494] the squeak of a door handle,[513] the snap of a trouser's button,[539] the rustling of silver foil,[540] the insipid notes of the pianola,[561] the ring of dancing bracelets,[562] the guttering sound of a gas jet.[568] In the street fight the altercation is accompanied by the bark of a stray dog[585] and the neighing of a horse.[590]

Even Molly's reverie is interrupted by the distant whistle of a train[739] speedily approaching Dublin[747] and the tolling of 2:00 A.M. from St. George's Church.[757]

Of course, the inclusion of sound effects could be achieved by any competent and conscientious realist. It is in the poetic rendition of these sounds that Joyce displays his genius. Foremost among these devices is that of onomatopoeia. The slow procession across the beach of the cockle-pickers is rendered by a succession of effortful verbs—"She trudges, schlepps, trains, drags, trascines her load."[48] (Verbs, incidentally, running the gamut of English, German, French, English, and Italian.) Assonance, rhyme, alliteration, and rhythm play their part in suggesting the surging tide:

In cups of rocks it slops: flop, slop, slap: bounded in barrels. And, spent, its speech ceases. It flows purling, widely flowing, floating foampool, flower unfurling.[50]

Repetition in reverse order is responsible for the striking musical effect of the loading of a beer van:

Grossbooted draymen rolled barrels dullthudding out of Prince's stores and bumped them up on the brewery float. On the brewery float bumped dullthudding barrels rolled by grossbooted draymen out of Prince's stores.[115]

The monotonous pounding of the presses is imitated by spaced repetition:

Sllt. The nethermost deck of the first machine jogged forward its flyboard with sllt the first batch of quirefolded papers. Sllt. Almost human the way it sllt to call attention.[120]

City traffic is successfully portrayed in a lengthy catalogue, with an interesting placing of verbs and adverbs:

Hackney cars, cabs, delivery waggons, mailvans, private broughams, aerated mineral water floats with rattling crates of bottles, rattled, rolled, horsedrawn, rapidly.[147]

The nauseating eating habits of the bums at the lunch counter are rendered by staccato alliteration—"Gulp. Grub. Gulp. Gobstuff."[168]

Even the intangible processes of thought are imitatively suggested in the circular or repetitious sen-

tence, as in Stephen's trailing thoughts of the past—
"When one reads these strange pages of one long gone
one feels that one is at one with one who once . . . . "[41]
—or in Bloom's reflections on the flow of life:

Always passing, the stream of life, which in the stream of life we
trace is dearer than them all.[85]

Closely associated with onomatopoeia is Joyce's
daring in word coinages and word linkings. His staggering vocabulary of 29,899 words is a philologist's
paradise. It is comprised of archaisms, neologisms,
puns; it illustrates almost every known law of word
formation.

Most frequent of Joyce's word formations is that of
combination. This is a native language trait, which
can be seen in the words "tomorrow," "redbrown,"
"bloodthirsty." A spot check of 5,000 words in Webster's *Collegiate Dictionary* beginning in *ca-* shows that
38 such unhyphenated compounds (without regular
suffixes) are included. The same section of the *Word
Index to Ulysses* shows that, of the 500 words Joyce
uses in the same section of the alphabet, 40 are unhyphenated compounds—ten times the proportion in
conventional English. That this compounding is increasing with the growing colloquialization of narrative style may be seen by the following figures for the
first ten pages of Fielding's *Tom Jones* (8), Dickens'
David Copperfield (15), Thackeray's *Vanity Fair* (14),
Hemingway's *For Whom the Bell Tolls* (19), John Dos
Passos' *Manhattan Transfer* (52), and Joyce's *Ulysses*
(64).

The principal effect of compounding is rhythmic
and can best be appreciated in the context. Yet, when

we read that Gerty's brows are "silkilyseductive,"[342] more is implied than each word separately would mean; so, too, the word "ardentbold,"[265] descriptive of Boylan, is perfectly in keeping with the proper satiric tone. The combined word "drumthumped"[250] exactly touches off the Highland band, while the narrator expresses his contempt for Bloom's racial features with the derisive "dunducketymudcoloured mug."[325] When we read that Davy Byrne "smiledyawnednodded all in one"[175] or that Miss Douce "smilesmirked supercilious,"[262] we feel that the phrasing is most felicitous.

Hundreds of passages could be cited as examples of the rhythmic effect of compounding, but one must suffice. Here the joining of words produces a blurred effect, as of a Corot landscape. Stephen gazes at the sea from the parapet of the tower:

Woodshadows floated silently by through the morning peace from the stairhead seaward where he gazed. Inshore and farther out the mirror of water whitened, spurned by lightshod hurrying feet. White breast of the dim sea. The twining stresses, two by two. A hand plucking the harpstrings merging their twining chords. Wavewhite wedded words shimmering on the dim tide.[11]

Closely related to the compounding of words is the word blend, in which the conclusion of the first member overlaps the beginning of the last. The two words, recognizable separately, are so married that neither is complete without the other. This trick, so common in modern journalism, is akin to the pun. Such is the "blandiloquence"[603] of the bum Corley, asking Stephen to get him a job. The "jocoserious"[661] tone of the late colloquy in Eccles Street is a true blend of the geniality of the host and the reticence of the guest. In

passing, one might mention the "abstrusiosities"[46] of
Stephen's medieval turn of mind and the "Malthusi-
asts"[416] discussed at the hospital.

Possibly most ingenious of Joyce's word devices is
the phonetic spelling of sounds. When we see "aw-
fullygladaseeragain,"[112] we may be a bit startled, until
we realize that it is merely a transcript of conversational elision. So the expanded form "Steeeeeeeeee-
phen"[21] resembles the stress of a high-pitched call. The
"zmells de bloodz oldz an Iridzman"[45] is clearly imi-
tative.

Readers will immediately recall the oddly spelled
whimper of the cat in Bloom's kitchen—"Mkgnao,"
"Mrkgnao," and "Mrkrgnao" in crescendo.[55] Such
phonetic spellings are found in profusion throughout
the book. Pigeons "roocoocoo" under the porch of the
bank.[225] The hushed whispering at confession is imagined by Bloom: "And I schschschschschsch. And did
you chachachachacha?"[81] The half-heard calls of a
vendor become the unintelligible "oot,"[92] the cry of a
lamb "maaaaaa,"[162] as those of cow and calf "moo"
and "meh."[168] A yawn is "Iiiiiiaaaaaaach!"[175] The
elements of phonetic spelling and of duplication in a
circular motion form a ludicrous imitation of a scratchy
phonograph record:

Kraahraark! Hellohellohello amawfullyglad kraark awfullyglad-
aseeragain hellohello amarawf kopthsth.[112]

Reduplication is an elemental speech trait, common
in the babble of children. We find in *Ulysses* "boya-
boy,"[377] "Burblblbrurblbl" (a beagle's call),[557] "chew-
chewchew,"[167] "dringadring" (chimes),[41] "haltyaltyal-
tyall" (bicycle bells).[428] Particularly effective uses of

this device are to be found in the melancholy phrase in which Molly's hair is described as Bloom imagines her dead, with her "wavyavyeavyheavyeavyevyevy hair un comb:'d,"[273] and in the sustained "endlessness-nessness"[271] of the empyrean.

Similar to reduplication is the process of sound gradation, seen in the principal parts of English verbs, such as "drink, drank, drunk." Joyce renders the sound of footsteps on the sand by "crush, crack, crik, crick."[38] A cloud covers the sun "wholly, slowly, wholly."[61] Stephen thinks contemptuously of the wailing "creecries" of the theosophists of the revival.[189]

Unusual effects are sometimes gained by forcing a word back into its original etymological significance, thus removing the blurred metaphorical effect of modern English. So the caretaker in the cemetery traverses the "dismal" fields,[110] bringing into sharp focus the basic significance of the word—"evil day." Joyce writes of the "crazy" windows of the funeral carriage[86] and, in speaking of the ringing of bells, describes the "bells with bells with bells acquiring."[195]

The pun is notorious now as the lowest form of wit, but it was not always so. In Elizabethan days it was considered a legitimate linguistic device, capable even of achieving effects of pathos. It plays an important part in the characteristic conceits of the metaphysical poets and can be found in profusion in Shakespeare, not only in the scenes of low comedy but in the sonnets and in some of the moving pasages of *Romeo and Juliet* and *Antony and Cleopatra*. Joyce's love for Elizabethan literature is well known; it colors Stephen's thought in both the *Portrait* and in *Ulysses*. With

the Elizabethans Joyce shares a love of language almost reaching the point of exhilaration; and he has,
too, that complex aesthetic response of wit, irony, and
pathos which has proved so foreign to readers of the
eighteenth and nineteenth centuries but which has
once again come into vogue, at least in sophisticated
circles, with the poetry of T. S. Eliot and W. H.
Auden, to mention only two of the modern metaphysical stylists.

The principal reason for the present low repute of
the pun is that it too often relies upon nothing more
than an inane word resemblance. Once the shock of
surprise has worn off, there is no insight or criticism,
such as distinguishes humor of higher quality. Of this
type—the garden variety of pun—we find a few examples in *Ulysses*. The custom of caning sailors is one
"more honored in the breach than in the observ-
ance";[323] a prostitute is described as a "lily of the
alley,"[501] though here a shade more of significance can
be observed. Even this type of pun may plausibly be
justified as a natural expression of play with words, a
sort of game in and of itself.

The higher levels of punning rest not merely on
verbal surprise but have a witty pertinence, often of a
blasphemous or parody-like effect. Note Stephen's
reference to "Lawn Tennyson,"[51] which ridicules perfectly the genteel effeminacy of the Victorian poet.
The dominance of commercial values today is suggested by the denomination of the opening of the
Bible as the "first chapter of Guinness's"[130] and by
the narrator's scorn for the "syphilisation" of the
British imperialist.[319] "Tramp, tramp, tramp, the
boys are . . . . parching"[417] indicates the nature of the

half-hypnotized recruit noticed by Bloom earlier in the day and implies that an army marches on little else than its stomach. Even more akin to the wit of the metaphysicals is Stephen's succinct summary of the infidelity of Shakespeare's wife: "If others have their will Ann hath a way."[189] Pun, parody, and pathos are combined in the statement "Greater love than this . . . . no man hath that a man lay down his wife for his friend,"[387] for it is just this situation that confronts Bloom.

The characters of *Ulysses* share a more than normal curiosity about phonetics. Mulligan notes that his name is comprised of two dactyls;[6] Stephen reflects on meter, of course,[38] and tries to imitate vocally the sound of the sea:

His mouth moulded issuing breath, unspeeched: ooeeehah: roar of cataractic planets, globed, blazing, roaring wayawayaway-awayawayaway.[48]

Bloom, too, thinks about poetry and music. He is fascinated by his wife's vocal accomplishments and contemplates a literary career. He notes that a lilting rhythm aids the memory.[58] Groping for a word to describe Molly's singing, he hits on "thrush" and "throstle"—

Beautiful on that *tre* her voice is: weeping tone. A thrush. A throstle. There is a word throstle that expressed that.[92]

He toys with rhyme, concluding that "that is how poets write, the similar sounds";[150] his disgust at the vulgar eating habits of those in the lunch-joint finds an amusing verbal outlet in imagined table talk—"I munched hum un thu Unchster Bunk un Munchday."[167] The silent *p* in "ptarmigan" amuses him — "Do ptake some ptarmigan"—as does the name Dube-dat.[173]

Connoisseurs of language will find hundreds of other examples in random reading of *Ulysses*, but the general reader will be more interested in the passages that demonstrate Joyce's harmony of meaning and style. Stuart Gilbert has identified more than eighty different rhetorical devices in the "Aeolus" chapter alone; we shall not follow in his footsteps.

A few characteristic quotations may serve to indicate Joyce's remarkable command of words, phrasal patterns, and tone. His use of the pause is striking. Note how the spacing of phrases suggests the rhythmic flow of the waves:

> They serpented towards his feet, curling, unfurling many crests, every ninth, breaking, plashing, from far, from farther out, waves and waves.[47]

In Stephen's meditation on the ancient history of Britain, a long rest prepares us for the final poignant cadence:

> Cease to strive. Peace of the druid priests of Cymbeline, hierophantic: from wide earth an altar.[215]

Similar is the periodic sentence, whose sustained meaning is released in its final phrase. An excellent example is that describing Bloom's erotic longings as he passes a lingerie shop:

> Perfume of embraces all him assailed. With hungered flesh obscurely, he mutely craved to adore.[166]

The naturalistic Joyce is equally perceptive and felicitous. Language almost attains to physical sensa-

tion in the description of the butcher wrapping meat
—"The ferreteyed porkbutcher folded the sausages he
had snipped off with blotchy fingers, sausagepink."[59]
The sound of a train interrupts Bloom in his mental
calculations of the profits in porter; aural, visual, and
psychological images are combined:

> An incoming train clanked heavily above his head, coach after
> coach. Barrels bumped in his head: dull porter slopped and
> churned inside. The bungholes sprang open and a huge dull flood
> leaked, flowing together, winding through mudflats all over the
> level land, a lazy pooling swirl of liquor bearing along wideleaved
> flowers of its froth.[78]

Verbal repetition is one of Joyce's most successful
musical effects. The echo quality it gives to his prose
makes his style unique, as would a new instrument
added to a conventional orchestra. On the broadest
scale this art is that of the Wagnerian leitmotiv, which
has been thoroughly analyzed in the earlier chapters
of this study. Joyce was attracted to this feature of
Dujardin's style, but he has carried it to a greater extent than any other novelist. In more restricted space
it is capable of unusual, haunting effects. The repeated
exclamation gives to the description of a fireworks
display a sense of mounting climax:

> And then a rocket sprang and bang shot blind and O! then the
> Roman candle burst and it was like a sigh of O! and everyone
> cried O! O! in raptures and it gushed out of it a stream of rain
> gold hair threads and they shed and ah! they were all greeny
> dewy stars falling with golden, O so lovely! O so soft, sweet,
> soft![360]

In the cemetery the increasing dominance of the white
pallor of tombstones is remarkable. They are first
viewed from a distance:

The stonecutter's yard on the right. Last lap. Crowded on the spit of land silent shapes appeared, white, sorrowful, holding out calm hands, knelt in grief, pointing. Fragments of shapes, hewn. In white silence: appealing.[98]

A page of conversation and reflection intervenes; meanwhile, the cemetery itself is glimpsed in passing:

The high railings of Prospects rippled past their gaze. Dark poplars, rare white forms. Forms more frequent, white shapes thronged amid the trees, white forms and fragments streaming by mutely, sustaining vain gestures on the air.[99]

More poetic is the successive variation of phrases picturing the swooping of the gulls into the Liffey to retrieve the crumbs thrown by Bloom on his way to lunch. Their motion is described five times in a page and a half, in each instance with slight variation in the phrasing or word order. Bloom first notices them "flapping strongly, wheeling"; his thoughts drift to drowning, and meanwhile they "wheeled lower." He next casts down the pamphlet *Elijah* "they wheeled, flapping."[150] He decides to feed them, whereupon "the gulls swooped silently two, then all, from their heights, pouncing on prey." As he leaves the bridge, "they wheeled, flapping weakly."[151]

The brilliant climax of Joyce's prose music is reached in the "Sirens" chapter, where thematic repetition, variation, and cadence are exploited to the full. This episode, like the Anna Livia chapter of *Finnegans Wake*, is the musical quintessence of *Ulysses*.

Lenehan still drank and grinned at his tilted ale and at Miss Douce's lips that all but hummed, not shut, the oceansong her lips had trilled.[261]

THE "Sirens" episode is the cadenza of *Ulysses*. We have already heard wave and tide; felt the music of the spheres; listened to the sounds of a city, living and breathing in the stentorian clangor of business, machinery, and traffic. Now these strains reach a crescendo of verbal virtuosity. The earlier themes are repeated and modulated, and the underlying tone of pathetic loneliness becomes dominant. The tempo marking is not given, but the scene in the Ormond bar is the *andante cantabile* section of the novel.

The chapter opens with an overture of themes— broken phrases that will recur in the context that follows. Though the full meaning of this page and a half is not apparent until the episode is read, it is a mistake to regard these lines as meaningless. Even without the ensuing narrative details, the spirit of music and the tone of pathos are apparent. The background of gaiety in the barroom flirtation is suggested by the marvelously phrased opening line: "Bronze by gold heard the hoofirons, steelyringing."[252] It is carried on by such fragments as "a jumping rose on satiny breasts" or "jingle jingle jaunted jingling." The secondary theme of loneliness is introduced by "cried to bronze in pity," developed with references to a "long and throbbing" and "longindying" call, pointed up in the contrast: "When love absorbs. War! War!" We hear undefined cries of "lost," "alas," "come," "far," before we reach the specific statement, "I feel so sad . . . . so lonely." Meanwhile, personal loneliness becomes gradually submerged by suggestions of a vaster, even cosmic, sense of loss; for we read of "a veil awave upon the waves," of a "moonlit nightcall," of the "cold seahorn" with its "plash and silent roar." This theme also becomes more explicit with the phrase "low in dark middle earth"[253] and the finality of "All gone. All fallen." The summation of these themes or, rather, the increasing dominance of the concept of universal loneliness is seen when the gay first statement is turned into questions:

> Where bronze from anear? Where gold from afar? Where hoofs?

Here is a clear anticipation of the final question of Bloom's day, the brief, unanswered, and significant conclusion of his peregrinations—"Where?"[722]

Like strange voices in a dream, these phrases come to us. Their exact meaning is not clear, but the tone is unmistakable. But is life itself, in its ultimate mystery, so unlike a dream? Glimpses of meaning occur from time to time, fragments of pattern seem to appear; but of positive proof or clear direction little is afforded. That *Ulysses* is an ambitious technical exercise is well known; that it is a naturalistic epic is equally clear; but it is less often recognized that the book is a fulfilment of King Lear's expectation, upon having been reunited with Cordelia, that they will

> take upon 's the mystery of things
> As if we were God's spies.

The chapter itself begins with the phrase "bronze by gold," recalled from the overture. The heads of the two barmaids are at the window, watching with excitement the passing of the cavalcade. Through a "halo of hurried breath" on the glass, they gaze in adolescent enthusiasm, in striking contrast to the subdued hatred and fear felt by the citizens in the conclusion of the "Wandering Rocks" episode. In half a page the bronze Miss Douce, silly and flirtatious, and the older and more sober Mina Kennedy are revealed. Miss Kennedy's weariness and disillusion provide the first sad note in the scene. Her mood is evoked in a passage of remarkable lyric beauty, the effect being based upon artful repetition and variation:

Miss Kennedy sauntered sadly from bright light, twining a loose hair behind an ear. Sauntering sadly, gold no more, she twisted twined a hair. Sadly she twined in sauntering gold hair behind a curving ear.
—It's them has the fine times, sadly she said.[254]

But with Joyce a moment of emotion or pathos is usually followed by the tart sting of irony. As if in mocking answer to her statement about the happiness of the male sex, Joyce turns our attention to the lonely and frustrated Bloom as he plods along Wellington Quay "bearing in his breast the sweets of sin," the book he rented for his wife, who is even now awaiting her assignation with Boylan.

An interlude of gaiety follows, the waitresses playfully scolding the boots who brings their tea. Then the cavalcade is again recalled. In broken rhythm the metrical pattern is suggestive of hoofbeats on the cobblestones:

Yes, bronze from anear, by gold from afar, heard steel from anear, hoofs ring from afar, and heard steelhoofs ringhoof ring-steel.[254]

As Bloom fumbles along the street after Boylan, the barmaids watch him with ridicule. The carefree humor of Miss Douce becomes contagious to her friend; "in a giggling peal young goldbronze voices blend-ed,"[256] and together, "bronze gigglegold," they throw their heads back in mirth:

Shrill, with deep laughter, after bronze in gold, they urged each each to peal after peal, ringing in changes, bronzegold gold-bronze, shrilldeep, to laughter after laughter.[256]

Here the duplication "each each," "peal . . . . peal," the reversal "bronzegold goldbronze," and the rhym-ing unison "laughter after laughter" convey the suc-cessive convulsions of humor.

Simon Dedalus and Lenehan stroll in, each flirting in turn with the receptive Miss Douce. The phrase "jingle jaunty jingle"[258] is the motif for the dapper Boylan, whom Lenehan expects to meet. The "jingle jaunty blazes boy"[259] is being shadowed by the timid Bloom—"Follow. Risk it. Go quick."

As the cavalcade passes from earshot, other sounds take its place. Miss Douce trills a phrase of a song;[257] a tuning fork is struck: "It throbbed, pure, purer, softly and softlier, its buzzing prongs."[260] Dedalus strums at the piano:

Brightly the keys, all twinkling, linked, all harpsichording, called to a voice to sing the strain of dewy morn, of youth, of love's leavetaking, life's, love's morn.[260]

The suspension of the last phrase echoes effectively the mood of the song which becomes dominant in the chapter—a song of lyric loneliness. Boylan approaches, his coin ringing on the counter; the cash register clangs, the clock whirs and strikes.[261]

The bronze-headed Miss Douce, eager for conquest, eyes the jaunty visitor—"sister bronze outsmiled her, preening for him her richer hair, a bosom and a rose."[260] The agitated Bloom secures a table in the near-by restaurant; indifferent to him and his cares, Lenehan and Boylan continue their flirtations. "Sparkling bronze azure eyed Blazure's skyblue bow and eyes";[262] and Lenehan induces the coy barmaid to sound the time by snapping her garters, "smackwarm against her smackable woman's warmhosed thigh." Miss Douce continues to admire Boylan, and Boylan, greedy-eyed, watches her figure disappear down the length of the saloon:

His spellbound eyes went after her gliding head as it went down the bar by mirrors, gilded arch for ginger ale, hock and claret glasses shimmering, a spiky shell, where it concerted, mirrored, bronze with sunnier bronze.[262]

With a reference to "bronze from afar" watching at the window, and "jingle a tinkle" jaunting,[263] we know that Boylan has left. Bloom, watching timidly, realizes what the departure means. His feelings are expressed in a sentence of singular poetic beauty, though with the inevitable overtone of mockery:

Bloom sighed on the silent bluehued flowers.[263]

Brief snatches portray the conquering progress of Boylan "with flick of whip, on bounding tyres,"[265] as he speeds to his assignation. Meanwhile, the songs of Dollard and Cowley come from the piano. One of them is ironically appropriate: "All Is Lost Now."[268] Bloom

dreams wistfully of the past, his thoughts lingering
on the beauty of sound earlier expressed in his meditations on the word "throstle":

A thrush. A throstle. . . . . Is lost. Rich sound. . . . . Echo.
How sweet the answer. . . . . All lost now. . . . . Fall, surrender,
lost.[268]

Bloom eats without relish, exchanging a few words
grudgingly with his table companion, Richie Goulding, but the music serves to console him. The tune,
"When First I Saw That Form Endearing," is blended
into Joyce's account of the feelings of the two diners:
"sorrow from them each seemed to from both depart
when first they heard."[269] The song of Lionel from
Martha continues, and Bloom thinks of when first he
saw Molly: "Luring. Ah, alluring."[271] Lionel cries in
"languor," in "lionel loneliness." With the climax of
the aria Bloom's frustrated desire reaches a breaking-
point. The style, with its sustained retard, indicates
a perfect identification of music, mood, and prose expression. The overtones of cosmic loneliness are
marked:

—*Co-me, thou lost one!*
 Co-me thou dear one!
Alone. One love. One hope. One comfort me. Martha, chest-
note, return.
—*Come!*
It soared, a bird, it held its flight, a swift pure cry, soar silver
orb it leaped serene, speeding, sustained, to come, don't spin it
out too long long breath he breath long life, soaring high, high re-
splendent, aflame, crowned, high in the effulgence symbolistic,
high, of the ethereal bosom, high, of the high vast irradiation
everywhere all soaring all around about the all, the endlessness-
nessness . . .
—*To me!*[271]

The ensuing applause is rendered in a passage of staccato phrases, word combinations, and exclamations:

—Bravo! Clapclap. Goodman, Simon. Clappyclapclap. Encore! Clapclipclap. Sound as a bell. Bravo, Simon! Clapclopclap. Encore, enclap, said, cried, clapped all.[271]

Bloom reflects on "Thou lost one," thinking of all the songs on that theme; and, filled with the pathos and cruelty of death, he remembers Dignam and has a panicky vision of Molly's corpse.[273] Halfheartedly he sets out to write to Martha, adding as postscript: "I feel so sad . . . . so lonely."[275]

In contrast, the playful Lydia Douce brings forth the spiked seashell that reposes on the bar, holding it for others to hear: "She held it to her own and through the sifted light pale gold in contrast glided."[276] A three-letter paragraph, "Tap," follows. It is the first sound of the blind piano-tuner's cane. It will recur with increasing frequency—the physical embodiment of loneliness. And the weird sounds of the shell bring indications of cosmic distance and the constant flux of nature, indifferent to the concerns of man. They hear "the plash of waves, ... a silent roar,"[276] and Bloom thinks of the universe within, the circulation through the body of the sea of blood with its "corpuscle islands."[277] Beyond, there is the eternal music of an ever changing nature:

Sea, wind, leaves, thunder, waters, cows lowing.[277]

The tap of the tuner's cane comes closer; the songs continue, the voice of "dark age, of unlove, earth's fatigue,"[278] then the awesome "croak of vast manless moonless womoonless marsh."[278] Voices of "warning,

solemn warning,"[279] of "penance and of grief," and
"the sighing voice of sorrow" remind the hearers, even
the carefree celebrants in the bar, of the ultimate destiny of man. The tap, tap, tap, approaches. Lydia
Douce—yes, even she, the bronze, the light of heart—
"gazed far away."[279] Bloom dreams of his lost son:

> All gone. All fallen. . . . . Last of his name and race.
> I too, last my race. . . . . Too late now. Or if not? If not? If
> still?
> He bore no hate.[280]

In mocking irony we are reminded that Bloom is at
this moment being deceived. He broods on "all things
dying," then on "all things born," and gazes pityingly
on the lovely bosom of Lydia Douce, symbol of life,
yet not so far from death:

> At each slow satiny heaving bosom's wave (her heaving embon)
> red rose rose slowly, sank red rose. Heartbeats her breath:
> breath that is life. And all the tiny tiny fernfoils trembled of
> maidenhair.[281]

Melancholy, the introspective little man leaves the
Ormond, sobered by reflection:

> By rose, by satiny bosom, by the fondling hand, by slops, by
> empties, by popped corks, greeting in going, past eyes and maid-
> enhair, bronze and faint gold in deepseashadow, went Bloom,
> soft Bloom, I feel so lonely Bloom.[282]

He feels ill, wishing "I hadn't promised to meet" (that
is, Cunningham, whom he is to meet at Kiernan's).
His meditations are exactly paralleled by the sounds
of the approaching blind man:

> Far. Far. Far. Far.
> Tap. Tap. Tap. Tap.[283]

Our attention is directed to the drinkers, now commenting on Bloom. The mockery continues. Joyce

likens a headless sardine, lying on a bier of bread, to Bloom.[284] The song, "When First I Saw That Form Endearing," is juxtaposed with a description of a frowsy prostitute.[285] The blind tuner, now at the Ormond in quest of his forgotten tuning fork, is portrayed sympathetically, only to be cruelly ridiculed:

Tip. An unseeing stripling stood in the door. He saw not bronze. He saw not gold. . . . . Hee hee hee hee. He did not see.[286]

In a dissonant finale, Bloom, a racial exile, thinks of the dying words of the patriot Emmet, representative of the nation in exile, Ireland. His recitation is interrupted by gas from his luncheon wine and the grating noise of a tram, symbols of the animality of man and of the chaos of an industrial society:

Seabloom, Greaseabloom viewed last words. Softly. *When my country takes her place among.*
Prrprr.
Must be the bur.
Fff. Oo. Rrpr.
Nations of the earth. . . . . Then and not till then. Tram. Kran, kran, kran. Good oppor. Coming Krandlkrankran. I'm sure it's the burgund. Yes. One, two. *Let my epitaph be.* Karaaaaaaa. *Written. I have.*
Pprrpffrrppffff.
Done.[286]

Thus concludes one of the most ambitious tone poems in modern literature. The gaiety of the barmaids, the effrontery of the boots, and the joviality of the guests contrast with the sentimental pathos of the songs and the aching loneliness of Bloom. As obbligato, the suggestions of the eternal mystery of life and the passing of all beautiful things—the cosmic loneliness of mankind; as ground bass, the constant echo of the sea, symbol of the ceaseless flow of nature.

The sea is, of course, appropriate to the Homeric "Siren" theme, as Stuart Gilbert has demonstrated. The maids drink tea beneath their "reef of counter";[254] they are likened to mermaids[257] and sing an "ocean-song."[261] Like creatures of the sea they appear in the half-light of the bar:

She drew down pensive. . . . about her bronze, over the bar where bald stood by sister gold, inexquisite contrast, contrast inexquisite nonexquisite, slow cool dim seagreen sliding depth of shadow, *eau de Nil*.[263]

The drinks are served "in depth of ocean shadow";[265] a dusty seascape hangs on the wall.[267] The fickleness of women is to Bloom like the flow of the sea,[268] and the ecstasy of love like a flood.[270] The shell seems to reproduce the "plash of waves,"[276] and Bloom thinks of "the sad sea waves" as he rises to leave.[280]

But the sea is to Joyce far more significant than as a mere Homeric correspondence. His early lyrics echo its wistful voice; Stephen's meditations on the beach further point to the meaning of the symbol; and in the "Sirens" scene the "endlessnessnessness" of the sea is clear. For the sea voices the eternal mystery of things. Like one of the songs sung by Simon Dedalus, it is "a moonlight nightcall, clear from anear, a call from afar."[274]

On the verbal level, Joyce's style reveals a joy in words for their own sake. As a narrative device, words become amazingly accurate for the rendition of the tones, impressions, and nuances of life. Ultimately, on the symbolic level, the music of words becomes a distant echo of the perennial music of the spheres.

as a competent keyless citizen he had proceeded energetically from the unknown to the known through the incertitude of the void.[682]

BLOOM'S careless failure to carry his house-key is symbolic in more than one way; and whatever comfort the reader might derive from the statement that the hero at last went from the unknown to the known must be dispelled: he has merely let himself into his house! The texture of *Ulysses* provides ample evidence that the book is intended to be a merciless exposure of the keylessness of modern man. Social institutions, be they religious, economic, political, or aesthetic, are subject to the most searching mockery. The mood may vary from the facetious to the sardonic; the intent is, nevertheless, the same. Joyce has no panacea to recommend; his task is diagnosis rather than therapy. But his diagnosis is brilliant and often prophetic.

Critics have hitherto concerned themselves so exclusively with the technique of *Ulysses* that no detailed study has yet been made of its devastating social analysis. Modern popular faiths are shown to be outmoded shibboleths. Bloom starts his day an innocent voyager in the modern world, with a complacency like Gulliver's. An average citizen, he does not question the tenets of society, albeit his notions are vague and confused. As the day wears on, however,

he, like Gulliver, begins to perceive the basic hollow-
ness of many of these premises.

Stephen had, even as a college student, felt the
tyranny of social ties in inhibiting individual development. In the *Portrait* he had exclaimed:

When the soul of a man is born in this country there are nets
flung at it to hold it back from flight. You talk to me of nationality, language, religion. I shall try to fly by those nets.[238]

The ardent admiration of the young Joyce for Ibsen
may seem a puzzle to those who conceive of the author of *Ulysses* as a mere technician. So different is
Ibsen's basically rational method of analysis, patient
uncovering of motives, study of cause and effect, from
the brilliant sparkle of Joyce's impressionism that
readers may well wonder what could lead the young
Irish writer to laud his predecessor, learn Norwegian
in order to read his work in the original language, and
write his first essay on the work of the dramatist.
Yet much the same purpose may be found in both writers, despite the divergence in their methods. The qualities of Ibsen that attracted Joyce are given in *Stephen
Hero*, where the young artist admires the mind of
the Norwegian as one "of sincere and boylike bravery,
of disillusioned pride, of minute and wilful energy."[41]

During the course of June 16, 1904, Stephen under-
goes little change of outlook. True, he renounces his
teaching position and abandons his occupancy of the
tower, as he had earlier renounced family and religion; but the mental preparation for these steps had
long since been made. It is in the case of Bloom that
one sees the growing awareness of new points of view,
an awakening or discovery or, to use Joyce's favorite

word, epiphany. It is the process toward this epiphany that constitutes one of the principal narrative directions of the novel. To those who remain convinced that *Ulysses* is devoid of philosophical and political content, a rereading of three chapters may be recommended, those in which Bloom discusses politics at Kiernan's and at Skin-the-Goat's and that describing his retiring at 7 Eccles Street (the question-and-answer chapter, termed by Joyce with whimsical affection "the ugly duckling" of the work).

At the outset it must be remarked that the conditions which Joyce reveals in Ireland of 1904 are not restricted to that country. Were that so, the book would have the limited appeal of a realistic study of local conditions. Such obviously is not the case. Ireland only demonstrates in aggravated fashion the characteristic diseases of modern social life. Not only in Ireland had politics become the plaything of careerists and the object of indifference and contempt by the populace. Not in Ireland alone had religion become a mere lip service to outmoded beliefs, incapable of effecting strong loyalties or positive social improvements. Dublin was not unique in having art commercialized and vulgarized or in seeing its major talents waste their efforts in sentimental trifles and wistful evocations of the past. Above all, the worship of money has been characteristic of modern society since the Industrial Revolution. Flaubert saw the same emptiness of social institutions in mid-nineteenth-century France; the English Victorian social critics—Carlyle, Ruskin, and Arnold—made the same indictment of their environment; Karl Marx used a similar diagnosis as the platform on which to erect his scaffolding of revolutionary prophecy.

Dublin in 1904 was the center of social atrophy and paralysis. The career of Parnell had been brought to an ignominious close; the terrorist tactics of the Invincibles were still the subject of hushed conversation, but the cause had been lost. Politics drifted into the hands of those who were willing to play the system for what they could get out of it for themselves, permitting moneyed interests to call the tune. The cry of "let well enough alone" was not heard in Ireland only, though here inaction was obviously disgraceful. Since no stimulus to creative social change was forthcoming, Dublin substituted a tradition of easy living as a mask for its political ineffectiveness. To a spirit such as Stephen's, with the glowing idealism of his youth, such an evasion is not possible. His *non serviam* is a grand, but ineffectual, gesture; his nihilism is the result of his own social disappointment. In *Stephen Hero* Joyce had voiced his contempt for the complacency of the Irish people, their "life of dull routine— the calculation of coppers, the weekly debauch and the weekly piety— a life lived in cunning and fear between the shadows of the parish chapel and the asylum!"[54]

Bloom feels uncomfortably aware of Stephen's coldness; he attributes it, in bourgeois fashion, to an unfortunate upbringing. Stephen's contemptuous remarks ("We can't change the country. Let us change the subject") seem curiously bitter to Bloom. Possibly the home "had not been all that was needful" or "he hadn't been familiarised with the right sort of people."[629]

The political history of Ireland is that of a nation struggling to assert itself, turbulent, impoverished, torn by factions. The disastrous famine of the 1840's had cut the population in half (1845: 8,295,000; 1901: 4,404,000). Policies of revolt, compromise, obstruction, treason, had been adopted. The story of these struggles often resembles the intrigue of romantic fiction, frequently descends to comic opera, sometimes reaches the level of tragedy.

Some main conflicts can be observed. The status quo was acceptable to the Anglo-Irish, especially the landowner. Catholics wished to be freed from the hated tithe to the Church of England but guarded zealously their rights of land tenure and extortionate rent (O'Connell's Catholic Committee of 1810). Protestants wished to abolish the Union to free Ireland from ruinous Empire taxes but feared Catholic domination. The glaring necessity for land reform became apparent during the dreadful famine of 1847, when thousands starved while millions of head of livestock were exported to England. And from the days of Wolfe Tone's Society of United Irishmen (1793) the call for independence had been raised.

The fight for freedom could be waged constitutionally, as Grattan, Butt, and Parnell attempted; but the results had been unpromising. It could be carried out by force, as Mitchel and his Young Irelanders (1841) or James Stephens' Irish Republican Brotherhood (1858) hoped. It could be attempted by terrorism, as in the Phoenix Park murders (1882) of the new chief secretary and undersecretary by the Invincibles; or by treason, like Robert Emmet's dashing

attempt to secure Napoleon's aid in 1803 or Roger
Casement's ill-fated alliance with Germany in 1916.

Many who began with the spirit of compromise,
willing to accept dominion status, only found themselves by-passed (as with so much of the Irish legisla-
tion of Westminster), blackmailed (as was Parnell in
the famous *Times* suit, based on forged documents),
or double-crossed (in the Irish repudiation of Parnell
after his involvement with Mrs. O'Shea).

On Joyce's political consciousness the shameful
treatment of Parnell left a permanent scar. The *Portrait* indicates how this issue rankled in his family
during his childhood; the joys of Stephen's first
Christmas dinner were poisoned by political bicker-
ing.[29] Consequently, the young artist conceived of his
role as one of utter impersonality, rejecting all political responsibility, content only to portray the world
as it is. Stephen's famous discussion with his college
friends in the *Portrait* concludes with the definition
of the artist as pure observer:

The artist, like the God of the creation, remains within or behind or beyond or above his handiwork, invisible, refined out
of existence, indifferent, paring his fingernails.[252]

The response of his friend Lynch is a striking revelation of the political despondency of Ireland:

—What do you mean . . . . by prating about beauty and the
imagination in this miserable God forsaken island? No wonder
the artist retired . . . . after having perpetrated this country.[252]

With the long history of Irish political failure in
mind, Joyce reached an attitude of "a plague on both
your houses." Hence the mocking re-enactment of

this history in "Circe" as an absurd Punch and Judy show:

Wolfe Tone against Henry Grattan, Smith O'Brien against Daniel O'Connell, Michael Davitt against Isaac Butt, Justin M'Carthy against Parnell, Arthur Griffith against John Redmond, John O'Leary against Lear O'Johnny, Lord Edward Fitzgerald against Lord Gerald Fitzedward.[583]

In such a frame of mind one is not apt to draw fine lines of distinction between conflicting parties. The truly revolutionary Easter Rebellion of 1916 (in which one of Joyce's boyhood friends was killed) seemed only another fiasco. On that "surprisingly bludgeony" Sunday, Joyce tells us in *Finnegans Wake*, the vile author Shem (Joyce) "kuskykorked himself up tight in his inkbattle house."[176]

Yet to take statements of political irresponsibility at their face value is as dangerous as to accept without qualification Joyce's presumed irreligious attitude. No one, least of all a sensitive artist, can completely wash his hands of his inheritance. Joyce is one of the most complex and ambivalent of modern authors. Against the concept of the artist as an indifferent God set Stephen's proposal of forging the conscience of the race; against Stephen Dedalus in *Ulysses* set the humanitarian Bloom. Does the phrase "inkbattle" suggest that Joyce is still waging, in a devious way, his fight for the liberation of humanity, or is it merely an especially outrageous pun? Or both? Is not the political indifference of the God paring his fingernails something, too, of a defiant gesture or dramatic pose, since it is such a grotesque exaggeration of Flaubert's idea of the artist's being, like God, everywhere present but nowhere visible?

The portrayal of the religious retreat, with its
searching pangs of conscience, occupies the central
place in the *Portrait*. Its vivid intensity suggests that
it was a traumatic experience for the young artist. To
a lesser degree Joyce's rejection of politics may be
traced to his feeling over the fall of Parnell. Neither
experience could be passed over lightly or be forgotten
in later life. Everything that Joyce rejected comes
back into his writing—family, country, religion, politics. Accordingly, one can see implicit throughout
Ulysses a criticism of Ireland for political and social
indifference, which suggests self-criticism at the same
time, for these are the author's own professed traits.

Of the Irish leaders contemporary with Bloom, the
most important were Michael Davitt (1849–1906)
and his friend Patrick Egan of the Land League,
championing revolution and the socialization of land;
Arthur Griffith (1872–1922), leader of the Sinn Fein
nationalists; Douglas Hyde of the Gaelic League,
urging the revival of patriotism through poetry, language, and legend; and the conciliatory John Redmond, advocate of dominion status.

In *Ulysses* we hear of Stephen's talks with Egan in
Paris;[43] the group in the newsroom discuss the Phoenix Park murders, but largely in terms of a journalistic scoop;[134] the Citizen at Kiernan's is reputed to
have got James Stephens away at the time of his ar-
rest;[311] and Bloom is rumored to have coined the
Irish slogan *Sinn Fein* ("We Ourselves").[329] Molly is
concerned about her husband's connections with the
dangerous and disreputable Sinn Feiners.[733]

But Bloom is far from being consistent as a patriot.

Joyce mocks the emptiness of political allegiance in a divided Ireland when he tells us that Bloom had been an adherent of the radical socialist program of Davitt but had also supported the constitutional agitation of Parnell and, to top all that, had advocated the reforms of Gladstone, who played a cat-and-mouse policy with the Irish throughout. In support of his political convictions, Joyce tells us, he had once "climbed up into a secure position amid the ramifications of a tree"[701] to witness a procession!

Most of the populace, however, would not even climb a tree. To them the solace of whiskey and the irrepressible spirit of Irish humor (so apparent in the minor characters) served as a refuge, albeit a poor one. Blasphemy stems from the same repression of constructive social vision; one may mock that which he cannot change or dare not openly attack. So Dublin lapses into a more or less gracious inertia, life goes on much as usual; but a rebellious spirit like that of Stephen's feels stifled, and, once his attention is called to the social void, an alert citizen like Bloom senses an undefined hankering for something more positive and meaningful in the society which he inhabits.

Possibly the most striking illustration of this inertia in *Ulysses* is the effect that the Russo-Japanese War has upon Dublin during the day. Easily the most significant historical event of the time, it occupies so small a place in the narrative that one could not expect a reader to recall that it had even been mentioned. It is discussed casually from time to time, arousing little interest in the minds of Dublin's provincial citizens. Unaware of the course of history,

Dublin carries on business as usual. The war is the subject of joke or anecdote or something to be noticed in newspaper headlines; only once is it subjected to political insight, and the remark is soon passed over and forgotten.

The war provides the framework of one of Simon Dedalus' imitations, the takeoff of the liquor dealer, O'Rourke.[58] Joe, hanger-on at Kiernan's, ventures a remark on Russian tyranny, which his confrere passes off with a request for another drink.[290] It is touched upon in intoxicated stupor and made an occasion for bragging, when Stephen's companions celebrate after leaving the hospital.[420] Skin-the-Goat, veteran of the Invincibles, now pub-keeper at the disreputable cabman's shelter, is the only character to whom the conflict of imperialisms means anything. He, incidentally, makes the most prophetic statement in the book. But his remarks that the "Germans and the Japs were going to have their little looking in," that the Boer War was the "beginning of the end," and that "brummagem England was toppling"—these remarks, incisive though they are, fall on indifferent ears.[624] The seaman Murphy, whose tall tales were more to the taste of the group, "heard these lurid tidings undismayed."[625] A battle headline catches Bloom's eye,[631] but that is all.

In the Ireland of this day statesmanship is a liability. The downfall of Parnell had been followed by a morose defeatism, lightened only by reverence for the memory of the departed leader—a spirit beautifully depicted by Joyce in one of the best of the Dubliner stories, "Ivy Day in the Committee Room." But Ivy

Day itself, we learn in *Ulysses*, is dying out, and even Parnell seems destined to oblivion.[109] We do hear of a foundation stone for him,[94] and Mrs. Riordan's hair-brushes, representing Parnell and Davitt, are mentioned,[665] as they were in the *Portrait*.[2]

The legendary hope that Parnell would again rise, voiced by Jack Power in the cemetery, is stoutly maintained by Skin-the-Goat to the silent dissent of his auditors.[633] But the prevailing pessimism about politics is expressed by Hynes as they walk by the chief's grave in Glasnevin:

—Parnell will never come again, he said. He's there, all that was mortal of him. Peace to his ashes.[III]

Bloom had once handed the leader his hat[634] and had long maintained his admiration for him.[701] He compares him to Garibaldi[161] and ponders the virtual anonymity of his surviving brother,[162] who idles away his time at chess.[245] In the "Circe" scene Bloom's political reflections give rise to a vision of grandeur, and, now Mayor of Dublin, he is hailed by the brother as Parnell's successor,[474] only to be driven from his post by the mob.[482] The shadow of Parnell's disgrace falls across the book; even Mr. Deasy, British as he is, compares Kitty O'Shea to Helen of Troy.[35] When we read of John Howard Parnell's looking intently at the viceregal procession, we sense the smoldering discontent of Ireland the slave.[249] And it is interesting to speculate as to whether Joyce intended any self-reproach when he has Skin-the-Goat recall the leader's advice:

His advice to every Irishman was: stay in the land of your birth and work for Ireland and live for Ireland. Ireland, Parnell said, could not spare a single one of her sons.[625]

A steady current of hatred for British imperialism flows through the novel. Stephen despises Mr. Deasy, the master of his school, on many grounds but, above all, because he belongs to the arrogant neighbor-nation:

The seas' ruler. His seacold eyes looked on the empty bay: history is to blame: on me and on my words, unhating.[31]

In response to the question just asked by Mr. Deasy about the proudest boast of an Englishman, he replies that it is that on his empire the sun never sets. Mr. Deasy haughtily corrects him and gives as his answer, "*I paid my way.*"[31]

In the library discussion Stephen sees in the Shakespeare who conceived the bloody finale of *Hamlet* the prototype of the British imperialist:

Not for nothing was he a butcher's son wielding the sledded poleaxe and spitting in his palm. Nine lives are taken off for his father's one, Our Father who art in purgatory. Khaki Hamlets don't hesitate to shoot. The bloodboltered shambles in act five is a forecast of the concentration camp sung by Mr Swinburne.[185]

Bloom is, of course, more moderate. He infuriates the debt-collector at Kiernan's by attempting to defend England and to preach brotherly love:

and Bloom trying to back him up moderation and botheration and their colonies and their civilisation.

—Their syphilisation, you mean, says the citizen. To hell with them![319]

A few minutes later the Citizen launches forth in another diatribe about the cruelty of the navy which represents that land whose citizens boast they will never be slaves. This portion of the narrative being the one which is interspersed with parodies, it is not surprising to find one of Joyce's most blasphemous parodies following soon after—the apostle's creed of the British imperialist.[323] But the humble Bloom is not wholly complacent. His mockery of British imperialism is characteristically disrespectful. He sees the label advertising Lemon's, confectioners to His Majesty, and smiles at the thought of the king, "sitting on his throne, sucking red jujubes white."[149]

Like Stephen Hero, who wondered how "such a poor scarecrow" as the liberty of the patriots (the revival of Gaelic and the creation of a bourgeois government) could bring "serious human beings to their knees in worship,"[61] Bloom sees the absurdity of much of the ineffectual home-rule agitation. He recalls with delight Editor Griffith's statement about the home-rule sun "rising up in the northwest from the laneway behind the bank of Ireland."[57] The debating societies which take such ardent interest in politics are to him somewhat like Salvation Army shelters, populated by half-fed enthusiasts.[161] The army recruits he sees in the street seem hypnotized, ready to defend the "overseas or halfseasover empire."[72] He is petrified by the fear of secret police,[160] a fact which later is seen to explain his extreme political caution.

Bloom realizes well enough that an "Irishman's house is his coffin,"[108] though he dares say little about it and certainly would not permit himself the license of the debt-collector, of Joe, of the Citizen, or of Skin-the-Goat. The debt-collector is a complete cynic; he is contemptuous of the Citizen's drunken boasts about the future of his country:

a new Ireland and new this, that and the other. Talking about new Ireland he ought to go and get a new dog so he ought.[300]

Few of the characters of *Ulysses* are as honest as this. For the most part they take refuge in political oratory. Dan Dawson's speech was undoubtedly admired by many. It is quoted (or, one fears, parodied) in the newspaper scene and provokes hearty laughs from Simon Dedalus, Ned Lambert, and Professor MacHugh when it is read,[122] as it had from Power earlier.[90] But Bloom is not so ready to laugh; it is "all very fine to jeer at it now in cold print but it goes down like hot cake that stuff."[125]

Professor MacHugh does not conceal his opinion of England. He points out that the Irish must not be misled by imposing sounds, such as "Rome" and "imperial":

The Roman, like the Englishman who follows in his footsteps, brought to every new shore on which he set his foot . . . . only his cloacal obsession. He gazed about him in his toga and he said: *It is meet to be here. Let us construct a watercloset.*[130]

When J. J. O'Molloy retorts that we also have Roman law, MacHugh's reply is final: "and Pontius Pilate is its prophet."[130]

But even these hardened critics can respond with the true Irishman's love of eloquence to the oratory of Seymour Bushe's defense in the Childs murder case[137] or to that of John F. Taylor's plea for Gaelic at the college historical society.[140] Stephen, who is now present, mentally thinks of the phrase "gone with the wind" to express his contempt and immediately makes a motion that they adjourn for drinks.[142] History is to Stephen, we recall, nothing but a collection of hollow shells.[30]

Religion occupies a less important place in *Ulysses* than it did in the *Portrait*. There Stephen's defection from the church was thoroughly analyzed; in this novel the decision has been reached, and only the qualms of conscience remain. It is, instead, Bloom who expresses the most important criticisms of the place of the church in the modern social order. As he walks to the bath in the morning, he drops into a service at All Hallows. His attention wanders, but he does reflect on the meaning of the ritual to those who, unlike him, have been raised under the aegis of Catholicism. He thinks that the Mass induces the same hypnosis in the communicants as he was later to observe in the army recruits.[79] Yet he is charitable enough to admit that it would be "more interesting if you understood what it was all about."[81] He recognizes the psychological validity and effectiveness of confession, though it immediately leads him into the direction of erotic imaginings.[81] The organization of the church[81] and its tremendous economic power are appreciated,[82] but that is all. For Bloom the longing in his heart cannot be assuaged by religion. Nor can he see that the last rites over Paddy Dignam do the deceased any good. To him the entire service seems perfunctory and mechanical.[102]

Yet he is aware of deeper stirrings than these superficial observations might indicate. He feels both the terror of death[104] and the silence of the infinite spaces beyond.[689] His respect for Stephen's learning leads him to inquire timidly about the theological explanation of the soul, but his friend's response is far from satisfying. Stephen replies that "on the best author-

ity" the soul is understood to be immortal, except
"for the possibility of its annihilation by its First
Cause, Who, from all I can hear, is quite capable of
adding that to the number of His other practical
jokes, *corruptio per se* and *corruptio per accidens* both
being excluded by court etiquette."[618]

Bloom's real religion, like that of most modern
men, is money. His mind buzzes with schemes for
getting rich. He contemplates the most profitable lo-
cations for pubs[57] and the profits in liquor[58] and
thinks of the immense checks he could write were he
a lord of distilling.[78] The profits of colonization in
Palestine attract him;[60] he concocts a maternity insurance scheme[159] and speculates on the possibility of
a new tram line to take cattle to the river.[96] It is no
exaggeration to say that "all kinds of Utopian plans
were flashing through his (Bloom's) busy brain."[642]
These plans are duly catalogued in the scientific chapter. They include a private telegraph system for race-
track betting, the discovery of gems or rare postage
stamps, hypothetical sums at interest over long peri-
ods of years, payments increasing in geometrical pro-
gression, breaking the bank at Monte Carlo, finding
buried treasure, and squaring the circle![702]

The scheme which recurs most frequently through
the day is that of writing a prize-winning story, such
as the one he read in the morning paper.[68] The words
"prize titbit," the title, "Matcham's Masterstroke,"
and the author's name, Philip Beaufoy, come to mind
constantly as leitmotivs of this commercial interest.
His first notion is to illustrate a proverb (a perfect indication of his bourgeois outlook on literature).[69] We

recall that he has often looked into Shakespeare for
moral guidance, though deriving "imperfect conviction from the text"![661] Next it is a poison mystery,
suggested by his lunch![172] As he blots his letter to
Martha in the Ormond, he is ready with an incident,
something a detective read off a blotter.[275] "The
Mystery Man on the Beach" is a title he concocts as
he walks at dusk.[369] He is accused of plagiarism by the
spirit of Beaufoy in the brothel;[450] and among the attractions which Stephen's acquaintance offers are
those of literary inspiration. By this time his imagination is on a bit more sophisticated level; now it is a
slice-of-life story he contemplates:

the coincidence of meeting, discussion, dance, row, old salt, of
the here today and gone tomorrow type, night loafers, the whole
galaxy of events, all went to make up a miniature cameo of the
world we live in, especially as the lives of the submerged tenth,
viz., coalminers, divers, scavengers etc., were very much under
the microscope lately. To improve the shining hour he wondered
whether he might meet with anything approaching the same
luck as Mr Philip Beaufoy if taken down in writing. Suppose he
were to pen something out of the common groove . . . . at the
rate of one guinea per column, *My Experiences*, let us say, *in a
Cabman's Shelter*.[631]

Indeed, Mr. Bloom is here well on the way to writing
Ulysses itself! Though one must add that it is very
unlikely that his expectations of affluence would be
fulfilled, judging from Joyce's lack of financial success.

Bloom's mind in the early morning is still revolving
around literary prosperity. Now the program centers
about editing schoolbooks, modeled on the themes he
recalls writing in his childhood. There seem to be in
this scheme "certain possibilities of financial, social,
personal and sexual success"![669]

This discussion of the range of Bloom's financial schemes should not lead one to believe that he is not just as eager about the possibilities in his own chosen work, that of advertising. He studies advertisements with a critically professional eye; he is always alert to new schemes about the writing or placing of them. Joyce deliberately builds up a picture of the commercial mentality with the express purpose of leading to one of his favorite satiric effects—the anticlimax.

Bloom scrutinizes advertisements with care; he is contemptuous of the notice of the cycle race, the cyclist doubled up like a cod in a pot (incidentally, this is perhaps an intentional prenatal symbol, coming as it does in the "Lotus Eaters" passage). His notion is to feature the wheel, with the hub carrying the message.[85] Another ludicrously poor advertisement was that of Plumtree's potted meat, placed under the obituaries in the morning paper! Read at a glance when the paper first arrived,[73] it seems more ridiculous to Bloom later,[152] and, finally, absolutely stupid.[169] On the other hand, he can appreciate with the artist's eye a good job of advertising. He considers the luminous crucifix one[149] and the signs placed on boats anchored in the Liffey another.[151] He speculates on the role of advertising as a reflection of social psychology; the marriage announcements are not decorated, while obituaries are.[112] Advertising, he thinks, has something in common with religion; there is the same use of persuasive repetition.[371]

He conceives of advertising stunts, such as showgirls on a float transported through the city.[152] His conversations about Molly's concert tour are good word-of-mouth advertisements, he feels,[170] and tie up with his dream of managing a big tour for her. Like the boats in the river or the street procession, a woman's mirror would be an ideal place for an ad.[365] Before retiring, we are told, his habitual meditations (his prayers to the god of money) were directed toward this subject:

> Of some one sole unique advertisement to cause passers to stop in wander [sic], a poster novelty, with all extraneous accretions excluded, reduced to its simplest and most efficient terms not exceeding the span of casual vision and congruous with the velocity of modern life.[705]

In the same chapter we are given a résumé of his thoughts on the art of publicity, with Plumtree again the horrible example.[668] A humorous twist is given to the trite phrase, "Beware of imitations," in the Plumtree ad. Joyce takes this in mock-seriousness, listing as possible imitations "Peatmot," "Trumplee," "Montpat," and "Plamtroo."[668]

The twin god to money is science, of which Bloom, a representative modern man, is a devout worshiper. He has a natural curiosity for abstract science, but his information is ill-digested and half-remembered. More to the point is the possibility of adapting science to material needs; it is invention and technology that really interest Bloom. Many of these have been discussed as schemes for making money, but Bloom's ingenuity is ever active. He thinks of an automatic switch to take some of the burden from the switchman he sees from the funeral carriage.[90] If corpses were buried in standing position, there would be more room in the cemetery,[107] and it would not be a bad idea to compel the piercing of the heart to avoid the danger of burial alive.[109] To perpetuate the memory of the dead, perhaps phonograph recordings should be made.[112]

He is also curious to know how things work and always ready to try experiments. The roughness of the cat's tongue fascinates him;[56] he wonders how the blind react to their environment.[179] Why do salt-water fish not have a salty taste?[151] We see this little man, squinting his eyes as he walks along the street, trying some experiment of vision, undoubtedly an amusing sight for passers-by.[164] He would be very much interested in making a sight-seeing trip through the brewery[150] (one can imagine the questions he would ask if the opportunity afforded!). He has often reflected on the immense volume of water on the globe.[614] But his scientific knowledge is both rudimentary and, one must admit, somewhat confused. Black (he is considering his funeral clothes) "conducts, reflects (refracts is it?), the heat."[57] And, on the way to the bath, thinking of floating in the Dead Sea, the law of floating bodies eludes him—

Couldn't sink if you tried: so thick with salt. Because the weight of the water, no, the weight of the body in the water is equal to the weight of the. . . . . It's a law something like that. Vance in high school cracking his fingerjoints, teaching.[71]

His curiosity is fair game to the grosser creatures of earth who surround him and to whom it is something of an aberration. Lenehan tells with great relish how he was able to make advances to Molly, while Bloom, oblivious to all but his beloved science, was pointing out the stars. And, much though we sympathize with the little man, we must admit that the story is a good one:

She's a gamey mare and no mistake. Bloom was pointing out all the stars and the comets in the heavens to Chris Callinan and the jarvey: the great bear and Hercules and the dragon and the whole jingbang lot. But by God, I was lost, so to speak, in the milky way. He knows them all, faith. . . . .

Lenehan stopped and leaned on the riverwall, panting with soft laughter.

—I'm weak, he gasped.[231]

It is the narrator in Kiernan's who has the greatest contempt for Bloom's intellectual curiosity, "with his jawbreakers about phenomenon and science and this phenomenon and the other phenomenon."[299] Bloom has the debt-collector addled with his legal discussion of Dignam's estate;[308] he is a "Mister Knowall"[309] who will always take the other side of any question:

Didn't I tell you? As true as I'm drinking this porter if he was at his last gasp he'd try to downface you that dying was living.[323]

It must be said to Molly's credit, however, that she respects her husband's knowledge. Characteristically, biology is the science she most admires: "still he knows a lot of mixed up things [she is right there!] about the body and the insides I often wanted to study up that myself what we have inside us."[728]

The picture of modern science given in *Ulysses* is that it constitutes a new folklore of a "believe-it-or-not" nature and that its principal appeal to modern man is as a materialistic aid to wealth or to the saving of effort. Moreover, though it is widely admired and respected, the average man has in his mind a mere flotsam of half-knowledge and an idle curiosity. As for the larger implications of science in modifying the world view of man, Joyce develops in the kitchen chapter the cold-blooded horror which a century of science has left in the human spirit; a new demon of blind scientific law has replaced the traditional God, and mere man is left a helpless victim in the tidal on-rush of forces he only vaguely understands.

The place of art in the modern world is no more encouraging. The true artist is suspected by the *bourgeoisie*, as is pointed out in *Stephen Hero:*

No-one would listen to his theories: no-one was interested in art. [The young men in the college] regarded art as a continental vice. . . . . It was a bad sign for a young man to show interest in anything but his examinations or his prospective "job." It was all very well to be able to talk about it but really art was all "rot": besides it was probably immoral; they knew (or, at least they had heard) about studios. They didn't want that kind of thing in their country.[34]

Sentimental songs, light opera, and music-hall turns serve for the rank and file. And the intelligentsia is really only slightly better. Their pleas of art for art's sake; their immature interest in the Irish revival; above all, their mystical nonsense of yogi and Mme Blavatsky, deserve nothing but contempt. Irish art is to Stephen "the cracked lookingglass of a servant."[8]

Joyce's own relationship to the revival is an interesting one and has been traced in some detail by Levin. Joyce was possibly unfair in his strictures; nevertheless, he was repelled by the essential triviality and amateurishness of the entire Abbey Theatre crowd, for he conceived of a deeper dedication to art than he felt they evidenced. The revival was to him basically an art of dilettantes. Moreover, it seemed to him to represent a surrender on the part of dramatists to popular taste. The hard-won victories of serious Continental dramatists, such as Ibsen and Hauptmann, were thrown away, and the day of the rabblement had come. In an essay of that title, published as a pamphlet in 1901, he had minced no words. Although written by a nineteen-year-old student, the essay reveals the stubborn integrity that never left Joyce:

the Irish Literary Theatre must now be considered the property of the rabblement of the most belated race in Europe. A nation which never advanced so far as a miracle play affords no literary model to the artist, and he must look abroad.

Ulysses contains many references to the Irish revival, none of them complimentary. J. J. O'Molloy asks Stephen in the newspaper office what he really thinks of that "hermetic crowd, the opal hush poets," and embarrasses him by mentioning that he had heard that Stephen was consulting A. E. about the planes of consciousness.[139] Bloom remembers with contempt the bohemian Lizzie Twigg, who had "no time to do her hair drinking sloppy tea with a book of poetry";[158] and a few minutes later A. E., "beard and bicycle," appears, with a woman disciple listening eagerly to his occultism:

Her stockings are loose over her ankles. I detest that: so tasteless. Those literary ethereal people they are all. Dreamy, cloudy, symbolistic Esthetes they are.[163]

It is in the library scene that the empty pretensions of the revivalists are most clearly set forth. The Quaker librarian who presides is the incarnation of all that is effeminate and self-consciously "literary" in the movement. Mr. Best is a perfect dilettante:

Mr Best entered, tall, young, mild, light. He bore in his hand with grace a notebook, new, large, clean, bright.[184]

With his "unoffending face"[185] and "innocent book,"[191] Best provides a running chorus of banality. He recalls that *Hamlet* seems so personal a full five minutes after Stephen has elaborated his theory;[191] remembers Coleridge's phrase, "myriad-minded";[203] makes an inane remark about the second-best bed;[201] pleads that nothing damaging be said about Richard, for that is his name.[206] His reaction to Stephen's thoughts on *Hamlet* is that they should be written up in dialogue form to make literary copy.[211] Stephen thinks of him as "Best of Best brothers"[208] and as "Mr Secondbest Best."[201] It is in his delight in Oscar Wilde that he shows most completely his effeminate dilettantism:

Of course it's all paradox, don't you know, Hughes and hews and hues the colour, but it's so typical the way he works it out. It's the very essence of Wilde, don't you know. The light touch.[196]

No wonder that his next appellation is "tame essence of Wilde," itself a neat paradox-pun.[196]

Synge is ridiculed both indirectly and by parody. Buck Mulligan identifies Shakespeare as "the chap that writes like Synge"[195] and a moment later engages in a hearty parody of his dialect rhythms.[197] A. E. is present for a while and protests that art must reveal "formless spiritual essences,"[183] a weak watering-down of Stephen's interpretation of the tragic personal tension which Shakespeare suffered while writing *Hamlet*. To Stephen's aggressive conception of the artist as a social rebel, he counters with a theory of revolution born of folk song.[184]

It is in Stephen's stream-of-consciousness that the most savage attack upon the Irish revival is to be found. He mocks the concept of revolution born of dreams and fantasy; "in the shadow of the glen he cooees."[183] The phrase "formless spiritual" is ludicrous to the bitter young poet,[183] and the mystical-spiritualistic atmosphere of the meeting of the group constitutes a "Yogibogeybox," where, "functioning on astral levels," the "hermetists await the light," "hesouls, shesouls, shoals of souls."[189]

Bloom is not so much concerned with culture in the strictly aesthetic sense of the word, but he has his own utopian dreams. These are principally elaborated in the question-and-answer chapter and consist of an unconsciously ironic prototype of the modern ideal of success, for this impecunious householder has his vision of suburbia. There he hopes to have a romantic cottage on a gentle eminence, some distance from neighbors but not over five minutes from tram or train. This will be completely furnished with wall-presses, a sectional bookcase containing encyclopedia and dictionary, as well as dinner gong, alabaster lamp, and telephone.[697] A summerhouse, rockery, garden, and "humane" beehive would be welcome additions.[698] In this cottage in Flowerville, Bloom would devote himself to gardening, "ameliorating the soil," to the hobbies of photography, studies of religions, amatory practices, and astronomy, "multiplying wisdom, achieving longevity."[699] He might become a gentleman farmer, then justice of the peace, and, finally, at the zenith of his career, reach "mention in court and fashionable intelligence"![700]

This complete digest of the ideals of a Babbitt fills seven detail-crammed pages and is as final a satire on bourgeois values as anything in modern literature. But Joyce's voice speaks out in less subtle terms in the "Circe" episode, where the mayoralty of Bloom is celebrated by the distribution of all that twentieth-century man holds most dear:

commemoration medals, loaves and fishes, temperance badges, expensive Henry Clay cigars,

and on through theater and tram-line passes (which Bloom had been itching to secure during the day) to cheap reprints of the World's Twelve Worst Books:

Froggy and Fritz (politic), Care of the Baby (infantilic), 50 Meals for 7/6 (culinic), Was Jesus a Sun Myth? (historic), Expel that Pain (medic), Infant's Compendium of the Universe (cosmic), Let's All Chortle (hilaric), Canvasser's Vade Mecum (journalic), Loveletters of Mother Assistant (erotic), Who's Who in Space (astric), Songs that Reached our Heart (melodic), Pennywise's Way to Wealth (parsimonic).[476]

We read that there was a general rush and scramble, as, indeed, there should be, for this is the day of the rabblement, and even the Muses have been renovated for the brave new world. They are, we are told, Commerce, Operatic Music, Amor, Publicity, Manufacture, Liberty of Speech, Plural Voting, Gastronomy, Private Hygiene, Seaside Concert Entertainments, Painless Obstetrics, and Astronomy for the People.[480] Each is represented in Bloom's preoccupations during the day, and again we see him as the typical man of the vulgar modern world. His own library, duly catalogued, reads much like the collection of the twelve worst books.[693]

We are told that Joyce delighted in popular reading matter, no matter how banal. In fashionable hotels he provided amusement to bystanders, who saw a most learned-looking man poring with nearsighted intensity over cheap fiction and comic books as though they were imperishable historical documents. Ezra Pound first called attention to the resemblance between *Ulysses* and Flaubert's unfinished encyclopedia of bourgeois futility, *Bouvard and Pécuchet*. Joyce's tone is difficult to analyze: at one time it seems to partake of the carefree gusto of Rabelais or the comic *esprit* of Sterne, again of the savage indignation of Swift (he compared himself to Swift indirectly in his play *Exiles*). But frequently it has the mood of the aging Flaubert, devoting his energy to the excoriation of human falsity and stupidity.

To return to the suburban utopia. It is for this that Bloom evolves his money-making schemes; it is for this that he treasures his securities, his insurance policies, and his bankbook.[708] Yet the bank balance is only eighteen pounds, the bonds nine hundred pounds; and immediately after the inventory we are asked to reduce Bloom "by cross multiplication of reverses of fortune" and find him progressively descending the social ladder to sandwich man, vagrant, inmate of a poor house, and, finally, "the aged impotent disfranchised ratesupported moribund lunatic pauper."[710] So thin, Joyce evidently is implying, is the ice of financial security upon which we build our dream mansions.

During the years following the publication of *Ulysses* Joyce continued his iconoclastic dissection of the institutions of our day. To attempt to do more than scratch the surface of the immense companion volume, *Finnegans Wake*, would clearly exceed any

reasonable limits of time and space. Yet this much
can be said. The basic conception of the later book—
that of a long nightmare—could be interpreted as
symbolic of the paralysis of modern civilization. Ireland has slumbered and, with it, the entire Western
world. Into the complex texture of the later style are
enshrined, often half-hidden under other layers of
meaning, some of the history of Ireland's ignominy.
To elucidate these in full detail would require an exhaustive knowledge of the minutiae of Irish history.

In *Finnegans Wake* Ireland is a stagnant fen, lying
under the curse of cultural sterility. It is "Echo-
land,"[13] a land dreaming of a fabulous past but incapable of stirring in the present. Its "phillohippuc
theobibbous paupulation"[140] is dedicated to an escape
from creative social activity. Indeed, the entire world
seems to be "flamend floody flatuous."[23] A study of
considerable extent might be made of the synonyms
for Dublin, all contemptuous. It is "Dyoublong" (reflecting Joyce's resentment at the neglect of his
work),[13] "dumplan,"[79] "Dumpling,"[215] "Devlin"[24]
(home of the devil?), "Diddlem,"[219] the home of "dul-
peners,"[193] to note only a few.

Politically adolescent, Ireland is "Errorland."[62] Its
slogan, *Erin go bragh* ("Ireland Forever") could more
accurately be rendered as "Ehren . . . . gobrawl,"[338]
or even better, considering its poverty, as "Erin gone
brugk."[347]

History, the nightmare from which Stephen had
wished to awake, is now a ludicrous farce produced by
"Thud and Blunder."[221] And the inevitable doom of
civilization, time's livid final flame, is rendered as a

concluding stage direction. The show begins with a community prayer, each for himself, and ends with "a chorale in canon, good for us all for us all us all all."[222]

To exhaust all the references in this huge monomyth might seem almost impossible. Since it has at least one-quarter as many more words as the 260,430 in *Ulysses*, with each word capable of two or more meanings, one could devote a lifetime to the project. It must suffice to call attention to the satire of war in the description of the Wellington Museum, where the guide's remarks fall into the rhythm of "The House That Jack Built,"[8] the satire on the bourgeois idea of progress in the libelous "Ballad of Persse O'Reilly," whose reforms are chanted in the manner of a W. S. Gilbert lyric:

He was fafather of all schemes for to bother us
Slow coaches and immaculate contraceptives for the populace,
Mare's milk for the sick, seven dry Sundays a week,
Openair love and religion's reform,
    (Chorus) And religious reform
            Hideous in form.[45]

One should also mention the ludicrous exegesis of Alp's Manifesto, a parody of scholarship;[107] the extended description of everyman;[126] the professor's lecture to his "muddlecrass" pupils;[152] the Swiftian fable of church schism, "The Mookse and the Gripes";[152] and the uproarious characterization of the extrovert imperialist brother Shaun, especially his Polonius-like speech to the girls' school.[429]

Here, indeed, is the nihilism which Carl Jung analyzed so brilliantly as the basic spirit of *Ulysses*. But the little advertiser is characterized with pity and sympathy. Bloom's basic humanity is ridiculed in the same way that the idealism of an earlier adventurer in the realms of the spirit, Don Quixote, is ridiculed; one starts to laugh at an eccentric but soon has a sobering second thought. Perhaps the absurdity of the hero is merely a reflection upon the inherent crassness of the world we inhabit.

THE OPPOSITE OF HATRED:
BLOOM'S HUMANITARIANISM

—Love, says Bloom. I mean the opposite of hatred.[327]

NOWHERE is Joyce's social criticism more searing than in his portrayal of Bloom's humanitarian philosophy. Essentially a man of good will, Bloom finds himself corrupted by a world given to crassly monetary values. This absurd little man has no difficulty in reconciling schemes for private profit with vague, general visions of human betterment. He reproduces on a primitive, prethought level the inconsistencies of the political and economic liberal, for, when freedom means merely freedom to exploit or freedom from responsibility, no positive social vision can emerge. Many high-minded souls (who, incidentally, castigate Joyce for lacking faith) are as bewildered as Bloom when they see how the ideal of brotherly love fares today. It is the fault of the church, say some; the fault of science, say others; the fault of the home, the fault of education. In their learned bewilderment they are only repeating, on a more imposing scale, the same confusion that besets Bloom.

In one sense the ideal of good will stands as a criterion by which Joyce may examine the world and vex mankind with his findings. It is a simple standard for such a learned and sophisticated writer, but it carries satiric overtones that the naïve do not see, for what is wrong with the world is not that it fails to live up to the ideal of good will but that it is impossible, under modern conditions, to do so. Bloom almost gets the point—indeed, comes closer than Stephen to seeing the point—and again proves that common sense may be a more reliable guide than sterile intellectuality.

Characteristically, Joyce hides his social insight so that it emerges only in glimpses. It is usually obscured by the heavier thunder of satire and parody. This mask of bitter humor is a protective grimace, which affords the author a refuge from the horror of the world as he sees it. The mask is practically never dropped in *Finnegans Wake*, though even there the strangely distant voice of charity is heard—the cries of the loving, pitying, forgiving mother of men, Anna Livia Plurabelle.

Out of the Pandora's box that is *Ulysses*, a small ray of hope emerges. The keyless citizen has one key left. It looks strangely out of place on the modern stage. Bloom is a man of good will. His notions are confused, inconsistent, muddled. He appreciates that his hope is naïve, yet does not know exactly what is wrong with it.

What is the fate of a man of good will in the modern world? Bloom's sympathy for others is ever present; yet he is imposed upon by his wife, mocked by his friends. Absurd though he is, this little creature is possessed of a warm heart. It is by the little-practiced ideal of brotherly love that he wishes to live. As a Jew, he realizes that society makes only a pretense of loyalty to this ideal. As an Irishman, he recognizes the role that force and economic exploitation play in the world at large. Yet, quixotically, he holds to his faith—ridiculous, laughable, lovable Bloom.

It is difficult for most readers, brought up on romantic fiction, to appreciate the mixture of the comic and the pathetic with which Bloom is portrayed. On one level, Bloom is a contemptible figure. Stephen judges him from that level, and one feels the unjustness of his lack of sympathy, for, with all his vulgarity, the modern Ulysses is a warmhearted creature. To those who would accuse Joyce of utter nihilism the first answer would be, "*Ecce homo*, Behold Bloom."

Our first view of this little man is one of his kindness and solicitude. He is downstairs getting breakfast for his wife (who does not deserve such consideration) and turns to feed the cat. He "watched curiously, kindly, the lithe black form."[55] He sets milk in a saucer for the cat, and then characteristically turns to scientific speculations about its feelers and the roughness of its tongue.

Consideration for animals is one of Bloom's dominant traits. He recalls his father's dog Athos with pity, "Poor old Athos,"[89] and treasures the pathetic solicitude of his father, in the suicide note.[708] He pities even the broken-down dray horses on the streets, "Good poor brutes they look," though he admits that their neigh can be very irritating.[76] Even at 1:30 A.M. he responds to a camel-backed nag pulling a street-sweeper and regrets that he has no sugar to feed it. To be sure, it was "just a big foolish nervous noodly kind of a horse," but "it was no animal's fault in particular if he was built that way."[646] We learn, too, that he had once brought home a little dog with a lame paw, a charitable act not appreciated by Molly.[641]

Bloom is himself a kindly animal. His embrace of Molly in the early morning is, we are told, "expressive of mute immutable mature animality."[719] Though his conceptions of love are largely physical, "a dream of wellfilled hose,"[362] he is ashamed of the sexual satisfaction he has derived from spying on Gerty Mac-Dowell:

What a brute he had been! At it again? A fair unsullied soul had called to him and, wretch that he was, how had he answered? An utter cad he had been. He of all men![360]

The ludicrous sentimentality of this passage should be interpreted again as a stylistic defense. Its intent is clear. Bloom realizes the tyranny that the flesh exercises over him.

Little acts of generosity mark his day. He is about to stop a youngster from smoking but is restrained by the thought that the child might as well have some fun, for his "life isn't such a bed of roses."[70] He would like to give the cabmen an odd cigarette, thinking of their drifting existence.[76] He thinks likewise of the dreadful life of sailors, some on "big brutes of ocean-going steamers floundering along in the dark, lowing out like seacows," others on smaller vessels "pitched about like snuff at a wake."[372] Lighthouse-keepers and coastguardmen also have a far from enviable existence.[373]

He considers the plight of children, prey to infectious diseases that are "canvassing for death."[89] He feels the pathetic fears of adolescence, which he had just experienced in the case of his daughter:

Her growing pains at night, calling, wakening me. Frightened she was when her nature came on her first. Poor child! Strange moment for the mother too.[373]

His heart quickens at suffering, wherever it is found. He is touched by the unhappy marriage of Martin Cunningham, whose drunken wife has been "leading him the life of the damned."[95] He notes with evident alarm a street urchin in tatters:

Good Lord, the poor child's dress is in flitters. Underfed she looks too. Potatoes and marge, marge and potatoes. It's after they feel it.[150]

Even the gulls in the Liffey, filthy as they are, are "poor birds" who deserve to be fed.[151] And his mind can never dispel the impression made upon it some years ago when he had had a job at the cattle market, of the stupid victims, unaware of their fate:

Wretched brutes there at the cattlemarket waiting for the poleaxe to split their skulls open. Moo. Poor trembling calves. Meh.[168]

It is he who straightens the hat of the solicitor Menton at the funeral, only to be scorned for his pains;[114] he who helps the blind piano-tuner across the street;[178] he who senses the enormity and injustice of the fate of the passengers on the "General Slocum" when it exploded in New York Harbor;[180] he who had the patience to wheel the aged Mrs. Riordan as far as the North Circular Road and wait while she gazed at passers-by through a spyglass.[664] It is no wonder that even the stupid Nosey Flynn admits that he has his good points:

—He's not too bad, Nosey Flynn said, snuffling it up. He has been known to put his hand down too to help a fellow. Give the devil his due. O, Bloom has his good points.[175]

Fastidious, delicate, and temperate (much to the debt-collector's disgust),[298] Bloom responds to others

with a smile.[92] He is opposed to faultfinding, it being
"proverbially bad hat,"[618] revising his earlier un-
sympathetic criticism of Simon Dedalus.[87] He even
represses his curiosity, a considerable triumph, in
hesitating to ask the proofreader, Nannetti, about the
pronunciation of *Voglio*, a word that has puzzled him,
for fear he might embarrass that worthy man.[119]

He feels most deeply the terror of death at the funeral and is eager to do all he can for the widow. His
generosity in contributing to the fund amazes Nolan,[243] and he is busy trying to arrange for the insurance when he is so ignominiously routed from Kiernan's. The pathos of death recurs to his mind throughout the day. He is sorry for widows and finds small
consolation in what "wise men say," that one must
outlive the other.[100]

The other important event of his day—the confinement of Mrs. Purefoy—touches his heart. He thinks
of the pains of childbirth with "heavy pitying
gaze."[156] Women have "no soft job," what with keeping house and raising children.[366] It is sympathy for
Mrs. Purefoy that leads him to the Holles Street
Hospital in the evening. He is sorry to hear of the
death of Doctor O'Hare[379] (earlier in the day he had
reflected that doctors were unappreciated).[159] Sitting
at the table with the drunken medical students,
"woman's woe with wonder pondering,"[382] he is sensitive about their ribald talk, "for that he rued for her
that bare whoso she might be."[383]

From the beginning of their acquaintance, he
adopts a paternal and protective attitude toward
Stephen. He is alarmed at Stephen's companions,[384]
indignant at their leaving him at Bella Cohen's,[598]

and "in orthodox Samaritan fashion"[597] does what he can to revive his friend's spirits, urging him to drink some coffee[619] and hoping to slip some money to him unobtrusively.

The ludicrous inadequacy of Bloom's gospel of reasonableness is most clearly seen in his discussions of politics. He is hard put to it to defend British imperialism from the onslaughts of the patriots at Kiernan's. He is not so ready to condemn British policy, yet his apologies for it are certainly lacking in conviction:

—Some people, says Bloom, can see the mote in others' eyes but they can't see the beam in their own.[320]

But such a soft answer fails to turn away the wrath of the ardent Citizen, who protests the spoliation of Ireland and the crimes of the British navy. Bloom again demurs, going so far as to blame the system, yet still holding to the ideal of brotherly love: "Wouldn't it be the same here if you put force against force?"[323]

The discussion at Kiernan's might be entitled "Bloom's Political Education," for here he is brought face to face with the appalling revelation that his doctrines of good will are inadequate as solutions for the chaos of modern industrialism and imperialism. Confronted with the entirely disrespectful Citizen and the cynical debt-collector, he is sensitive enough to feel the naïveté of his outlook. His embarrassment leads him to a ridiculous definition of a nation—"the same people living in the same place . . . . or also living in different places."[325]

The uncompromising spirit of his associates is contagious; and, in impassioned protest against anti-

Semitism, his words throb with the intensity of his feeling:

—Robbed, says he. Plundered. Insulted. Persecuted. Taking what belongs to us by right.[326]

And when the Citizen scornfully asks whether he is talking about the new Jerusalem, he replies simply: "I'm talking about injustice."[327]

The basic paradoxes of modern political creeds are clearly revealed in the saloon discussion; for the intransigent nationalists are just as jingoistic as the England they despise, and the limitation of their vision is clearly seen in their own anti-Semitism. The protest against anti-Semitism plays a more important part in *Ulysses* than most critics have recognized. Stephen objects to Mr. Deasy's prejudice. The schoolmaster had held that the scourge suffered by the Jews is accounted for by their sinning against the light, to which Stephen gives as his reply the provocative question "Who has not?"[35] We feel throughout the book the burden of loneliness and scorn that Bloom carries on his shoulders. And to the Citizen's contempt for Bloom as the new Messiah for Ireland, Martin Cunningham's reply is final:

—Well, they're still waiting for their redeemer. . . . . For that matter so are we.[331]

Inherently Bloom is not stupid in regard to the nature of social forces. He notes that the police are seldom to be found in the rougher districts of the city, where they are most needed, "the obvious reason being they were paid to protect the upper classes."[599] Despite his dreams of enlightened good will, he is aware that force governs society. Irish patriotic pride is merely wishful thinking. To the boasts of Skin-the-Goat in the cabman's shelter about the strength of Ireland and the decline of English power, he is sensible enough to realize that the British, "unless they were much bigger fools then he took them for, rather concealed their strength than the opposite."[625]

His ideas on government are permeated by two inconsistencies. The ineffectuality of good will in a world dedicated to the use of force, overt or hidden, is a common oversight among liberals. Equally common is the incompatibility of cheap dreams of material progress with finer visions of social betterment. If man's hopes are limited by the horizons of petty commercial schemes, if his outlook remains primarily monetary, no satisfactory conception of the good life is possible. Yet Bloom muddles along, trying honestly to reconcile what his eyes reveal to him and what his heart hopes for.

It is in the cabman's shelter early in the morning that Bloom shows most clearly his divided state of mind. He betrays a silent admiration for revolutionaries, such as Skin-the-Goat, one of the Invincibles, a living reminder of Ireland's bloody past. Yet he admits that he would not have the courage to be one; and, his innate bourgeois caution coming to the fore, he feels the danger of associating with such characters. His inconsistency is strikingly apparent in his meditation. He "couldn't help feeling, and most properly, it was better to give people like that the goby unless you were a blithering idiot," since there was always the chance of someone's "coming forward and turning queen's evidence." Then, his law-abiding nature asserting itself, "he disliked those careers of wrongdoing and crime on principle." But is it wrongdoing to take social action? And is not social action necessary? He cannot repress his admiration for the courage of the patriot:

Yet, though such criminal propensities had never been an inmate of his bosom in any shape or form, he certainly did feel, and no denying it (while inwardly remaining what he was), a certain kind of admiration for a man who had actually brandished a knife, cold steel, with the courage of his political convictions though, personally, he would never be a party to any such thing.[626]

For readers who might be troubled by the syntax of this sentence it is only fair to remark that it appears in the chapter devoted to exaggerated satire of the involved modifiers, subordinate clauses, and circumlocutions of conventional English.

As he holds forth to Stephen on his ideals of government, one can easily see the uncertainty and hesitation which color his innate faith in tolerance, freedom, and opportunity. He believes that progress must come gradually, that revolutions, almost without exception, tend to be abortive. He pours out his heart in the shelter:

It is hard to lay down any hard and fast rules as to right and wrong but room for improvement all round there certainly is though every country, they say, our own distressful included, has the government it deserves.[627]

Going on to suggest that "with a little goodwill all around" much could be done, he states that "I resent violence or intolerance in any shape or form." Moreover, violence is usually self-destructive: "It never reaches anything or stops anything." Revolutions must come, in Bloom's commercial phrase, "on the due instalments plan." And then concluding, some-what inconsecutively, he argues that "it's a patent ab-surdity on the face of it to hate people because they live round the corner and speak another vernacular, so to speak."[627] Good old Bloom!

As the discussion turns to the downfall of Parnell, Bloom continues to reveal his unusual forthrightness and understanding. He feels the injustice of "seventy-two of his trusty henchmen rounding on him with mu-tual mudslinging"[634] and is ready to forgive the chief his misdemeanors with Kitty O'Shea:

the simple fact of the case was it was simply a case of the hus-band not being up to the scratch with nothing in common be-tween them beyond the name and then a real man arriving on the scene, strong to the verge of weakness, falling a victim to her siren charms and forgetting home ties.[635]

The large-mindedness of this statement should be ap-parent to all who note the parallel between the unfor-tunate captain and Bloom himself.

Bloom's dreams, we read in the homecoming chap-ter, were "at the critical turningpoint of human ex-istence . . . . to amend many social conditions, the product of inequality and avarice and international animosity."[681] In his youth he had been an ardent radical, going further than Michael Davitt on the peasant landownership question.[641] But now, on the threshold of middle age, his political outlook is more conservative. As an important political figure (an-other of his dreams) he plans to hold a course that lies "between undue clemency and excessive rigour"; to be "loyal to the highest constituted power in the land"; to aim for "the strict maintenance of public order," while advocating a gradual elimination of

abuses.[700] These mildly Fabian tactics are not such as
to arouse enthusiasm, either in the stubbornly un-
political Stephen or in the belligerent patriots with
whom Bloom comes in contact during the day. And
when he turns to the Gospel for authority and argues
that Jesus was a carpenter and the first socialist,
Molly has another cause for annoyance.[728]

The inconsistencies of his political views are made
ludicrous in the visions of the "Circe" scene. We may
reconstruct the background of the episode by a few
hints. Bloom apparently had been holding forth on
his political and social gospel (a little out of place at
Bella Cohen's, but such is Mr. Bloom), and his words
lead to a drunken delusion of grandeur. As Lord May-
or he is hailed by the multitude and expresses his
program:

I stand for the reform of municipal morals and the plain ten
commandments. New worlds for old. Union of all, jew, moslem,
and gentile. Three acres and a cow for all children of nature.
Saloon motor hearses. Compulsory manual labor for all. All
parks open to the public day and night. Electric dishscrubbers.
Tuberculosis, lunacy, war and mendicancy must now cease.
General amnesty, weekly carnival, with masked licence, bonuses
for all, esperanto the universal brotherhood. No more patriotism
of barspongers and dropsical imposters. Free money, free love
and a free lay church in a free lay state.[480]

Ridiculously bourgeois, one must admit, stated in
this absurd fashion, but merely a grotesque perversion of Bloom's essentially humane outlook, distorted
by his petty bourgeois outlook. He confesses to Stephen that he wants to see everyone, "all creeds and
classes *pro rata* having a comfortable tidysized income, in no niggard fashion either, something in the
neighborhood of £300 per annum." And continuing,

eloquently but inconsecutively, he defends his position:

That's the vital issue at stake and it's feasible and would be provocative of friendlier intercourse between man and man. At least that's my idea for what it's worth. I call that patriotism. *Ubi patria*, as we learned a small smattering of in our classical day in *Alma mater, vita bene*.[628]

And then, perhaps sensing Stephen's indifference to his discourse, he translates, an act which is scarcely necessary when talking with the brilliant graduate of University College: "Where you can live well, the sense is, if you work."[628] Stephen murmurs about "*Christus* or Bloom"[627] but remains passive and unresponsive:

listening to this synopsis of things in general, Stephen stared at nothing in particular. He could hear, of course, all kinds of words changing colour like those crabs about Ringsend in the morning, burrowing quickly into all colours of different sorts of the same sand where they had a home somewhere beneath or seemed to. Then he looked up and saw the eyes that said or didn't say the words the voice he heard said—if you work.

Count me out, he managed to remark, meaning to work.[628]

With this cold reception Bloom's finest statement of humanitarianism in political life is received, just as his earlier definition of love had been followed by a parody:

Love loves to love love. Nurse loves the new chemist. Constable 14A loves Mary Kelly. Gerty MacDowell loves the boy that has the bicycle. M. B. loves a fair gentleman. . . . . You love a certain person. And this person loves that other person because everybody loves somebody but God loves everybody.[327]

One cannot help feeling that Joyce has difficulty in repressing his innate idealism and that he engages in this sort of byplay and ridicule to ease his own un-

happy heart. But to accuse the novel of being uncom-
promisingly nihilistic is to fail to sense the presence
of the buried hopes of humanity that lie concealed in
its pages.

One must not go so far as to interpret Joyce as a
humanitarian liberal. He is too clear-eyed for that.
It is as though he were setting himself the task of
showing what a small part Christian idealism plays in
the modern world and raising the question of why it
has proved so ineffectual, not to say ridiculous.

It is significant of Joyce's social sympathy that he
adopts as the major figure of his story a character not
far above the proletariat in social position, and treats
him so sympathetically. The identification of Joyce
with Stephen has often been made, but the creator of
Bloom is far more tolerant than Stephen, the silent
and cynical accuser of all phases of modern life.
Stephen's only faith had been in the world of art.
But in a society which admires Philip Beaufoy and
feels that the Abbey Theatre represents the culmination of culture, it is impossible for him to forge the
conscience of the race. One must be content to picture
life as it is, without illusions, without hope.

But is Stephen the author of *Ulysses?* Indifferent
to the bustling life of the city all about him, devoid of
humor, contemptuous of his companions, the young
poet is lost in memory and meditation. Bloom, confused as he is, is far more positive. Joyce expressed a
personal interest in him, and he is, after all, for better
or for worse, the modern Ulysses. As the author confessed slyly to a friend in Paris, most commentators
overlook the fact that the *Portrait* was entitled the

portrait of the artist as a *young* man. The young Stephen Hero had walked through Dublin only to observe the crassness of the people:

There was no face that passed him on its way to its commercial prison but he strove to pierce to the motive centre of its ugliness.[30]

But the mature author of *Ulysses* cannot be accused of such disdain. He has done more than merely to uncover ugliness; he has seen the soul of the little man beneath its mask. Bloom is ridiculous, but only because man's hopes have been vulgarized by a competitive society into matters of suburban homes (who will live in the city when everyone leaves it for suburbia?), insurance policies, and get-rich-quick schemes. It is not so much the ideal of good will that is ludicrous as it is its incompatibility with the values of the modern world. In such circumstances no other fate could be expected than that which is accorded Bloom's ideals.

Humiliated and ridiculed as he is, he is both product and victim of his environment. His very efforts to escape that environment are ludicrously inadequate. Kindness and good will are oddly out of place in a society alien to the better impulses of man. More than that, they themselves become grotesque in taking on the coloration of the society in which they still survive feebly. Finally, good will is incapable of providing the dynamic necessary for social change.

Bloom is not so absurd as he appears, just as he is far from being as hopelessly vulgar as Stephen thinks him. He is sensitive enough to feel the emptiness of the modern world and the inadequacy of his hope. He

knows that he is a victim of society, just as Charles
Bovary, a much more stupid character, finally comes
to a realization of his own limitations. But, in contrast to Bovary, who is ridiculously banal, Bloom
approaches the level of the tragic hero. If not a great
man by conventional reckoning, he is at least great of
heart, and he suffers greatly. The burden of loneliness
is his in no small measure. Neglected, despised
("When in doubt persecute Bloom"),[455] this Wandering Jew carries in his soul the secret of love.

At times the burden becomes almost intolerable.
The debt-collector cannot understand his reactions.
"And then he collapses all of a sudden, twisting
around all the opposite, as limp as a wet rag." But
finding the acceptance of defeat intolerable, Bloom
rises to a final eloquent appeal:

—But it's no use, says he. Force, hatred, history, all that.
That's not life for men and women, insult and hatred. And
everybody knows that it's the very opposite of that that is
really life.

Even the carefree Alf Bergan is touched, albeit bewildered, by this appeal, and asks, wonderingly,
"What?" to which Bloom gives the simple response:

—Love, says Bloom. I mean the opposite of hatred.[327]

XIV INELUCTABLE MODALITY: *THE RHYTHMS OF LIFE*

Ineluctable modality of the visible: at least that if no more, thought through my eyes. Signatures of all things I am here to read, seaspawn and seawrack, the nearing tide, that rusty boot.[38]

JOYCE was both naturalist and symbolist, social realist and mystic visionary. His keen observations of the contemporary scene are permeated by a feeling for the panorama of history and a vision of the mysteries beyond. Unlike the social reformer, whose attention is directed exclusively to the immediate scene, he is constantly attracted to the ultimate problems of existence itself. If *Finnegans Wake* is anything more than a *jeu d'esprit*, a monument of Dadaist trifling with words or giant jokebook, it is a philosophical poem on the essence of history. Its basic themes revolve about the recurrent patterns of life, the effect of the long shadow of the past in creating a sort of collective unconscious for mankind. Like Sir Thomas Browne three hundred years before him, Joyce had a mystic sense of man's place in history. Of the past we have only imperfect records, of the future we know nothing. The pages of history rapidly pass from view, and each generation, in turn, writes its records. But the pages are palimpsests on which we can barely trace the half-erased writing of our predecessors. Naught is permanent but the fact of change and the constant rhythm of individual life— birth, growth, and death. We repeat the patterns of our forebears with slight modification, and, as we pass on, it is difficult for our descendants even to identify us as individuals.

Ulysses is thus an important point of mid-passage between the personal concern of the *Portrait* and the cosmic preoccupations of *Finnegans Wake*. For the moment, personal, social, and cosmic perceptions merge. If Joyce is not, after all, a critic and reformer like Shaw, it is because his interests are already headed toward larger perspectives. His major concern is metaphysics. A constant undertone in the *Portrait*, it plays an important role in *Ulysses* and dominates *Finnegans Wake*. *Ulysses* shows the compulsive drift of the author's mind toward the ineluctable.

It is probable that Joyce read with sympathy the following passage from Browne's *Religio medici* (1643), for it not only expresses the philosophy of *Ulysses* and *Finnegans Wake* but also contains one of the important thematic words of the earlier novel:

For, as though there were a metempsychosis, and the soul of one man passed into another, opinions do find, after certain revolutions, men and minds like those that first begat them. To see ourselves again, we need only look for Plato's year: every man is not only himself; there have been many Diogeneses, and as many Timons, though but few of that name; men are lived over again; the world is now as it was in ages past; there was none then, but there hath been some one since, that parallels him, and is, as it were, his revived self.

Finnegans Wake is a complete incarnation of this vision of history. The characters merge and overlap, appearing now in the guise of ancient heroes, now as modern Dubliners. We read of how "idlers' wind" turns "the leaves of the living in the boke of the deeds,"[13] how the world "is, was and will be writing its own wrunes for ever."[19] The central theme of this gigantic problem child of modern literature is "a theory none too rectiline of the evoluation of human society and a testament of the rocks from all the dead unto some the living."[73] When H. C. E., the hero, is sometimes the legendary Finnegan, sometimes Tristan, sometimes Adam, sometimes the Hill of Howth (scene of Bloom's proposal), again the concept of Space or the spirit of Civilization, we see that the book is truly a "continuous present tense integument" slowly unfolding "all marryvoising moodmoulded cyclewheeling history."[186]

The diction of the book, fascinating, bewildering, or exasperating, as the case may be, is nonetheless an illustration of the "fadograph"[7] that is man's culture. Medley of parody, pun, echo of music-hall song, legend, and buried etymology, it is the despair of readers.

The key conception, that of the constant recurrence in history, is repeated with variations. We read: "This ourth of years is not save brickdust and being humus the same roturns."[18] Later it is "Teems of times and happy returns. The seim anew."[215] It recurs in babytalk in the schoolroom chapter as "We drames our dreams tell Bappy returns. And Sein annews."[277] It is prophetically modulated into

—Booms of bombs and heavy rethudders?
—This aim to you![510]

In beginning the cycle over again, it becomes "Themes have thimes and habit reburns. To flame in you."[614] And its last appearance becomes the weary "Time after time. The sehm asnuh."[620]

One other theme demands reference because of its pertinence to *Ulysses*. It is the oft-repeated, variously stated rendition of the rhythm of the life-span of man. We read that they "lived und laughed ant loved end left";[18] again we are asked, "Have you whines for my wedding, did you bring bride and bedding, will you whoop for my deading . . . .?"[24] And the cycle is endlessly repeated, for "on the bunk of our bread-winning lies the cropse of our seedfather."[55] Men's "weatherings and their marryings and their buryings"[117] go on and on. It is always a case of "harry me, marry me, bury me,"[414] and even "the nice little smellar squalls in his crydle what the dirty old bigger'll be squealing through his coughin."[444] In more cynical mood we read of the cycle as "eggburst, egg-blend, eggburial and hatch-as-hatch can."[614] Such are the four stages of man.

This conception of flux, which dominates *Finnegans Wake* to the extent of determining its style and structure, is one of the important integrating themes in *Ulysses*. The plan of the book—that of tracing the dance of the hours on one day—implies that any other of the thousands of days in history would show, *mutatis mutandis*, a similar pattern. The metaphor buried in the phrase "stream-of-consciousness" suggests that life consists of a constant flow of impressions, ideas, experiences, associations. Temporarily halted by, or rather submerged in, sleep, the continuity of existence is resumed on the following morning. Thus there is some truth in the contention that *Ulysses* could begin anywhere and end anywhere or, more accurately, has neither beginning nor end. But it is by the isolation and segregation of eighteen hours of human history in one small locality that Joyce imposes an arbitrary unity upon his investigation and implies the larger flow of life before and after, as well as outside, the time and place that he selects.

The two major characters are preoccupied with this conception. Stephen is led by his mother's death to speculate on the mystery of human personality and its destiny after death. The simple phrase "Where now?" pierces through one of his first soliloquies, which continues with the eloquence of the idea of his mother's personality, now "folded away in the memory of nature."[11] But the living are also constantly changing in character; change through continuity, or continuity through change, marks the strange nature of individual destiny. So Stephen reflects, recalling his youth at school, "I am another now and yet the same."[13] Our bodies are woven and unwoven, "their molecules shuttled to and fro";[192] yet man's physical features remain relatively constant throughout life.

Another interesting speculation is no less directly related to Stephen's own experience. Feeling alienated from his father by temperament and from his mother by religious conviction, he scrutinizes his relation to his parents, and, his generalizing tendency being what it is, the wider problem of generation itself is touched upon. Birth seems to be in the hands of a fate far more extended in scope than the parents' own will and instinct; the mystery of birth goes back to the eternal mystery. "The cords of all link back" to an unascertainable first cause, who "from before the ages" willed the creation of each individual.[39] Thus "paternity may be a legal fiction," Stephen concludes in his meditations in the library;[205] that is, blood relationship has no bearing upon spiritual kinship: "Who is the father of any son that any son should love him or he any son?"[205]

In the changing world of form and appearance, the soul itself is the greatest mystery. It is the "form of forms,"[27] yet none can know it truly. Its relation to the body is indefinable; it walks, a strange companion, with Stephen on the beach.[45] Possibly the body is only its temporary guardian, and the soul-stuff is transmitted to others:

Endless, would it be mine, form of my form?[49]

Physical change and psychic change, the links of generations, the utmost destiny of man and his metaphysical significance, it is no wonder that "darkness is in our souls."[49] Soliloquizing in the library, Stephen speculates that, since "molecules all change," "I am other I now"; yet the soul somehow mysteriously remains the same:

But I, entelechy, form of forms, am I by memory because under everchanging forms.[187]

As Stephen turns from metaphysics to history, the same problem recurs. Those turning-points of destiny, where the direction of the future is determined, what of them? Are they merely the result of a blind chance, or is there an inherent design which man cannot probe?

Had Pyrrhus not fallen by a beldam's hand in Argos or Julius Caesar not been knifed to death. They are not to be thought away. Time has branded them and fettered they are lodged in the room of the infinite possibilities they have ousted. But can those have been possible seeing that they never were? Or was that only possible which came to pass?[26]

The thought of what might have been, "possibilities of the possible as possible," continues to perplex Stephen as he observes on the library shelves rows of books—thoughts of the past, embalmed and preserved.[191] Earlier, as he had contemplated his literary career while walking on the beach, Stephen had an acute sense of kinship with thinkers long since deceased:

When one reads these strange pages of one long gone one feels that one is at one with one who once. . .[41]

These tantalizing problems of human existence permeate Stephen's subconscious throughout the novel. But even Bloom, materialist though he is, is aroused to similar speculations. His reasoning is, of course, more factual, less nebulous, and less philosophical. The word "metempsychosis," used by Sir Thomas Browne, is called to his attention in a typically banal episode. Molly has stumbled across the word in her reading (and we recall what her literary taste is!):

She swallowed a draught of tea from her cup held by not-handle and, having wiped her fingertips smartly on the blanket, began to search the text with the hairpin till she reached the word.
—Met him what? he asked.
—Here, she said. What does that mean?
He leaned down and read near her polished thumbnail.
—Metempsychosis?
—Yes, Who's he when he's at home?
—Metempsychosis, he said, frowning. It's Greek: from the Greek. That means the transmigration of souls.
—O rocks! she said. Tell us in plain words.[64]

The word, with Molly's illiterate variant, "met-him-pike-hoses," lingers in Bloom's consciousness through the day. It pops into his mind as he thinks of another Greek word, *parallax*, on his way to lunch.[152] It arises in connection with the "General Slocum" disaster;[180] the smell of liver at the Ormond suggests it (he had been frying kidney for breakfast);[265] it is recalled as he dreams of Molly's beauty[280] and as he carries the *Sweets of Sin* with him;[283] at twilight on the beach he thinks of it[371] and again remembers it as one of the incidents of the day.[375] At the hospital[402] it recurs twice,[407] as it does in "Circe," first as Dignam's ghost,[464] then as one of the new goddesses (Bloom had stopped at the museum after lunch).[480] In showing Molly's photograph to Stephen, Bloom thinks of the word,[037] and it is listed as one instance of Molly's ignorance[670] in the catechism chapter. Molly recalls it as she lies in bed.[738]

These fifteen appearances of the word would not be listed were it not such a good instance of Joyce's verbal technique. No thought exists singly in Joyce; it is connected by multiple ramifications and associations with many others. By observing these recalls one can see that it is connected with an odor, that of the kidney; an object, book; a person, Molly; its origin, Greek; and, by extension, with the Greek statues seen in the museum. Joyce repeats his thematic words with psychological validity as well as with philosophical intent.

Not only the word but the conception that lies behind it comes before Bloom's mind. He, like Stephen, feels the constant flux of life, though in more concrete terms. The funeral is sufficient for him to wonder at the mystery of life. On his way to the cemetery he realizes that funerals are taking place all over the world at the same moment;[100] the universality of death is also suggested as he lists mentally the many burial customs of past and present.[113] The life-cycle comes to his attention as he hears of Mrs. Purefoy's confinement:

Trams passed one another, ingoing, outgoing, clanging. . . . . Things go on same; day after day: squads of police marching out, back: trams in, out. . . . . One born every second somewhere. Other dying every second. Since I fed the birds five minutes. Three hundred kicked the bucket.[162]

And, continuing, Bloom characteristically descends to the humorously vulgar as he thinks of the three hundred born, being washed in the blood of the Lamb (a recall of the evangelistic pamphlet just given him). Further, he recalls the saying that landlords never die; despite the vicissitudes of life and death, the accumulation and inheritance of money continue.

The funeral also brings to Bloom's consciousness the fact of decay, and a rat seen in the cemetery lingers in his mind. Thinking of the disintegration of the body, he reflects:

Of course the cells or whatever they are go on living. Changing about. Live for ever practically. Nothing to feed on feed on themselves.[107]

An interesting chain of thought occurs in the newspaper office. Noticing the necessity of proofreading backward as the paper is made up, Bloom remembers his father's reading his Hagadah book backward, then turns to thoughts of Jacob's sons. The very thought of the chain of thought leads to an expression of the

law of survival phrased in the style of the nursery
tale of "The Old Woman at the Stile":

And then the lamb and the cat and the dog and the stick and the
water and the butcher and then the angel of death kills the butcher and he kills the ox and the dog kills the cat. Sounds a bit silly
till you come to look into it well. Justice it means but it's everybody eating everyone else. That's what life is after all.[121]

This notion reaches a climax of revulsion as he turns
away in disgust from a filthy eating-joint—"Eat or
be eaten. Kill! Kill!"[168]

In the impersonal catechism chapter the question
is raised as to whether Bloom thought man infinitely
perfectible. In answer, the inevitable conditions of
mortality are set forth, including "the necessity of
destruction to procure alimentary sustenance," "the
painful character of the ultimate functions of separate existence, the agonies of birth and death," and
culminating in the conception of "vital growth,
through convulsions of metamorphosis, from infancy
through maturity to decay."[681]

The last phrases suggest the stages of existence as
given so many times in *Finnegans Wake*. There are
two statements in *Ulysses*, however, which come even
closer as anticipations of the "harry me, marry me,
bury me" formula; for Stephen on the beach mouths
the phrase "bridebed, childbed, bed of death,"[48] and
in the manner of Francis Bacon one passage in the
hospital scene reads:

The aged sisters draw us into life: we wail, batten, sport, clip,
clasp, sunder, dwindle, die: over us dead they bend.[387]

The passing of the generations in uninterrupted
flow is called to Bloom's mind by his thoughts of

Palestine. The land itself is old, its history buried in the past; but the Jews have wandered over the earth "multiplying, dying, being born everywhere."[61] The De Quincey passage in the hospital scene reaches into the realm of the spirit. Carrying on Bloom's thoughts of the death of his son, we read that "silently the soul is wafted over regions of cycles of cycles of generations that have lived."[407]

Life is likened to flowing water by both Stephen and Bloom, a concept that permeates *Finnegans Wake* especially in respect to Anna Livia Plurabelle, a symbol both of the River Liffey and of the eternal feminine. Stephen, walking by the sea, thinks that it represents the spirit of nature. He has been closing his eyes, thinking of the ultimate nothingness, and, upon opening them again, sees the ocean carrying on its endless task:

There all the time without you: and ever shall be, world without end.[38]

Echoes of St. Ambrose, of Matthew Arnold's "Dover Beach,"[50] of the *Tempest* and of "Lycidas," come to mind as he broods over the never ending cycle of nature and the brevity of man's existence. He then thinks of the sea-change that is life—"God becomes man becomes fish becomes barnacle goose becomes featherbed mountain"—and reflects that even as he walks he is breathing dead breaths and treading dead dust.[51]

So, too, does Bloom think of the stream of life, "always passing, the stream of life, which in the stream of life we trace,"[85] a passage which seems to be deliberately phrased in an interacting fashion—that is, our little lives are but eddies in the larger tides of existence. The phrase and the idea recur as he leans over the O'Connell Bridge to feed the gulls:

It's always flowing in a stream, never the same, which in the stream of life we trace. Because life is a stream.[151]

Howth Hill, which plays an important role in *Finnegans Wake*, enters *Ulysses* as the scene of Bloom's proposal.[173] It comes to mind frequently, and Bloom thinks of the change in his relationship to Molly since those happy days, sixteen years ago. At one point the thought of Howth merely brings forth the brief but moving "I. He. Old. Young"[267]—in reference to Boylan, who is at the very moment enjoying Molly's favors. In melancholy mood on the beach, Bloom thinks of the passing of time (it is twilight), and Howth once again comes to mind:

All quiet on Howth now. The distant hills seem. Where we. The rhododendrons.[370]

And he thinks of "all that old hill has seen," concluding with the pathetic notion that "names change: that's all."[370] The twilight scene is described, with an ironic mockery of the deceived Bloom:

Twittering the bat flew here, flew there. Far out over the sands the coming surf crept, grey. Howth settled for slumber tired of long days, of yumyum rhododendrons (he was old) and felt gladly the night breeze lift, ruffle his fell of ferns. He lay but opened a red eye unsleeping, deep and slowly breathing, slumberous but awake. And far on Kish bank the anchored lightship twinkled, winked at Mr Bloom.[372]

In the city proper it is the incessant rounds of the trams that suggest the never ending cycle of life.

Trams are noted throughout the day. One slides between Bloom and a woman mounting a carriage and thus prevents a sight of well-filled hose.[73] A tram passes while Bloom meditates in church.[82] The clatter of the vehicles impinges upon his thoughts twice, much to his annoyance, once when he is trying to recollect a name,[153] once as he is recalling the last words of Robert Emmet, the Irish rebel.[286] The passing of the trams suggests to Bloom the concept of the stream of life.[162] One feels that this is a deliberate symbol on Joyce's part; for one chapter, the newspaper-office scene, begins and concludes with descriptions of the tram routes. Only twice during the day are the trams silent and unmoving, once because of a short-circuit[147] and in the afternoon for the viceregal procession.[249]

But, most important of all, the basic pattern of the book is a microcosm of the stream of existence. The functions of life are dramatized in successive sections. The novel traverses the whole of experience—birth, in the hospital scene; education, in the school; young manhood, in the scene at Martello Tower; religion, in the "Lotus Eaters"; philosophy, in Stephen's soliloquy on the beach; music, at the Ormond; journalism, at the *Freeman* office; literature, in the library; city life and the interweaving of characters, in the "Wandering Rocks"; sex, in Molly's soliloquy; science, in the catechism chapter; politics, at Kiernan's; and death, at Paddy Dignam's funeral. June 16 is the prototype of any modern day. Not for nothing was Joyce bred in medieval scholasticism.

An epic range and integration are achieved, as has

been shown throughout this study. Themes extend beyond the chapters in which they are introduced. In *Ulysses* thoughts, characters, events, hopes, fears, and memories are woven into an intricate strand, constantly changing color with the changing moods of the principal figures. One sees the ineluctable modality not only of the visible but of the audible, the psychological, the intellectual, and the emotional.

XV PARENTHESIS OF INFINITESIMAL BREVITY: *THE COSMIC OVERVIEW*

*socalled fixed stars, in reality evermoving from immeasurably re-
mote eons to infinitely remote futures in comparison with which the
years, threescore and ten, of allotted human life formed a parenthesis
of infinitesimal brevity.*[683]

FROM the conception of the basic biological rhythms
of life contrasted with the apparently never ending
forces of nature—the tides of the ocean, the flow of
the Liffey—it is only a step to a view of human life
from the perspective of astronomical time and space.
And we see that June 16 is projected against the great
backdrop of infinity.

Just as Mann achieves an extra-dimensional scope
to the tale of *Joseph and His Brothers* by his brilliant
introductory chapter, musing with philosophical reverence upon the endless coulisses of the past, so Joyce
projects Bloom's day against the infinite spaces beyond. It is to the cosmic plane that *Ulysses* finally
reaches.

It must be remembered that Joyce's early discipline
in scholastic thinking led him inevitably to this point.
The cosmic perspective is to be found in each of his
major works, and in each with an increasing emphasis,
until in *Finnegans Wake* cosmic background and realistic foreground are but two aspects of the same material.

Harry Levin, alone among commentators on Joyce,
has called attention to this phase of *Ulysses*. His

treatment is perceptive, though brief. Several of the illustrations used in this chapter are mentioned by him and brilliantly interpreted. It is hoped to do more than repeat or paraphrase his analysis; and to that end the references will be more fully given and the implications drawn more closely to the themes treated earlier. It is especially interesting to trace the relationship of Joyce's point of view to traditional religious skepticism.

The cosmic point of view is found in the *Portrait of the Artist* and *Dubliners*, it colors one chapter in *Ulysses*, and it becomes dominant in *Finnegans Wake*. Even as a schoolboy, Joyce tells us in the *Portrait*, Stephen had sensed the relativity of man's place in nature. In his geography textbook he had written:

> *Stephen Dedalus*
> *Class of Elements*
> *Clongowes Wood College*
> *Sallins*
> *County Kildare*
> *Ireland*
> *Europe*
> *The World*
> *The Universe*[11]

From the point of view of the universe, what is Stephen Dedalus, that it should weep for him, or, indeed, what is Ireland itself? A fragment of Shelley, "Art thou pale for weariness," with its evocation of the moon's sense of the loneliness of heaven and earth, lingered in Stephen's mind: ·

Its alternation of sad human ineffectualness with vast inhuman cycles of activity chilled him, and he forgot his own human and ineffectual grieving.[108]

As he suffers the pangs of religious remorse, the vision recurs to him. In a passage striking for its psychological insight, Joyce tells how the algebraic symbols on his school page faded from the young boy's vision, then emerged as eyes and finally as glimmering stars. A dizzying sensation came upon him, and he felt drawn into a mystic trance: "The vast cycle of starry life bore his weary mind outward to its verge and inward to its centre, a distant music accompanying him outward and inward," the music of Shelley's lines.[116] Soon the vision faded, and "cold darkness filled chaos."

Similarly, as he had walked along the bay below Dublin, the city itself seemed to recede into cosmic perspective:

Like a scene on some vague arras, old as man's weariness, the image of the seventh city of christendom was visible to him across the timeless air.[194]

In melancholy mood he turned his face toward the sky, and the clouds floating through the heavens seemed infinitely remote and mysterious—"They were voyaging across the deserts of the sky, a host of nomads on the march, voyaging high over Ireland, westward bound."[194]

Such meditations may be turned in the direction of pathos or of ridicule or of both, depending upon the tone and sympathy of the attitude. Removal from the immediate scene can be an effective satiric device, as the travels of the outlanders Gulliver, Candide, Rasselas, or, indeed, of any of the other imaginary satiric visitors of literature will show. There is much of this satiric tone in *Ulysses*. It is implicit in the very minuteness with which Joyce chronicles one day in a modern city. If human life be reduced to such a microscopic degree of analysis, what values can be found in it? From the standpoint of the eternal, how petty, trivial, ridiculous, are the daily acts of man!

But a keen sense of religious melancholy may also be evoked. How small mere mortals are when compared to the vastness beyond, how pitiful their plight! The vanity of human life has been a common theme in religious literature from the time of Ecclesiastes. It was reiterated throughout medieval literature. During the Renaissance a new impetus was given it by the discoveries of physical science. On the one hand, science seemed to upset the convenient anthropomorphic world view of the Middle Ages, thus paving the way for skepticism and atheism. Quick to sense the danger, the church used the very weapon of skepticism to lead the way back to revealed religion, for the greater man's supposed knowledge, so the argument ran, all the greater is his sense of helplessness in the face of cosmic forces. The gnawing sense of unbelief provoked by science can be used as a dire warning of the dangers of skepticism. The argument appears in Montaigne, in the essay on Raymond Sebond, longest of the essays. In answer to the presumption of philosophers, he cites the physical frailty of man, the relativity of knowledge, the untrustworthiness of science, and concludes that man may elevate himself only "by forsaking his own means, and suffering himself to be elevated by heavenly means."

The conception colors all the work of Sir Thomas Browne and forms the core of Dryden's *Religio laici*, but its most pertinent expression is in Pascal's meditation on "The Misery of Man without God." "Would that man," he exclaims, "consider what he is in comparison with what is; that he would regard himself as lost in this last outpost of nature." And, reflecting upon the new universe of science, he cries out: "The silence of these infinite spaces terrifies me." Carrying out the analysis of man's position "between the two abysses of infinity and nothingness," that is, between the infinitely large spaces of the universe and the infinitesimal spaces of the atom, he feels that, without God,

we waver over a vast middle ground, ever uncertain and ever adrift, driven from one course to the other. Whatever the bourne where we think to find rest and a firm refuge, it gives way and eludes us; if we follow, it evades our grasp. . . . . Nothing for us is ever at rest. Such is our state of nature, and ever utterly at conflict with our inclination; we burn with desire to discover a firm seat and a foundation fixed and lasting whence we may raise a tower which shall pierce infinity, but the foundation shudders and the earth yawns even to the abyss.

Stripped of its religious implications, the same trend of thought forms the moving climax of *Ulysses*. Lacking religious faith, Joyce can view the spectacle of man's futility only with pity. But the pity is touched with ridicule, too—another instance of the ambivalent attitude which he so often adopts and which confounds his interpreters. Almost as though to protect the armor of his objectivity, Joyce presents this thought in the most impersonal chapter of the book, the scene in Bloom's kitchen. The question-and-answer technique fits perfectly with the concept of impersonality and, at the same time, provides a vehicle for parody of the jargon of science.

There are earlier preparations for this revelation. It is intimated in Stephen's soliloquies during the morning. Bloom conceives of the process of evolution on a cosmic scale as he speculates on the nature of time:

Gasballs spinning about, crossing each other, passing. Same old dingdong always. Gas, then solid, then world, then cold, then dead shell drifting around.[164]

At twilight he thinks of magnetic movement and the force of gravity.[367] In the hospital the medical student, Lynch, expresses his confidence that ultimately science will be able to explain "both natality and mortality, as well as all other phenomena of evolution, tidal movements, lunar phases, blood temperatures, diseases in general, everything, in fine, in nature's vast workshop from the extinction of some remote sun to the blossoming of one of the countless flowers."[412]

The pervasive emphasis on the concept of flux leads directly to the cosmic perspective which makes its first ironical occurrence when Bloom falls down into the areaway to let himself into his house. The question "Did he fall?" is answered with a record of Bloom's exact weight, as recorded on scales on May 12, 1904, followed by other calendar calculations:

(jewish era five thousand six hundred and sixty-four, mohammedan era one thousand three hundred and twenty-two), golden number 5, epact 13, solar cycle 9, dominical letters C B, Roman indication 2, Julian period 6617, MXMIV.[652]

Such a passage might be interpreted merely as an example of Joyce in a mood of pedantic humor, were it not shortly followed by other indications of the perspective of relativity. As he draws water from the faucet in order to prepare cocoa for his uncommunicative guest, the exact details of the flow of water are recounted in half a page of scrupulous accuracy, followed by Bloom's reflections on water. He thinks of "its universality," "its democratic equality and constancy," "its vastness in the ocean of Mercator's projection: its unplumbed profundity," and "the restlessness of its waves and surface particles"[655] (another reiteration of the conception of the eternal flux of nature). Driving the point to its extreme, the disquisition runs on for more than five hundred words, touching upon the preponderance of water on the globe, the phenomena of erosion and alluvial deposits (possibly an echo of the striking metaphor of the waste of time in Shakespeare's sonnet 64), and its metamorphoses as "vapour, mist, cloud, rain, sleet, snow, hail."[656]

These phrases recall the poignant climax of the story entitled "The Dead," in *Dubliners*, when Gabriel Conroy, having learned of his wife's early infatuation for the dead boy, Michael Furey, whom he had never seen, feels the awesomeness of life as he gazes at the snow falling outside his hotel window:

Yes, the newspapers were right, snow was general all over Ireland. It was falling on every part of the dark central plain, on the treeless hills, falling softly upon the Bog of Allen and, farther westward, softly falling into the dark mutinous Shannon waves. It was falling, too, upon every part of the lonely churchyard on the hill where Michael Furey lay buried. It lay thickly drifted on the crooked crosses and head-stones, on the spears of the little gate, on the barren thorns. His soul swooned slowly as he heard the snow falling faintly through the universe and faintly falling, like the descent of their last end, upon all the living and the dead.[287]

And with this prose poem the volume concludes.

At the time this story was written, between 1902 and 1905, Joyce could still dare to be lyrical, even sentimental in the style of the aesthetes of the nineties. But after haggling with publishers for nine years over the issue of *Dubliners*, Joyce undoubtedly felt a well-merited contempt for the timidity of the public. Here was silence, to be sure; exile was already his; cunning alone remained. Never again would he wear his heart on his sleeve. Hence the calculated irony and objectivity of *Ulysses*.

The pathos and ridicule which surround Bloom throughout the book are particularly apparent in his final homecoming. As he steps outside with Stephen to the privy (a characteristically naturalistic touch), he observes the stars. In Joyce's lushly evocative phrase, "the heaventree of stars hung with humid nightblue fruit."[683] His thoughts correspond exactly with Pascal's. He reflects on "meditations of evolution increasingly vaster"; on the phases of the moon; on the Milky Way; on Sirius, "10 lightyears (57,000,000,-000,000 miles) distant and in volume 900 times the dimension of our planet"; on Arcturus, Orion, the nebulae, and novae; and, rising to a magnificent climax,

of our system plunging towards the constellation of Hercules: of the parallax or parallactic drift of socalled fixed stars, in reality evermoving from immeasurably remote eons to infinitely remote futures in comparison with which the years, threescore and ten, of allotted human life formed a parenthesis of infinitesimal brevity.[683]

Then, turning from the infinite to the infinitesimal, as Pascal had over two centuries before, Joyce directs Bloom's thoughts to an equally detailed exegesis "of the myriad minute entomological organic existences concealed in cavities of the earth."[683]

Earlier in the day, as he sat in the Ormond and watched the waitresses listening as they put a seashell to their ears, Bloom had reflected on the structure of the blood:

> The sea they think they hear. Singing. A roar. The blood it is. . . . . Well, it's a sea. Corpuscle islands.[277]

Passing over the inaccuracy of his explanation, we find the blood described as a cosmos of the infinitesimal:

> the universe of human serum constellated with red and white bodies, themselves universes of void space constellated with other bodies, each, in continuity, its universe of divisible component bodies of which each was again divisible in divisions of redivisible component bodies, dividends and divisors ever diminishing without actual division till, if the progress were carried far enough, nought nowhere was never reached.[683]

"Nought nowhere was never reached"—a ludicrous, but surprisingly pertinent, use of the triple negative! From this cosmic point of view it is no wonder that Bloom alone should earlier have been compared to a sardine on a bier of bread under the sandwich-bell! For the cosmic is not so unrelated to the comic after all. Stephen Leacock's excellent study of humor concludes with a suggestion that the utmost in humorous detachment is probably reached only when men are able to view all of human life *sub specie aeternitatis*. Then all the ills of life, faded into the distance, mellowed by retrospect, would become humor in the finest sense of the word.

True to form in his daring shifts of point of view, Joyce's next questions swing from the cosmic through the comic to the soberly pessimistic mood of Ecclesiastes. In answer to the question as to why Bloom did not carry his calculations further, we are told that to write out the "9th power of the 9th power of 9" would fill "33 closely printed volumes of 1000 pages each"[684] (the author of the study has not verified the assertion!). Surely a beautiful *reductio ad absurdum* of mathematical inquiry! And his speculations about the possibility of life on other planets are concluded with the thought that if such life were present, beings such as they were would probably "remain inalterably and inalienably attached to vanities, to vanities of vanities and all that is vanity."[684]

Other indications of cosmic relativity abound in this chapter. We have an extended mathematical disquisition on the relationship of Stephen's and Bloom's ages, toying with proportions and projecting them until we must have Stephen live until 3072 A.D. and Bloom born in 81,396 B.C.[663] Here is a case of parallax with a vengeance!

The word "parallax" has puzzled Bloom through the day. It first occurs as he thinks of a book about astronomy that he had read some time before, adding: "I never exactly understood."[152] He thinks of visiting the observatory and plans to find out, but not by direct question, which would certainly lead to a "Show this gentleman the door."[164] In the De Quincey dream vision at the hospital, parallax stalks behind the hopes of the day, goading them toward oblivion.[407] Chris Callinan (with whom Bloom had discussed astronomy while Lenehan petted Molly) appears in "Circe" to ask Bloom about "parallax,"[478] and the word is uttered by the grotesque spirit of Bloom's father later on in the brothel scene.[501]

Bloom finally retires to the bed, which is described in echo of Stephen's reflections on the beach[48] and in anticipation of the cycle of life in *Finnegans Wake*. For the bed is "the bed of conception and of birth, of consummation of marriage and of breach of marriage, of sleep and of death."[716] Before retiring, he had thought of the various members of the funeral party and where each was at that time. Each, in turn, is listed, with the parenthetical "(in bed)" following his name, until we reach "Paddy Dignam (in the grave)"[689]—eloquent understatement of the mystery of existence. At the conclusion of Bloom's day we are faced with the ultimate question.

Bloom had speculated on the infinite spaces, we are told, and had reached the following conclusions:

That it was not a heaventree. . . . . That it was a Utopia, there being no known method from the known to the unknown: an infinity, renderable equally finite by the suppositous probable apposition of one or more bodies equally of the same and of different magnitudes: a mobility of illusory forms immobilised in space, remobilised in air: a past which possibly had ceased to exist as a present before its future spectators had entered actual present existence.[686]

As he dresses for bed, he thinks of "companions now in various manners in different places defunct," feels "the cold of interstellar space"[689] and "the apathy of the stars."[719]

The exact position of Bloom in bed is given, but

though apparently at rest, we are told that husband
and wife were being "carried westward, forward and
rereward respectively, by the proper perpetual motion of the earth through everchanging tracks of
neverchanging space."[721] Last seen in prenatal pose,
Bloom sleeps:

> Womb? Weary?
> He rests. He has travelled.[722]

As the final climax of the 667 pages devoted to placing Bloom socially, psychologically, temporally, geo-
graphically, and cosmically, the last question:
"Where?" is followed (in the earlier editions) by a
large black dot! The paragon of animals has indeed
been reduced to the quintessence of dust.

In turning the pages of Thom's *Directory* for 1904,
with their closely printed lists, house by house, seeing
Thomas Johnson, professor of botany, living next to
Cecil Moore, retired registrar, near the Association
for the Relief of Distressed Protestants, and just
down the block from the Dublin Tramways Stables,
one feels, as Joyce undoubtedly felt when he consulted
the same directory, that one is viewing the world
from a distant perspective. "Where bronze from
anear? Where gold from afar?"[253] Where, now, Thomas Johnson and his neighbor, the retired registrar?
Yet commentators have held that it is vain to seek
a philosophy in Joyce! The "cursed jesuit strain" is
certainly there; but in place of revealed religion,
Joyce has no faith to offer. Here is truly the plight of
the man without God. Skepticism, if you will, but
not mere cynical indifference. In a characteristic vein

of understatement Joyce concludes one extended disquisition on constellations with the touching phrase
"obscurity of terrestrial waters, pallor of human beings."[685] With all the wistful and ridiculous pathos of
Bloom's dreams of wealth, wisdom, and love, despite
his absurd efforts at self-improvement, mental and
physical (*Physical Strength and How To Obtain It* and
Short but Yet Plain Elements of Geometry were among
his books),[694] this man is willing to accept his lot,
even the fact of his wife's adultery; for Molly's activities were "as natural as any and every natural act"[717]
and, "more than inevitable, irreparable."[718]

He is even able to view his utopian daydreams with
common sense: "As a philosopher he knew that at the
termination of any allotted life only an infinitesimal
part of any person's desires has been realised."[704] And
though he, like the Wandering Jew himself, would
ever "wander selfcompelled, to the extreme limit of
his cometary orbit" as far as "the extreme boundary
of space, passing from land to land, among peoples,
amid events," yet "somewhere imperceptibly he
would hear and somehow reluctantly, suncompelled,
obey the summons of recall."[712]

Ulysses thus anticipates the thought of *Finnegans
Wake* that "we are circumveiloped by obscuritads,"[244]
or, in more comic vein: "We are once amore as babes
awondering in a wold made fresh where with the hen
in the storyaboot we start from scratch."[336] But in
the later dream-novel the comforting voice of Anna
Livia is also heard, cognizant of the fate of men and
sympathetic to her offspring. So throughout Joyce's
career a heartbreaking pity throbs behind the façade
of impersonality.

This is the world of *Ulysses*—a world hurrying through the infinite spaces of the universe at staggering speed, its residents unaware of their destiny. In a small city, the central point of a small island, adrift in the midst of the limitless expanse of the seas, they live in their little orbits, and the generations of man are as grass. Their economic schemes petty, their religions tangled masses of dogma, their art superficial, men of twentieth-century Dublin would be ridiculous if they were not so pathetic.

It is a sorry world that is so mercilessly depicted. Without the saving graces of sympathy and humor, the book would be intolerable. Even so, the patient accumulation of evidence conveys to most readers a feeling of protracted and unrelieved weariness. They forge on doggedly through a never ending jungle of words, ideas, impressions. Observations are thrown upon the page with bewildering rapidity. *Ulysses* is a mosaic of psychological recalls, topics of the day, Dublin landmarks, social, political, and cultural themes, mystic correspondences and philosophical concepts. Its tone changes with kaleidoscopic rapidity—from irony to pathos to ridicule to poetry. In its cubistic arrangement of contrasting planes and perspectives it is a perfect art form for the modern era. As an art form it has been variously praised and attacked; its content has never received the consideration it deserves. Even those who have analyzed its meaning have been prone to regard it as full of scattered insights, but lacking purposeful direction.

Yet *Ulysses* marks an important stage in the development of the most accomplished writer of this century. It confronts the poetic and philosophic artist with the common man and the vulgar values of society and projects his vision toward the symbolic plane later to be attained in *Finnegans Wake*. Thus, beneath the complex of ribaldry and sentiment, blasphemy and aspiration, mockery and tenderness, so strangely compounded, there lies a deeper purpose. Joyce had himself been ineffectual in attaining the prophetic mission he envisioned in the *Portrait*. In *Ulysses* he has set himself the task of analyzing the reasons why his hopes have been buried. The nature of his dream is more clearly stated in *Stephen Hero* than elsewhere in his writing: he "would live his own life according to what he recognized as the voice of a new humanity, active, unafraid and unashamed."[194] But humanity has been corrupted by its environment; man has degenerated through timidity, through the cheap acceptance of shams; he has welcomed his own fetters.

By the very scope of its indictment and the bleakness of its atmosphere, the novel constitutes a most powerful challenge to commercialism, vulgarity, ignorance, prejudice, and inertia.

Ulysses is a modern *Hamlet;* but it is a *Hamlet* without the last three acts.

APPENDIX A

THE TEMPERAMENT, PERSONALITY, AND OPINIONS OF LEOPOLD BLOOM

OF THE hundreds of characters in literature or life, none do we know so intimately as Montaigne, Pepys, Samuel Johnson, Rousseau, and Proust, different though they are. Leopold Bloom may seem a humble addition to this august circle, but Joyce has earned for him "a place i' the story." The following list should demonstrate that the little man of Eccles Street is undoubtedly the most completely characterized figure in the history of fiction, if not in all literature. Approximately 530 references are given here, though the list could be considerably extended.

A few remarks may be made in regard to the findings about Bloom's character. The predominance of practicality and scientific curiosity is apparent. One may note, too, the essential Christianity of his spirit, his pity, sympathy, and respect for others, and this despite two handicaps—the ridicule which dogs him everywhere, even in his home, and the hopeless inadequacy of his associates, which Bloom is too clear-eyed to overlook. Of his friends, only Cunningham seems deserving. It is impossible not to conclude that Bloom is superior to his environment. His sensuality, which has been unduly emphasized as an aspect of *Ulysses*, is largely a matter of sex frustration and, even so, is not so apparent as other qualities. The inadequacy of his education is most clearly seen in his reactions to art and literature, though his feeling for *Hamlet* reveals a fine untrained taste. In conclusion, there can be noted the deep melancholy which colors his political and religious opinions and pervades his philosophy.

Theme words are given in small capitals, with letter in parentheses indicating proper appendix; the dash is used to indicate an opinion, either spoken or subconscious.

Throughout all appendixes Bloom, Stephen, and Molly (Bloom) are referred to by initials—"B.," "S.," and "M."

I. PERSONAL HABITS

A. Life:

Childhood:
Stories of father's travels, 709; Bible reading, 75; childhood, 406; first love, 406; flirtation with Mrs. Breen, 437; grammar school, 76, 693, 697; high-school days, 535; athletic career, 665.

Married life:
Home life important, 629; M.—loves to potter around house, 737; erotic habits, 730, 758. Cf. BLOOM, MARION (B).

Homes:
Lombard Street—when at Thom's, 153; M. twenty-three when left (1894), 165; Milly three (1892), 364; there in 1891 and 1892, 651. Ontario Terrace—Milly eight (1897), 677; Mary Driscoll, 724. Holles Street—when B. was down and out, 264, 363; Milly six (1895), 677; M. thought of posing to earn money, 738; M. played piano in shelter, 264, 366, 619. Raymond Terrace—when Rudy was conceived (1893), 88. City Arms Hotel—in 1893–94, 168, 300, 366, 371, 664; when at Cuffe's, 742. Cf. RIORDAN, MRS. (B).

Jobs:
Hely's (1883–94), 153. Unemployed (1894); (cf. Holles Street, *above*). Thom's (1894), 153; printers, 336. Cuffe's (1894) (cf. City Arms, *above*), 59; butcher, 96; talked back to grazier, 309.

Financial condition:
Expected commission, Keyes's ad, £2, 8s., 177; paid June 16, £1, 7s., 6d., 696; day's budget, 696; insurance, 707; bank balance, 707; Canadian bonds, 708.

B. Appearance:
Funeral suit, 57; stork's legs, 65; brown hair, 68; body soft, 91; oyster eyes, 157; sad face, dark eyes, 351; ashamed of profile, 363; contents of pockets, 430; size of clothes,

695; body measurements, 706; description, 712; M.—handsome when young, 728. Cf. KEY, POTATO, SOAP (all in D).

C. Health:

Constipation, 68; body soft, 91; kneecap hurts, 102; short of breath, 181; gas on stomach, 283; kidney trouble, 433; stitch in side, 427; sciatica, 516; somnambulism, 677; patent medicines, 706. Cf. BEE STING, SANDOW'S (D).

D. Taste in food:

Inner organs, 55, 265; cigar cooling, 77; vegetarianism, 163; vegetables, 168; raw pastry, 172; teetotaler, 298. Cf. BURGUNDY (D).

E. Thrift:

Secondhand coat, 56; pass to see Milly, 67, 78; pass to theater, 91; pass for brewery, 150; secondhand glasses, 164; pass for trip, 610.

F. Household:

Library, 693; contents of drawers, 705; furniture, 690. Cf. OWL (D).

G. Plans:

Seaside vacation, 66, 150, 177, 373; garden, 67; visit Milly, 67, 98, 365; loves travels, 610; plans about S., 631, 647, 680; schemes, 643; self-help, 650; mnemotechnic, 694; suburban dream, 697; managed concert, 733; M.—plans absurd, 750. Cf. TOUR, AGENDATH (D).

II. INTELLECTUAL OUTLOOK

A. Practicality, money-making schemes, ingenuity:

Respect for Tweedy's shrewdness, 56; profitable positions for pubs, 57, 97; profits in liquor, 58, 78; profits in writing, 68; profits in pills, 87; automatic switch, 90; by-products of meat, 96; bury standing, 107; fertilizer, 107; coffins waste wood, 108; law to pierce heart of dead, 109; benefits of post mortems, 110; gramophone records of voice, 112; waste paper, 119; Carlisle's wealth, 158; maternity clinics, 159; inventors' institutes, 177; dummy pianos, 274; sunburn lotion, 277; traffic routes, 612; food inspection, 619; schemes, 643; inventions, 667; education of M., 671; money-making schemes, 702; ads, 85, 149, 151, 152, 169, 318, 365, 371, 667, 705, 760. Cf. TOUR, TRAMLINE, BEAUFOY, MATCHAM, TITBIT (all in D).

B. Scientific curiosity:

How I look to cat, 55; feelings of mice, 55; cat's whiskers, tongue, 56; pronunciation, cf. VOGLIO; color and heat, 57, 435; metempsychosis, 64; electricity from cat, 67; weight in water, 71; gravity, 71; moisture in air, 73; *Hamlet* problem, 75; eyestrain and indigestion, 77; life in monastery, 81; drugs, 83; lotions, 83; why blighted real estate, 94; decomposition, 97; how funeral horses feel, 99; ends of coffin, 101; feelings of priest, 103; feeling of cemetery caretaker, 106; feeling of death, 109; methods of burial, 113; would love to teach, 118; sound of press, 120; proofreader reads backward, 121; phosphorescence, 149; interest in brewing, 150; taste of swan meat, 151; why salt fish not salty, 151; visual experiment, 164; sunspots, 164; feeding on tabloids, 168; taste of human flesh, 169; odd foods, 172; X-ray, 177; sensation of blind, 178; weight and volume, 179; embryos, 232; mathematics of music, 274; acoustics, 278; ventriloquism, 281; instruments, 285; science, 295, 299; law, 308; Mr. Knowall, 309, 311, 323; hoof-and-mouth disease, 309; magnetism, 367; heat and perfume, 368; nature of perfume, 368; light rays, 369; mirage, 370; burning glass, 371; determination of sex, 411; left hand smaller, 445; color affects women's characters, 515; sunspots, 535; extent of water on globe, 614, 655; why newspapers pink, 616; Bacon theory, 618; dietetics, 657; M.—knowledge of anatomy, 728; M.—B. would explain arsenic, 729; M.— discusses Spinoza, 754. Cf. BALL, BLACK, PARALLAX, SQUARING CIRCLE, SPINOZA, THIRTY-TWO (all in D).

C. Common sense:

Agendath not romantic, 57; not feasible, 60; East barren, 61; popular literature silly, 68; effect of uniform, 71; pretense of aristocracy, 72, 158; impossibility of mission work, 79; Latin stupefies, 79; hats absurd, 79; communion wine aristocratic, 80; money in church, 82; gambling silly, 84; effect of name "hospital for incurables," 96; popular love of lurid, 99; pomp of funeral, 99; vanity of Victoria, 101; priest has to say something at funeral, 103; oblivion of dead, 109; charity wiser than tombs, 111; does anybody pray for dead? 111; occupational inscription of tombs wiser, 111; marriage ads not beautified like funeral ones, 112; ads sell paper, 117; journalists unreliable, 124; oratory popular, 125; Catholics versus birth control, 149; women unfair sex, 156; women's questions, 158; radicals become civil servants, 161; sham pretense of women in politics, 161; absurdity of Irish revival, 163; poetry depends on diet, 163; chewing old thoughts, 168; pretense of aristocratic menu, 172; salesmanship, making the unwilling buy, 285; repetition in prayer, like ads, 371; M.—says absurd things, 739. Cf. UNIFORM (D).

D. Political opinions:

Recalls conspirator, 68; army discipline, 71; halfseasover empire, 72; Irishman's house a coffin, 108; oblivion of Parnell, 109; machines rule world, 117; detectives, 160; home rulers absurd, 161; radicals become civil servants, 161; German trade shrewd, 164; law, 180; inequality in Mozart's day, 277; litigation squabbles, 284; moderation in political argument, 319, 320, 323, 327; versus anti-Semitism, 336, 627, 628, 642, 676; injustice of large estates, 470; new Bloomusalem, 475, 480; realistic on British rule, 625; moderate reform, 627, 628; land question, 641; M.—socialism is undesirable, 728. Cf. HOME-RULE SUN, GLADSTONE (D).

E. Religious opinions:

Kingdom-of-God-within idea good, 80; community in religion, 80; organization of church, 81; effect of confession,

81; Salvation Army blatant, 82; money in church, 82; cleverness of theology, 82; funeral perfunctory, 102; resurrection absurd, 104; bloodiness of evangelicalism, 149; problem of evil, 180; religion pays, 256; asks S. about soul, 617; ridicules provinciality of Christianity, 642; disbelief, 650; M.—irreligious, 726; M.—wide knowledge of religions, 756.

F. Opinions of people:

Admires Tweedy, 56; O'Rourke cute, 58; Dedalus humor (cf. HUMOR); M'Coy a sponge, 75; Lyons dirty, 84; Dedalus self-centered, 87; Power nice, 92; Goulding a card, 103; Cunningham sympathetic, 95; Breen a fool, 157; Flynn stupid, 171; Dodd dirty Jew, 180; Costello missing link, 400; Mulligan a sponger, 615; Dedalus talented, 604.

III. TEMPERAMENT

A. Pity and sympathy:

Cat, 55; circus cruel, 64; Dignam, 69, 82; boy, 70; horses, 76; cabbies, 76; disease dreadful, 89; dog pathetic, 89; beggar, 92; suicide, 95; pathos of death, 100; Dignam's son, 101; filling the grave, 109; dead bird, 112; underfed child, 150; gulls, 151; Mrs. Purefoy, 156, 159, 366, 382; cruelty of hunting, 158; doctors humane, 159; time to aid mothers instead of oratory, 159; vegetarianism, 163; cattle, 168; aids blind, 178; ship disaster, 180; for dying and born, 281; humane methods of slaughter, 310; migrating birds, 371; sailors, 372; lighthouse-keepers, 372; sorry about doctor's death, 379; maternity, 380; ashamed of smutty jokes at hospital, 383; Costello insensitive, 400; tram driver, 428; pleads, "I am doing good," 445; scolded tram driver for cruelty, 446; prostitute, 617; charity shelters desirable, 619; for S., 640; brought home lame dog, 641; horse, 646; Mrs. Riordan, 664; M.—polite to old women, 723. Cf. ATHOS (D).

B. Respect for others:

Not disturb M., 57; black suit for funeral, 57; not disturb children, 76; hesitates to embarrass, 119; politeness to as-

tronomer, 164; to librarian, 198; shame at Gerty episode,
360; pays S.'s bill, 545; aids S., 597; not intrude, 600; duty
to S., 630; handed Parnell hat, 634; sympathetic, broken
marriages, 635; annoyed at cabmen's blatant jokes, 639;
forgives Boylan, 717; M.—polite to old women, 723; M.—
timid about proposal, 728; M.—liked lovemaking, 732; M.
—sympathy with women, 767.

C. Sociability:

To O'Rourke, 58; to one who does not see him, 60; to cabmen, 76; to Hornblower, 85; sociable smile, 92; in funeral
carriage, 93; to intern, 96; straightens Menton's hat, 114;
to astronomer, 164; represses anger habitually, 401; stops
to say kind word to nurse, 416; not pugnacious, 641; hospitality, 661.

D. Family love and loyalty:

Cf. BLOOM, MILLY; BLOOM, MARION; BLOOM, RUDY; VIRAG
(all in B).

E. Fastidiousness:

Breakfast, 56, 63; cleans chair, 62; straightens bedspread,
63; house in disorder, 68; bath, 68; care of trousers, 68, 69;
paper cup sanitary, 78; Lyons dirty, 84; polished shoes,
100; kneels on newspaper, 102; notes threads on suit, 108;
caretaker well dressed, 109; S. careless in dress, 145;
lunch-joint disgusting, 166; Ormond clean, 266; hates
rumpled stockings, 622; washes hands, 656; loves order,
694.

F. Humor:

Our daily bread (van), 57; home-rule sun, 57; Dedalus'
humor, 58, 102, 107, 116, 156, 163; on earth (street-cleaner), 60; counting-house (privy), 68; blind faith (snoring in
church), 80; length of sermons, 81; happy returns (at
grave), 92; cock robin (at funeral), 102; caretaker looking
for customers, 109; tell death, try next door, 109; prayers,
109; king sucks subjects like candy, 149; Elijah is coming
(pamphlet thrown into river), 149; M.'s wit, 152; women

unfair sex, 156; legal wigs show gray matter, 124; Methodists, 158; pigeons, 160; police out to graze, 160; Moore, 160; landlord never dies, 162; first Irish convert choked to death, 167; born with knife in mouth, 167; taste of humans, 169; dog returning to vomit, 177; chamber music, 278; God made country, 280; Pick and Pocket, attorneys, 284. Cf. BARRELTONE, ONE AND EIGHT, PLUMTREE, ROCK, (all in D).

G. Melancholy:

Inertia of East, 78, 80; of monastery, 81; of bath, 85; thought, if we were suddenly someone else, 109; thought, no one is anything, 162; mood of gray twilight, 407; resignation, 489; increasing loneliness, 651; impossibility of perfection, 681; desire to go away, 711; M.—in bad mood, 727; M.—sexually cold, 762. Cf. BLOOM, RUDY; VIRAG (B); LOST ONE, RAT, RIP VAN WINKLE (D).

H. Sensuality:

Woman on car, 72; girl fixing garter, 73; church fine for meeting girl, 79, 80; unbuttoned trousers, 82; love among tombs, 106; lingerie, 166; pornography, 233; mermaids, 259, 277; Gerty, 360 ff.; nymphs, 533; "Circe" visions, *passim;* smutty photos, 706; erotic ambitions, 707. Cf. BLOOM, MOLLY (B); EMBON (D); FRILLIES (D); GARTERS (D); NYMPH (D); PERFUME (D); POLO MATCH (D); RAOUL (D); SWEETS OF SIN (D); MAID AT WOODS'S (D); PLASTO'S (D); SEASIDE GIRLS (D).

IV. IMAGINATION

A. Taste in literature:

Likes moral, 68; admires *Hamlet*, 107; Robinson Crusoe, 108, 151, 485; mixes Wordsworth and Gray, 111; rhyme and blank verse, 150; absurdity of revival, 163; Enoch Arden, 608; not enthusiastic about literature, 650; morals in Shakespeare, 661; poetic attempts, 662; library, 693. Cf. HAMLET, MAFFEI, SPINOZA (all in D).

B. Taste in music:

Hums, 76; recalls song, 77; M.'s singing, 81; Mercadante, Mozart, Palestrina, 81; love of vocal music, 92; Kelly song, *Saul*, 96; "Mater misericordiae," 99; hums at cemetery, 103; *Lucia*, 109; *Martha*, 116, 270, 407, 645; voice of Morkan, 160; Meyerbeer, 166, 286; voice, 268, 272; music everywhere, 277; discusses with S., 645. Cf. ANTONIO, ASIA, DANCE OF THE HOURS, DON GIOVANNI, LÁ CI DAREM, LOVE'S OLD SWEET SONG, SEASIDE GIRLS, WHEN FIRST I SAW (all in D).

C. Taste in art:

Statues, 174, 621. Cf. MUSEUM, PHOTO BITS, NYMPH (all in D).

D. Interest in language:

Words, 70; quite, 80; I.H.S., 80; strange names, 173; meaning of *teco*, 177; names, 255; Goodwin's name, 280; admires Italian language, 606; rhythm, 58; words, 167.

E. Philosophy:

Cycle of life, 61, 96, 107, 117, 121, 151, 162; birth, 88; life, 88; frequency of death, 100, 103, 112; once dead you're dead, 104; cruelty of death, 273; wheels within wheels, 160; cosmic cycle, 164; survival of fittest, 121, 168; time, 256; age, 267, 370, 406; sea of blood, 277; extent of water, 655; astronomical meditations, 683, 689. Cf. METEMPSYCHOSIS, DANCE OF THE HOURS, STREAM OF LIFE (all in D).

APPENDIX B

A BIOGRAPHICAL
DICTIONARY OF *ULYSSES*

JOYCE'S novel creates a miniature world. Hundreds of characters appear throughout the narrative, often seen in brief glimpses as they pass through Dublin on June 16, 1904. To aid the reader in identifying the major figures and in tracing their many appearances, this index has been prepared. Since the most interesting characters have been discussed in this study, no extensive description is given here. The principal characters are identified, their major activities summarized, and the theme words associated with each are given.

Leopold Bloom and Stephen Dedalus appear so frequently in the novel that their names have been omitted. Characters appearing in only one episode, though they are as interesting as the debt-collector at Kiernan's or the seaman at the cabman's shelter, are also omitted, since it is easy for the reader to find them in the text. A few characters which do not appear directly in the novel are included because of the many references to them by other characters. Notable among these are historical figures, such as Aristotle, Shakespeare, Tennyson, Wilde, Wordsworth, and the contemporary leaders of Irish politics and literature.

Since Joyce has used some twenty-five characters which appeared in his earlier works, these identifications are made. The appearances in the visions of the "Circe" episode are placed within parentheses. Words in small capitals indicate additional references under verbal motifs in Appendix D.

It may be of interest to note that 150 characters are listed here, of which 122 appear in person or in vision. The total number of cross-references is over 900.

A. E., mystic poet of Irish revival.—Molloy ridicules as master-mystic, 139; B. ridicules affectation, 158; seen discussing occult with slovenly disciple, 163; as oracle in library discussion, 183; leaves library, 189; S. ridicules, 183, 189, 193; B. recalls seeing, 366; in parody, 391; (as Mananaan Maclir, mutters mystic nonsense, 499).

Antisthenes.—Cf. Appendix D.

Apjohn, Percy, one of B.'s childhood companions.—B. recalls, 160; (one of halcyon days, 535); friend of B., 651, 701; killed, Boer War, 689; facial expression cited, 722.

Aristotle.—FORM, POSSIBLE. S.—possibilities of history, 26; S.—once a schoolboy, 183; S.—neither he nor Plato would tolerate him, 184; S. balances cane, experiment of, 190; a Shakespeare anachronism, Ulysses quotes, 209; his biology text titillates B., 232; B.—biology, 404; B. tells S. he was pupil of a rabbi, 671; M. thinks of as Aristocrat, 757.

Arius.—Cf. Appendix D.

Artifoni, Almidano, Italian teacher (in *Stephen Hero*).—Talks with S., 225; walks, 246; sees procession, 251; (to S., 507).

Averroes.—Cf. Appendix D.

Ball.—Cf. Appendix D.

Bannon, Alec, student, now at Mullingar.—Buck's brother visiting, comments on Milly, 25; Milly's card, 66; parody, 390; hospital, 395; mention, 410; (beatitude, 498).

Beaufoy.—Cf. Appendix D.

Bergan, Alf, legal clerk and practical joker.—B.—probably wrote insulting card, 157; at Kiernan's, 293 ff., convulsed about Breen, shows hangman's letters, discusses fighting, laughs at smutty photographs, tries to pacify Citizen; (in sandwich board with inscription of Breen's card, 438).

Blake.—Cf. Appendix D.

Best, Richard, dilettante.—In library, 184 ff., with notebook, eager to agree, brightly vacuous, loves Wilde, beautiful in sadness, jokes about name, interested in folklore, wants S. to write theory; (quotes "A thing of beauty," 499).

Never thought I'd be named Bloom. Adolescence. 747: Train whistle. Scorn of highbrow women. 748: I know more than any-one about men. Cold winters. 749: B.'s late hours, his ordering breakfast. Marketing, picnics. 750: *Sweets of Sin*, B.'s schemes. 751: Jealousy of Milly, sly like B. 752: B. foolish about father. 753: Once snubbed at races. Servants. Stephen, recall of Simon. Did B. tear pants getting in? 754: Beginning to menstruate. B.'s intellectual talk. Sad lot of women. Boylan's eroticism. 755: Perhaps I'm ill; contempt of doctors. 756: Meeting B., his politics, his lack of religion. 757: Gets up. B.'s homes and jobs, Raymond Terrace, Ontario Terrace, Lombard Street, Holles Street, City Arms, Thom's, Hely's, Cuffe's, Drimmie's. Bells— 2:00 A.M. B. in bed like baby. 758: B. ordering breakfast, his erotic habits, funeral, his disreputable friends. 759: I'll defend B. from teasing. Sorry for Mrs. Dignam. Dollard, Dedalus sing-ing. What sort is S.? I saw him eleven years ago, in mourning for Rudy. 760: Cards predicted fair visitor; would be change from B.'s business concerns. 761: Probably lovely like statue. Will try fortune, will study, will marry S. Boylan not up to S.; but he couldn't help admiring me, I wish I were a man. 762: Sex not disgusting, it's only nature. B. cold. I'd like to pick up sailor. 763: B. covers too much of bed; he had bad fate in cards. Break-fast. Women ought to rule world. Rudy. 764: Used to love com-ing home late. Women a bad lot. Too bad S. didn't stay; we'd travel together. 765: Marketing. I'll defy B., tell him all. Adultery not evil. 766: I'll get money from B. 2:15 A.M. I'll decorate if S. returns; will accompany S. 767: I love flowers, na-ture; atheism is absurd. Proposal at Howth; I liked B.'s sym-pathy. 768: The glory of Mulvey's kiss.

tion, 678; drawing kept, 705; legatee of insurance, 707; M.—nursing, 739; M.—her card, 743; M.—B. sent away because of Boylan, 751.

Bloom, Rudy, dead son of B.—B.—midwife hopeless over, 66; B.—death, 88, 109; B.—never enjoyed copulation after, 165; B. mourns, 280, 407; (593); his shroud, 384, 725, 763.

Boylan, Blazes, concert manager, lover of M.—JINGLE. On Milly's card, 62; M. to sing with, 63; B. reads card, 66; B.—his wealth, 69; seen from funeral carriage, 91; B. wonders if sandwich men are employed by, 152; Flynn mentions, 170; B. dodges into museum to avoid, 180; buys flowers, flirts with clerk, 224; secretary phones—to meet Lenehan, 226; Rochford mentions, 229; walks, 243; Dignam's son sees, 247; forgets to salute cavalcade but salutes ladies, 250; B. sees, 259; Lenehan waits for, 258, 259; meets, 260; toast to races, 261; Douce flirts with, 262; leaves Ormond, 263; jauntily on way to M., 265, 272, 277, 278; narrator comments on tour, 314; Lenehan mentions bet, 320; (550 ff.); Corley asks B. for job with, 602; Du Boyes in paper, 631; lover of M., 716; M. thinks of, 725, 727, 729, 732, 734, 746, 748, 749, 751, 758.

Brady, Joe, conspirator in Phoenix Park murders.—Discussed, 134 ff., 299.

Brayden, William, barrister.—116; (571).

Breen, Denis, victim of insulting card.—U.P. To lawyer's office, 237; sees procession, 250; passes Kiernan's, 293; going to detective, 315; (pursues B., 571).

Breen, Josie Powell, Bloom's childhood sweetheart, wife of Denis Breen.—To B. about husband, 154 ff.; sees procession, 250; B.—her girlhood, 362, 366; (accuses, 435, pursues B., 571); B. pleased at impression made on, 707; M. suspects, 727, 758; recalls, 746.

Burke, Andrew, one of M.'s lovers.—Discussed, 300, 309, 329; (478); (pursues B., 571); M.'s lover, 716; M.—750.

Burke, O'Madden, editor (in "A Mother," *Dubliners*).—At news office, chatting in lighthearted mockery, 130 ff.; to write about Abbey, 227; discussed, 258; (ridicules B., 480).

monious toward Mrs. Sheehy, schoolboys, one-legged sailor, sur-
prises Lenehan with girl in field; Cunningham has written, 242;
Lenehan recalls being surprised by, 409; (to S., 548, 564); one of
B.'s possible careers, 674.

Conroy, Father.—Had confessed Paddy Dignam, 248; conducts vespers, 352; (461).

Conroy, Gretta, wife of journalist (in "The Dead," *Dubliners*).
—B. recalls M. asking about, 69; husband mentioned as on
Express, 124.

Corrigan, Father (in "Two Gallants," *Dubliners*).—At funeral,
632; asleep, 689; M.'s lover, 716; M.—confession. 726.

Costello, "Punch," medical student.—At hospital, 382 ff.; (483,
495); (beatitude, 498).

Cowley, Father.—Talks with Dedalus, 236, 240; at Ormond,
264 ff.; (pursues B., 571).

Crawford, Myles, editor.—In office, 126 ff., gossips about Deasy, Phoenix Park murders, great lawyers of past, insults B.; B.
to speak to, 318; to ask about ad, 374; (450); (jury, 461).

Crofton, political appointee (in "Ivy Day," *Dubliners*).—Mentioned, 92, 330 ff.; (at B.'s inauguration, 479); (pursues B., 571).

Cuffe, Joseph, packer.—B.—job with, 96; B.—fired, 309; mentioned, 392; (B. gives as reference at trial, 457); (pursues B.,
571); job with (1893–94), 664; M.'s lover, 716; M. thinks of B.'s
jobs, 737.

Cunningham, Martin (in "Grace," *Dubliners*).—B.—79; at
funeral, 86 ff., laughs at Kernan, pities child corpse, suicide; B.
thinks of his Shakespearean face, his drunkard wife, 95; refers
to break about suicide, 100; B.—his spelling conundrum, 120;
discusses fund for widow, 242 ff.; B. asks for at Kiernan's, 298;
at Kiernan's, defends Jews, 330 ff.; (jury, 461); (Shakespeare becomes Cunningham, 554); B.—promised pass to B., 610; listed
in newspaper, 632; asleep, 689; M. despises, 758.

D'Arcy, Bartell, tenor (in "The Dead," *Dubliners*).—B.—M.'s
singing with, 154; Lenehan—singing, 230; (pursues B., 571); one
of M.'s lovers, 716; M.—730, 759.

Dillon, Joe, auctioneer (in "An Encounter," *Dubliners*).—B. looks for Keyes at, 128; B. sees Dilly at, 149; Dilly at, 233; (527).

Dillon, Mat, alderman.—Menton danced with M. at home of, 105; B. recalls meeting M. at, 113, 271, 370; (B. recalls, 530); B.'s discussions with M. at, 651; B. met S. at, 664; clock wedding gift of, 692; M.—courtship at, 743.

Dixon, interne (in *The Portrait*).—B.—dressing a sting, 96, 160; at hospital, 380 ff.; (483); (beatitude, 498).

Dlugacz, butcher.—B. on way to, 56; B. at, 58; B.—his voice, 68; Boylan passes, 275; (456).

Dodd, Reuben J., solicitor.—B. tells story of drowning son, 92; B.—son swallowed water, 150; B. hates, 180; female about to enter office, 248; B.—story, 283; discussed, 316; (Rochford recalls story, 465); (as Iscariot, 487); (as Antichrist, 495).

Dollard, Ben, "base barreltone."—Power laughs at Kernan's extravagant admiration for voice, 89; Flynn—171; Lenehan—230; B.—has fine voice, 237; Cowley waiting to see, 240; meets Cowley, 241; sings at Ormond, 263 ff.; (ridicules B.'s suburban utopia, 479); (sings, 510); (pursues B., 571); one of M.'s lovers, 716; M.—759.

Doran, Bob, loafer and drunkard.—M'Coy—72; at Kiernan's, 293 ff., maudlin over Dignam's death, asks dog for paw, expresses regrets to B., drunk at 5:00 P.M.; (asks dog for paw, 446); (pursues B., 571).

Douce, Lydia, barmaid.—Sees cavalcade, 242, 249; at Ormond, 252 ff., shows sunburn, laughs at B., flirts with Dedalus, Lenehan, Boylan, Lidwell, listens to shell; (550).

Doyle, Jimmy, tenor (in "The Race," *Dubliners*).—To sing with M., 63; B.—tour, 92.

Driscoll, Mary, servant.—(Defends herself, 451 ff.); M. discharged for dishonesty and flirting, 724.

Dudley, Earl of, lord-lieutenant of Ireland.—Wife of, 136; procession, 248 ff.

Goulding, Richie, law clerk, S.'s uncle.—Dedalus ridicules, 87; B.—practical joker, 157; walks, 228; sees procession, 248; eats silently with B. at Ormond, 261 ff.; B.—363; (439, 517).

Griffith, Arthur, political leader.—S.—Egan's talk of, 44; B.— humor of, 57; B.—steady but not dashing, 161; mention, 328; (583); M. thinks little of, 733.

Grogan, Mother, figure in Mulligan's joke.—Mulligan tells joke, 14; casts in ribald play, 214; parody, 397; (481).

Haines, folklore student from Oxford.—With S. and Mulligan at tower, 6 ff., S. thinks of as usurper, Mulligan ridicules as fanatic; leaves library, 184; Eglinton ridicules, 184; to go to George Moore's, 190; at D.B.C. with Mulligan, 244 ff.; sees procession, 249; at hospital, 405.

Hornblower, porter at college.—B. speaks to, 85; sees procession, 250; (pursues B., 571); M.—758.

Hynes, Joe, reporter.—Takes down names at funeral, 110; at news office with account, 117; B.—177; at Kiernan's, 287 ff., more interested in drink than in discussion; B.—369, 374; (463, 477, 479); (pursues B., 571); B. reads funeral account of, 631; in bed, 689.

Kelleher, Corny, undertaker's assistant.—B.—got job for undertaker, 70; funeral, 89 ff.; B.—possibly a spy, 161; Conmee passes, 218; making accounts, 221 ff.; parody, 296; advised Breen, 315; rescues B. and S., 570 ff.; B.—glad of rescue, 598; paper, 632.

Kennedy, Mina, barmaid.—At Ormond, 253 ff., more melancholy than Douce; (550, 552).

Kernan, Tom, tea merchant (in "Grace," *Dubliners*).—TRENCHANT, RETROSPECTIVE. B. to get tea from, 70; funeral, 88 ff., Cunningham ridicules his extravagant admiration for Dollard's voice, discusses insurance, admires Anglican burial service; B. forgot to ask, 159; B.—good at salads, 169; walks, pleased with order he got, 234; sees procession, 248; at Ormond, 272 ff., delighted with Dollard's song; (jury, 461); (474); in newspaper, 632; in bed, 689; 711; B. forgot to ask for tea, 714; M. hates, a vile drunk, 758.

MacDowell, Gerty, adolescent.—Sees procession, 249; in parody, 327; on beach, 342 ff., dreaming of romance, marriage, clothes, domesticity, religion, sex experience, sympathizing with B.; (leers at and accuses B., 434).

MacHugh, Hugh, scholar.—ANTISTHENES. At news office, 122 ff., criticizes Rome, praises Greece, says Antisthenes claimed Penelope more lovely than Helen; 258; (cross-examines B., 454).

Maginni, Denis, dancing master.—B.—151; walks, 217, 232; sees procession, 250; (conducts dance, 560).

Maid at Woods.—Cf. Appendix D.

Maimonides.—Cf. Appendix D.

Mastiansky, Julius, grocer.—B.—60, 107; (as Jew, 487); (at wailing wall, 532); (pursues B., 571); B.'s discussions with, 651; lover of M., 716; M.—734.

Menton, J. H., solicitor.—At funeral, 101 ff., wonders why M. married B., B. recalls rivalry, snubs B.; Dollard saw, 241; sees procession, 249; (B. mentions as his solicitor, 447); (jury, 461); (mention, 464, 488); (pursues B., 571); in newspaper, 632; in bed, 689; lover of M., 716; M.—724.

Moore, George, novelist.—To have literary group at home, 190; Eglinton refers to his mannerism of using French, 209; Mulligan ridicules as lecturer on French culture, 212; group returns from, 398.

Mulligan, Buck, medical student.—AENGUS, BEASTLY, CORONATION, DOGSBODY, EPI ONIPA PONTON, JESUIT. At tower, 5 ff., ridiculing S.'s Jesuit pride, self-concern; S.—31, 36, 40; Dedalus thinks a rotter, 87; S.—132, 183; at library, 190 ff., ridicules religion, Irish revival, laughs at B., sentimental conception of Shakespeare, S. suggests ribald play; at D.B.C., 244 ff., ridiculing S.; sees procession, 249; B.—256; at hospital, 390 ff., ribald; (beatitude, 498); (pronounced B. sexually abnormal, 565); B. warns S. about, 604; B.—691.

Mulvey, Lieutenant, M.'s first lover.—B.—M.'s kiss, 364; in coda, 375; 677; M. recalls ecstasy of love, 716, 746, 767.

Power, Jack (in "Grace," *Dubliners*).—At funeral, 86 ff.; B.—160; Dedalus—235; with Nolan, 242 ff.; at Kiernan's, 330 ff.; (jury, 461); in newspaper, 632; in bed, 689; M. hates, 758.

Purefoy, Mrs., delivered of child at 10:00 P.M.—Mrs. Breen to B., 156 ff.; B.—pity, 232, 276, 281, 366; hospital, 391, 414 ff.; B.—visit to, 444; (pursues B., 571); (Goddess of sex, 583); résumé, 713; M.—72.

Riordan, Mrs., invalid at City Arms Hotel, formerly at Dedalus' (in *The Portrait*).—B.—96, 172; narrator ridicules B.'s sympathy for, 300; (disappointed in B., 481); (pursues B., 571); S. and B. reminisce about, 664; M. thinks B. silly for sympathy with, 723.

Rochford, Tommy, jockey.—At Byrne's, 175 ff.; with Lenehan, 228 ff.; sees procession, 249; Lenehan—263; Bergan—294; (465); (wins race, leaps into void, 583).

Rumbold, H., hangman.—Letter of, applying for job, discussed, 298; (to hang B., 462, 578).

Sabellius.—Cf. Appendix D.

Sandwich men, advertising H, E, L, Y, 'S.—B. sees on way to lunch, 152, 153; Boylan sees, 224; walk, 226; halt for procession, 250; (Breen appears in sandwich boards, 438); example of B.'s possible decline to pauperhood, 710.

Sceptre, race horse.—Lenehan picks, 126; Flynn—171; Lenehan drinks to, 261; Lenehan—320; 408; (races, 558); in newspaper, 632.

Shakespeare.—HAMLET. Mulligan—S.'s theory, 19; S.—Mulligan on, 29; Deasy quotes maxim, 31; Cunningham's face like, 95; B.—150; S. discusses in library, 183 ff.; Mulligan—S. on, 245; B. quotes, 276; in parody, 292; S.—425; B.—439; S.—494; (shouts nonsense, 553); B. interested in Baconian theory, 618; B. looks for moral maxims in, 661.

Sheehy, David, M.P.—B.—Dedalus' ridicule, 163; Conmee ingratiating to wife, 216.

Sinico, Mrs., suicide (in "A Painful Case," *Dubliners*).—B. last in cemetery at funeral of, 113; B. asks S. if he knew, 680; B.

APPENDIX C

A DIRECTORY OF SHOPS, OFFICES, PUBLIC BUILDINGS, PROFESSIONAL AND CIVIC PERSONAGES

THE exhaustiveness with which Joyce creates his setting is apparent from the 220 actual addresses listed below. The wide range of occupations and landmarks described gives another clue to the comprehensiveness of his picture of contemporary civilization.

Addresses are taken from Thom's *Official Directory* (1905). Parentheses indicate those not identified.

1. Advertising
  M'Glade, 43 Abbey

2. Antiques
  Marks, 16 Ormond Q.
  Reddy, 19 Ormond Q.

3. Astronomers
  Joly, C. J., Royal astronomer, Dunsink

4. Auctioneers
  Dillon, Joe, 25 Bachelor's W.

5. Authors
  A. E. [G. W. Russell], Rathgar
  Moore, George, 4 Ely

6. Bakers
  Rourke, 138 Britain, gt.

7. Banks
  Hibernian, College Green

8. Barristers and solicitors
  Barry, R. F., 21 Wellington Q.
  Brayden, W., Sandymount
  Bushe, S., 15 Ely
  Collis and Ward, 31 Dame
  Dodd, Reuben J., 34 Ormond Q.
  Greene, R., 11 Wellington Q.

  Menton, J. H., 27 Bachelor's W.
  O'Donohoe, M., 23 Wicklow
  White, D., 29 Kildare

9. Baths
  (O'Brien, J. P.), Tara Street

10. Bazaar
  Marks Penny, 42 George's

11. Booksellers
  Clohisey, 10–11 Bedford Row
  Combridge, 18 Grafton
  Connellan, 51 Dawson
  Fitzgerald, F., Merchant's Arch, Metal Br.
  Gill, 50 Sackville
  Ponsonby, 116 Grafton

12. Bottle works
  Wallace, Ringsend Road

13. Butchers
  Buckley, Dorset, up.
  (Dlugacz), Dorset, up.
  Mangan, 1 William
  Olhausen, 72 Talbot

14. Cabdrivers
  Barton, Donnybrook

15. *Caretakers*
   O'Connell, Glasnevin

16. *Cattle dealers*
   Cuffe, L., 5 Smithfield

17. *Chemists*
   Sweny, F. W., 1 Lincoln Pl.

18. *Churches*
   All Hallow's, 46 Westland
   (Bethel, House of), Lombard?
   St. Agatha's, William
   St. Francis Xavier, Gardiner
   St. George's, Hardwicke Pl.
   St. Joseph's, N. Strand Road
   St. Mark's, 40 Brunswick, gt.
   St. Mary's Abbey, Capel
   St. Nicholas Without, Francis
   Three Patrons, Rathgar

19. *Clergy*
   Coffey, F., 65 Dalymount
   Conmee, J. S., Gardiner, up.
   Conroy, B., Sandymount
   Malone, C., Rathgar
   O'Hanlon, J., Sandymount

20. *Clothiers*
   Henry and James, 1–3 Parliament

21. *Clubs*
   Catholic, 42 Sackville, up.
   Freemason's Hall, 17–18 Moles-
      worth
   Kildare Street, 1–3 Kildare

22. *Confectioners*
   Gray, 18 Dawson
   Lemon, 49 Sackville

23. *Consuls*
   Austro-Hungarian, 26 Waterloo

24. *Convents*
   Tranquilla, Rathmines

25. *Cycles*
   Rover, 23 Westmoreland

26. *Dancing instructors*
   Maginni, D., 32 George's

27. *Dentists*
   Bloom, M., 2 Clare

28. *Distillers*
   Dublin, 21–32 Watling
   Guinness, James Gate

29. *Drapers*
   Arnott, 11–15 Henry

30. *Dyers*
   Prescott, Corn Market

31. *Editors*
   Griffith, A., 15 Fownes

32. *Florists*
   Thornton, 63 Grafton

33. *Furniture*
   Spring, 15–17 Dorset

34. *Gas works*
   Buckingham Street

35. *Grocers*
   Cassidy, 44–45 Gardiner
   Donohoe, 4–5 Green
   Kavanagh, 27 Parliament
   Mullet, 12–13 Bridge
   O'Bierne, 62 Mabbot
   O'Rourke, 72–73 Dorset, up.

36. *Hairdressers*
   Drago, 17 Dawson
   Gillen, 64 Talbot
   Kennedy, P., 48 James

37. *Hardware*
   James, 30 Henry

38. *Hatters*
   Plasto, 1 Brunswick, gt.

39. *Hospitals*
   Industrious Blind, 41 Sackville
   Mercer's, William
   National Maternity, Holles
   Our Lady's, Harold's Cross
   Sailor's Home, 19 Rogerson's Q.
   Stewart Institution, 40 Moles-
      worth
   Ward for Incurables, Eccles

40. *Hotels*
   City Arms, 54 Prussia
   Dolphin, 34 Essex
   Edinburgh Temperance, 56 Sack-
      ville
   (Finn's), Waterloo

40. Hotels—continued
Grosvenor, 5 Westmoreland
North Star, 26–30 Amiens
Ormond, 8 Ormond Q.

41. Ice cream
Rabaiotti, 65 Talbot

42. Insurance
Drimmie, David & Sons, 41 Sackville
Patriotic, 9 Sackville

43. Jewelers
Carroll, 29 Wellington Q.
Figatner, 26 Wellington Q.
Moulang, 31 Wellington Q.
Sexton, 118 Grafton
Wine, 33 Wellington Q.

44. Librarians
Best, Richard, National Library
Lyster, R. W., 10 Harcourt Terrace

45. Linseed
Leask, 14–19 Rogerson's Q.

46. Livery stables
Sewell, 60 Mount

47. Lumber
Meade, 159 Brunswick, gt.

48. Millers
Shackleton, 35 James

49. Milliners
Doyle, 33 Wicklow

50. Music
Butler, 34 Bachelor's W.
Pigott, 112 Grafton

51. Needlework
Monypenny, 52–53 Grafton

52. Neighbors
Citron, J., 17 St. Kevin's Parade
Doyle, Luke, 41 Kevin
Mastiansky, P., 16 St. Kevin's Parade
Woods, R., 8 Eccles

53. Newspapers
Evening Mail, 37–38 Parliament
Evening Telegraph, 4–8 Prince's
Express, 37–38 Parliament
Freeman's Journal, 4–8 Prince's
Irish Times, 31 Westmoreland

54. Offices
Commercial Buildings, Dame

55. Opticians
Werner, 31 Merrion Sq. n.
Yeates, 2 Grafton

56. Pawnbrokers
Claffey, 65–66 Amiens
White, M., 32 Arran Q.

57. Physicians
M'Ardle, 7 Merrion up.

58. Piano teachers
Levenston, 35 Frederick

59. Plumbers
Miller, 17 Duke

60. Political officers
Dillon, Valentine [Lord Mayor, 1894–95], Bachelor's W.
Dudley, Earl of [Lord Lieutenant], Viceregal Lodge
Falkiner, Sir Frederick [Co. court judge], 4 Earlsfort Terrace
Isaacs, Rufus [M.P.], London
Nannetti, Joseph [M.P.], 18 Hardwicke
O'Reilly, R. [alderman], 9 Parliament
Parnell, J. H. [city marshall], 3 Dame
Sheehy, D. [M.P.], 2 Belvidere

61. Potted meat
Plumtree, G. W., 23 Merchant's Q.

62. Printers
Cahill, 35–37 Strand, gt.
Hely, 27–30 Dame
King, 36 Ormond Q., up.

63. Public buildings
Ballast Office, Westmoreland
Bank of Ireland, College Green
City Hall, Cork Hill
Customs House, Beresford Place
Four Courts, King's Inn Q.
Metropolitan Hall, Abbey
Morgue, 3 Store

Museum and National Library, 9
    Kildare
Post offices
    General, Sackville & Prince's
    Branches:
        18 Westland
        4 Molesworth
        34 Ormond Q, up.
        18 Rogerson's Q.
        9 Westmoreland
    Public library, 106 Capel
    Sheriff's office, 2 King's Inn Q.

64. *Public houses and restaurants*
    Bergin, D., 46 Amiens
    Bolton, 36 Westmoreland
    Burton, 18 Duke
    Byrne, D., 21 Duke
    Clarence, 6–7 Wellington Q.
    Conway, 32 Westland
    D.B.C. [Dublin Bakery Co.]
        ["Damn Bad Cakes"], 33 Dame
    Dock, 1 Store
    Dolphin, Essex
    Doran, J., 10 Dawson
    Empire, 29 Nassau
    Harrison, 29 Westmoreland
    Kiernan, B., 8–10 Britain
    Long, J., 52 Dawson
    (Lyman), Essex?
    M'Aulay, T., 82 Dorset
        (*Maison Claire*), ?
    Ormond, 8 Ormond Q., up.
    Ship, 5 Abbey, lower
    (Signal House)?
    Tunney, Ringsend

65. *Publishers*
    Falconer's *Railway Guide*, 53 Sack-
        ville, up.
    Thom's *Directory*, 87–89 Abbey

66. *Railroads*
    Dublin and Kingstown, Westland
    Great Northern, Amiens

67. *Rectifiers*
    Kennedy, J., 31–32 Mary's Abbey

68. *Rubber*
    Elvery, 46–47 Sackville, lower

69. *Schools*
    Civil Service College, 51 Sackville
    National, 121–24 Brunswick, gt.
    St. Joseph's, 81–84 Dorset, up.
    Trinity College

70. *Silk*
    Brown, Thomas, 15–17 Grafton
    Clery, 21–27 Sackville, lower

71. *Stationers*
    Daly, Ormond

72. *Statuary*
    Bassi, J., 18A Wellington Q.
    Ceppi, 8–9 Wellington Q.

73. *Statues*
    Crampton Memorial Fountain,
        College
    Goldsmith, Trinity College
    Gray, Sackville
    Matthew, Sackville
    Moore, College Green
    Nelson's Pillar, Sackville
    Parnell, Rutland Sq.
    Tone, Grafton at Stephen's Green
    William III, College Green

74. *Stonecutters*
    Baird, 16–25 Talbot
    Dennany, Glasnevin

75. *Tailors*
    Mesias, 5 Eden Q.

76. *Tea merchants*
    Belfast and Oriental, 6 Westland
    Crimmins, 27–28 James
    Moses, 30 Essex
    O'Neill, J., 29 Essex

77. *Theaters*
    Antient Concert Rooms, 42 Bruns-
        wick, gt.
    Empire Palace Theatre of Vari-
        eties, Dame
    Gaiety, 48–49 King
    Lowry's Music Hall, Essex
    Queen's, 209 Brunswick, gt.
    Rotunda, Rutland Sq.

78. *Tobacco*
    Daly, T., 1 Ormond Q., up.
    Grogan, 16 N. Strand Rd.
    Lundy Foot, 26 Parliament

79. Undertakers
Nichol's, 26 Lombard
O'Neill, Newcomen Bridge

80. Wallpaper
Dockrell, 47–50 Stephen

81. Watches
Anderson, 30 Parliament

82. Wine merchants
Cantwell and M'Donald, 12 Wellington Q.
Kavanagh, 27 Parliament

ALPHABETICAL INDEX OF APPENDIX C

[References to preceding directory are in parentheses. Other figures refer to
Ulysses or to proper appendix.]

APPENDIX D

AN INDEX OF VERBAL MOTIFS

COMMENT on Joyce's use of the verbal motif has been frequent, but no attempt has yet been made at an exhaustive list of such theme words. For the convenience of the reader, words associated with Leopold Bloom have been separated from those of Stephen Dedalus. The references total about 700.

Contrary to what might be the usual impression, the motifs for Bloom are both greater in number and also more ingenious and varied in elaboration. This fact testifies that, though Stephen's mind may be more profound in the generally accepted sense of the word, it is not more interesting. His thought is complex, but the complexity rests on one level, that of metaphysical speculation. Bloom's is ever alert, ranging over the whole of experience. He is, like his counterpart Ulysses, a man "of many devices," as Homer always epitomizes him.

MOTIFS ASSOCIATED WITH LEOPOLD BLOOM

Agendath (*13*), *name of Zionist colony.*—B. reads brochure, 60; recalls after breakfast, 68; suggested by silk shop, 166; by thoughts of food, 172; feels brochure in pocket, 181; Boylan passes shop where B. got it, 275; coda of themes, 375; in meditation of disillusionment, 407; (B. defends self by claiming to own, 456); (in mock genealogy, 485); (B. to be persecuted in, 487); B. burns brochure, 691; one of B.'s schemes for wealth, 703.

Antonio (*2*), *character of popular song.*—B. hums, 96; B. associates with tattoo artist, 616.

Asia (*2*), *phrase from bawdy song.*—B. recalls Mrs. Cunningham's drunken song, 95; (Mrs. C. sings, 554).

Athos (*3*), *B.'s father's dog.*—B. recalls father's dying plea for, 89; (516); in suicide note, 706.

Ball (4), astronomer.—B.—book is fascinating, 152; B. imagines meeting, 164; (B. says he was just chatting with, 457); one of B.'s books, 693.

Barreltone (5), M.'s description of Dollard's voice.—B.—M.'s wit, 152; B.—sex of singers, 266; mentioned at Ormond, 278; (in stage directions, 510); M. recalls, 759.

Beaufoy (8), author of "Matcham's Masterstroke."—B. sees in paper, 68; B. envies income of, 69; B. mixes with Purefoy, 156, 444; associates with visit to Mrs. Purefoy, 366; (accuses B. of plagiarism, 450 ff.); B. plans to write sketch like, 631, 669.

Bee sting (8).—B. stung on Whitmonday, 68; medical student dressed, 96; Dixon, who dressed it, at hospital, 160; soreness nearly gone, 166; B. recalls, 371; (B. tells of, 504); details given, 695; M.—749.

Black (2).—B. recalls learning of heat absorption of, 57; (converses about, 435).

Breakfast (7).—B. prepares for M., 55 ff.; B. recalls, 168; B. gives M.'s cream to S., 661; one of rites of day, 713; M. thinks B. nervy to ask her to get, 723, 749; M. thinks of getting for S. and B., 763 ff.

Burgundy (8).—B. orders, 169; arouses his senses, 173; B. thinks good to pick one up, 177; causes gas, 285, 286; (B. invites watchman to have, 448); (evidence for prosecution against B., 454); B. staunch believer in, 599.

Callan (4), one of deceased during day.—B. sees in paper, 90, 274; B. murmurs as he addresses letter to Martha, 275; (given by B. as reference during trial, 456).

Castile (9), Lenehan's pun on opera.—Lenehan puns, 133; in overture to "Sirens" scene, 252; Lenehan calls barmaid, 260; coda of B.'s thoughts, 281; recall of barmaids, 285; in mock list of famous characters, 291; B. recalls, 419; (B. mentions to watchman, 447); (B. springs joke, 481).

Coombe (4), song sung by sluts in slum by that name.—Song suggested by pin, 77; religious picture suggests, 78; B. associates with Doran's intoxication, 165; (hags, 539).

"Dance of the Hours" (*3*), *light concert piece.*—B. recalls hearing, thinks of day being like, 69, 368; (561).

"Elijah" (*11*), *evangelistic pamphlet.*—Given to B., 149; B. throws into Liffey, 150; floats downstream, 223, 236; in bay, 246; B. recalls, 275; B.'s exit from saloon parodied, 339; parody of evangelistic oratory, 420; (announces end of world, 496); (B. recalls, 537); a tip for race, 660.

Embon (*3*), *phrase from novel "Sweets of Sin."*—B. reads at bookstall, 233; used in description of barmaid, 281; recall of themes, 375.

Epitaph (*3*), *last words of patriot Emmet.*—B. recites, 286; Bello quotes, 531; (Nannetti quotes, 537).

Frillies (*4*), *phrase from "Sweets of Sin."*—B. reads, 232; satirically used in description of B., 283; recall of themes, 375; (one of Daughters of Erin, 488).

Garters (*5*).—B. recalls M.'s violet, 57; thinks of buying petticoat to match, 177; catalogued among household things, 715; M. recalls, 725, 735.

"Giovanni, Don" (*5*), *the opera.*—B. hums aria from, 177; hears minuet from, 277; (M. hums, 434); B. whistles, 486; among B.'s favorites, 645.

Gladstone, W. E. (*3*), *the prime minister.*—B. recalls prayers for, 79; B. had been ardent supporter of in 1885, 701; B. has kept prophecy he wrote on consequences of 1886 bill, never passed, 705.

Gulls (*4*).—B. feeds, 150; B. recalls, 275; (445); (B., at trial, uses as example of kindness, 463).

Heigho (*5*).—B. thinks of as bells toll, 69; B. recalls while glancing at paper, 274; (463); prostitutes bracelets sound, 562; B. hears at 2:00 A.M., 688.

Hely's (*5*), *store in Dublin.*—Lambert mentions B.'s job in, 105; B. recalls man who died there, 112; B. recalls getting job year he married, 153; M. remembers B.'s losing job, 738; M. thinks his losing job typical of his uselessness, 757. Cf. SANDWICH MEN (B).

Mackintosh, man in, seen in cemetery (*9*).—In cemetery, 108; B. to reporter, 110; sees procession, 251; in parody, 327; B.—a mystery man, 369; (475); (Virag dressed in, 500); in paper as M'Intosh, 632; mystery of day, 714.

Maffei (*2*), *villain of gothic romance.*—B. sees illustration of, 64; (446).

Maid at Woods (*3*).—B. sees on street, 59; B.—provocative swagger of, 71, 275.

Mairy (*4*), *phrase of vulgar song.*—B. recalls sluts singing, 77; B.—275, 362; (sluts sing, 539).

"Matcham's Masterstroke" (*4*), *novelette in magazine.*—B. reads, 68; B.—Mrs. Purefoy, 156; B.—prize story, 276; (author appears, 450).

Metempsychosis (*15*).—M. asks definition of, 64; B. recalls with amusement, 152; B.—disaster in New York, 180; B.—M.'s pronunciation, 265; B.—280; in description of B., 283; in description of twilight, 371; in B.'s recall of day, 375; description of medical students, 402; in Coleridge parody, 407; (Dignam ghost says, 464); (description of Venus, 490); B.—M.'s asking about, 637; instance of intellectual inadequacy of M., 670; M.—738.

Moustache cup (*5*).—Given B. by Milly, 62; on shelf, 659; S. uses for tea, 661; listed, 679; M. to use for breakfast, 765.

Museum (*7*).—B.—on visiting, 174; B. enters, 180; B. recalls day, 373; (keeper appears, 480); B. mentions visiting, 621; B. recalls while showing M.'s picture, 637; one of rites of day, 713.

Nymph (*4*).—Chromo over bed, 64; in parody, 335; (accuses B., 532 ff.); M.—vulgar, 738.

One and eight (*5*), *anecdote of Simon.*—Dry wit of Simon, 93; B. recalls, 150, 283; B. quotes, 445; (quoted, 527).

Owl, stuffed (*3*), *a wedding present from Alderman Hooper.*—B.—dead bird pathetic, 112; B. used to teach Milly, 678; in room, 692.

Papli (*6*), *baby nickname of B., used by Milly.*—Salutation on Milly's card, 65; B. recalls poignancy of love, 88; B. recalls, 373;

(Milly addresses B., 530); (Bello says, scoffingly, 531); B. has saved childhood drawings of Milly addressed, 705.

Parallax (6).—B.—Ball's book, 152; B. thinks of asking about, 164; in parody, 407; (Callinan, with whom B. had discussed astronomy, asks meaning, 478); (Virag uses in gibberish, 501); in essay on cosmic relativity, 683.

Patience (3), phrase of Martha's letter.—B. reads, 77; B.—90, 275.

Pensive (4), phrase of Dawson's grandiloquent speech.—Speech ridiculed in news office, 122; B. thinks more sensible to do something for poor rather than speak so, 159; in B.'s erotic meditations, 364; (O'Molloy uses in defense speech at trial, 456).

Perfume (7), phrase of Martha's letter.—Martha asks about what kind M. uses, 77; B.—78; suggested to B. as he orders lotion, 83; suggested to B. taking soap out of pocket, 122; B.—placing of ad in paper, 158; in love meditation, 270, 271.

"Photo Bits" (3), cheap magazine.—Picture of nymphs taken from, 65; (nymphs accuse B., 533); M. has thrown away, 739.

Pineapple rock (4), confection.—B. sees displayed, 149; B. thinks of as end of world, 164; Boylan passes, 267; (distributed as gift to followers by Mayor Bloom, 476).

Plasto's (5), label in hatband.—B. notices slip of paper behind, 56; B. sees it still there, 70; B.—91; B. thinks of deceiving M., 275; B. notes as he leaves Ormond, 282.

Plumtree (5), potted-meat advertisement in morning paper.—B. reads jingle in ad, 73; a silly ad, especially under obituaries, 152; B.—169; empty pot of, in kitchen, 659; example of poor ad, 668.

Polo match (2), scene of one of B.'s flirtations.—B. recalls haughtiness of woman at, 72; (woman accuses B., 458).

Potato (11), good luck piece in B.'s pocket.—In pocket, 56; found while dashing into museum, 181; not a remedy for rheumatism, 418; B.'s mother's panacea, 428; B. feels, 430; (mother speaks of, 431); (Mrs. Bellingham mentions, 457); taken by prostitute, 467; (one of Daughters of Erin, 488); B. asks for as relic, 517, 542.

Quoits (5), jingling decoration on bed.—M. rattles on awakening, 56, 63; (461); B. mentions, 534; B. gets into bed carefully because of, 715.

Raoul (8), phrase from "Sweets of Sin."—B. reads at stall, 232; B. dreams erotically, 233; in mock description of B., 254; B.—fears of Boylan, 256; B. sees portrait of mermaid, 259; mock description of lovelorn B., 283; coda of themes, 375; (Marion addresses Boylan as, 551).

Rat (5), seen in cemetery.—B. sees, 112; B. thinks of as symbol of disintegration, 117; B. wonders where it is, 279; in parody, 405; (465).

Retrospective (7), phrase of Kernan's praise of Dollard.—Kernan ridiculed for, 90; Kernan thinks of word, 237; in mock description of Kernan, 273; describing B. reminiscing, 406; (B. uses, 437); B. thinks of nature of love, 636; in reminiscence of B.'s father, 709.

Rip Van Winkle (5), symbol of passing of B.'s happy youth.—B. recalls charade on, 370, 371; (485, 529); B. thinks of as lost lover, 608.

Rocks (3), M.'s expression of scorn at B.'s learning.—M. answers B.'s description of metempsychosis, 64; B. recalls her wit, 280; (464).

"Ruby" (3), title of sensational cheap novel.—B. glances at as M. asks about metempsychosis, 64; (villain accuses B., 446); M. recalls, 736.

Sandow's (4) patent exerciser.—B. must begin exercises again, 61; (B. says he must use, 428); possible aid to rejuvenation, 665; B.'s chart of measurements, 706.

Seaside girls (12), phrase of popular song.—B. glances hurriedly at Milly's card, 62; B. reads, 66; B. thinks of romantic times with M., 67; B. applies to maggots in corpses, 107; B. recalls seaside, 177; B.'s erotic dreams, 270; B. thinks of as seashell is held to ear of barmaid, 277; B. recalls, 280; B. applies to Gerty, 365; B. applies to experience with Gerty, 366; (Milly appears as, 530); (descriptive of dance in brothel, 562).

Soap (13), purchased for M.—B. sees, 83; B. buys, 84; B. uncomfortable with, in pocket, 86; B. puts in coat, 99; B. puts in trousers, 122; B. feels, 181; feels sticky, 282; B. smells, 369; not paid for, 369; B. feels, 430; (433); (one of Daughters of Erin, 488); B. washes with, 656.

Spinoza (5).—B. quoted to M., 280; B. claims as great Jew, 336, 672; B. has book of, left by father, 693; M. ridicules B.'s interest in, 754.

Squaring the circle (3), example of B.'s scientific curiosity.—(Father refers to, 503); discouraged B. from extensive calculations, 684; a scheme of getting rich, 703.

Stream of life (3), B.'s meditation on cycle of life.—B. thinks of, always passing, 85; B. recalls, passing river, 151, 153.

"Sweets of Sin" (14), pornographic book for M.—B. sees at stall, 232; B. buys, 233; in mock description of B., 254; in B.'s erotic dreams, 256; in mock description, 283; B. feels in pocket, 430; (said by wreaths of smoke, 444); (one of Daughters of Erin, 488); (bookseller of pursues B., 571); avoids showing to S. as he finds M.'s picture, 636; S. writes Irish characters in cover, 672; B. mentions to M., 720; M. thinks of, 750, 754.

Thirty-two feet per second (7), law of gravity.—B. tries to recall law, 71; B. thinks of dropping *Elijah* to gulls, 150; parody, 302; (workmen, 475); (B. quotes, 477, 516); (B. recalls in memory of proposal on Hill of Howth, 537).

Throwaway (5), tip on races.—Descriptive of Elijah, 149; floats downstream, 223, 236, 246; as tip, 660.

"Titbit" (10), magazine.—B. takes to toilet, 67; B. reads, 68; B. thinks of writing, 69, 172, 275, 369, 631; (evidence in trial, 454); a scheme of getting rich, 643, 669.

Tooraloom (5).—B. hums, 70; B.—at cemetery, 104; (B. sings, 481); Kelleher sings, 588; descriptive of escape from street fight, 592.

Tour (9), M.'s concert trip with Boylan.—B.—to M'Coy, 74; to Power, 92; to Flynn, free ad, 170; to crowd at Kiernan's, 313; as way of getting seaside vacation, 611; money-making scheme, 643; unavoidable aid to M.'s unfaithfulness, 717; M.—732, 748.

Tramline (*6*), *a get-rich-quick scheme.*—B. thinks of cattle tram, 58; B.—to crowd in funeral carriage, 96, 97; (as Mayor, advocates, 469); 611; get-rich scheme, 703.

Trenchant (*3*), *phrase of Kernan's praise of Dollard.*—Laughed at, 90; Kernan says, 282; (B. uses of *Leah*, 439).

Uniform (*2*).—Seeing recruiting poster, B. thinks makes it easier to drill, 71; (B. quotes, 447).

Up (*2*).—B.—M. not up yet, 74; B.—M. not up, 92.

U.P. (*10*), *mocking postcard sent to Breen.*—Mrs. Breen tells B., 156; B. thinks Bergan or Goulding wrote, 157; B. associates with Mrs. Purefoy, whom Mrs. Breen had been also discussing, 276; Bergan laughs about, 293, 294; O'Molloy discusses libel suit, 315; B. associates with idea of trick, 374; (Bergan appears wearing letters, 438); (O'Connell—465); (B.—477).

Valise (*3*).—B. fears M'Coy wants to borrow, 74; B. recalls M'Coy, 277, 362.

Voglio (*7*), *phrase of one of M.'s songs.*—B. wonders if M. pronounces it right, 63; B. hums, 76; B. thinks M. probably humming, 92; B.—could ask Nannetti about, 119; (B. asks about, 434); (Mrs. Breen exclaims, 438); B. quandary mentioned, 606.

"When First I Saw" (*4*), *phrase from song.*—Dedalus sings, 269; B.—first seeing M., 271; in mock description of prostitute, 285; (B. sings, 511).

Woman getting on car (*2*).—B. hopes to see ankles, 73; B. thinks of sophisticated women like, 158.

"Yorkshire Girl" (*6*), *popular song.*—Band plays during procession, 250; prostitute is, 489; accompaniment of dance in brothel, 559, 560, 563; (pursues B., 583).

MOTIFS ASSOCIATED WITH STEPHEN DEDALUS

Adiaphane (*2*).—In reflections on beach, 38; in parody of Sir Thomas Browne, 387.

Aengus (*3*), *Mulligan's nickname for S.*—Mulligan calls S., 212; S.—214; Mulligan repeats, 245.

Coronation (2), phrase of one of Mulligan's songs.—Mulligan sings, 13; (Edward VII sings, 579).

Dogsbody (4), Mulligan scorns S. as.—Mulligan—to S., 7; S.—8; S., seeing cur on beach, 47; (Mulligan says, 565).

Epi oinopa ponton (3), Homeric phrase describing sea.—Mulligan—enthusiasm for pagan culture, 7; S.—48; (Mulligan says, 565).

Fabled (2).—S. thinks of history, 25; S. recalls as he insults privates, 572.

Fathom (3).—Boatman speaks of drowned man, 23; S. associates with "Lycidas," *The Tempest*, 50; S. speaks of Prospero burying his book, 209.

Form (4).—S. reflects on soul, 27, 45, 49, 187.

Fox (6).—S. springs riddle on schoolboys, 28; S. associates with mother, 29; S.—with dog on beach, 47; (544, 545, 557).

Hamlet (57).—Mulligan—S.'s theory, 17, 19; Haines—tower like Elsinore, 20; S.—recall of Mulligan on, 29; S.—recall of phrase on cliff, 38; nipping airs, 39; S. "very like a whale," 41; S.—Elsinore, 45; S. "sable silvered," 48; S.—Hamlet hat, 48; S. "my tablets," 48; S. "sandal shoon," 50; B.—Ophelia's suicide, 75; B. "refuse Christian burial," 95; B.—gravediggers, 107; MacHugh, 125; S. "porches of ear," 138, 194; B. "I am thy father's spirit," 150; B. "could a tale unfold," 160; B. "look on this picture," 167; S. expounds theory, 182-212; librarian "sea of troubles," 182; S. "list, list," 185; S. "sledded poleaxe," 185; S. "if thou didst ever," 186; S. "I am thy father's spirit," 186; S. "art thou there, truepenny," 187; S. "by cock, she was to blame," 189; S. "beaver is up," 194; Eglinton "by Saint Patrick," 196; Mulligan "play's the thing," 206; S. "no more marriages," 210; Best "all save one," 211; S. "gall his kibe," 212; Mulligan—Haines missed S. on, 245; B. "sweets to the sweet," 268; B. "on his daughter," 268; B "to be," 276; Nolan "custom more honoured in the breach," 325; B. "for this relief,'" 366; in parody, 381, 387; B. "witching hour," 438; (Dignam quotes ghost, 464); B. "to be," 489; B. "frailty, thy name," 534; S., to have or not, 542; S.—French title, 545; prostitute paraphrases ghost, 547; Lynch, 553; S. recalls French, 556; S. "Hola, hilly-ho," 557; S. "break my spirit," 567; S. cries Hamlet, revenge, 579; B. refers to Baconian theory, 618; "consummation devout-ly," 625; to enter or not, 652.

Heresiarch (*3*).—In meditation on heresy, 22; S.—39; S. uses in library, 205.

Hising (*2*), *phrase from Mulligan's song.*—Mulligan sings, 15; S. associates with waves on beach, 50.

Ineluctable (*9*).—S. meditates on modality of visible, 38; of audible, 38; S.—on soul, 49; S.—visible, 49, and audible, 49; S.—at brothel, 494, 546; in discussion on Eccles Street, 682.

Jesuit (*6*).—Mulligan calls S., 5, 6, 10, 18, 213; in tavern, 418.

Key (*5*).—S. has, 13, 19; S. guards jealously, 21; gives to Mulligan, 24; symbol of homelessness, 45.

Liliata (*5*), *phrase from deathbed prayer.*—S.—death of mother, 12; S. thinks as he walks, 24; S.—188; (choir—564); S. thinks as bells ring at 2:00 A.M., 688.

Livid flame (*4*).—S. in school, 25; S. on beach, 44; S. at hospital, 385; (description of breaking of chandelier, 567).

Maimonides (*4*), *Jewish philosopher.*—S.—on mathematics, 29; in parody, 383; (485); B.—as great exile, 671.

Nebrakada (*3*), *words of charm.*—S. reads, 239; (M. quotes, 432); B. quotes, 540.

Nightmare (*2*), *S.'s conception of history.*—S. to Deasy, 35; S.—135.

Noise in street (*4*), *S.'s definition of God.*—S. to Deasy, 45; S. thinks in library, 184; in brothel, 494, 559.

Omphalos (*4*).—S. thinks of new paganism of Mulligan, 9; Mulligan says, 19; S. ridicules theosophical, 39; Mulligan to name fertilizing farm, 396.

Orient (*2*).—S.—on fruitfulness, 39; S. —238.

Photius (2), banished ecclesiastic.—S.—on heretics, 22; S. in library, 195.

Possible (3).—S.—were other events possible, 26, or only that which happened, 26; S. thinks of buried thoughts in library, 191.

Quarrons (2), phrase from seventeenth-century lyric.—S.—on beach, 48; S.—to prostitute, 582.

Rosewood (3), descriptive of mother's corpse.—7, 12, 28.

Sabellius (2), heretic.—S.—on heretics, 22; S. quotes in library, 205.

Shells (4).—S. sees in Deasy's room, 30, 31; S. thinks of people as, 42, 51.

Socrates (5).—Eglinton mentions, 188; S. in discussion of Shakespeare, 200; S. quotes Maeterlinck on impossibility of escaping self, 210; S. recalls, 214, 425.

Übermensch (2).—Mulligan calls self, 24; at tavern, 417.

Void (5).—S. thinks of passing of glory, 22; church founded on, 205; (in *Götterdämmerung*, 583); applied to B. and S. in their activities, 682; in description of stellar space, 683.

Weave (6).—S. thinks of passing of history, 22, 26; suggests Blake's rhyme on harlot's cry, 34; S. in library, life a weaving of bodies, 192; (dance in brothel, 562); recall of Blake, 582.

INDEX